DATE DUE

			PRINTED IN U.S.A.

Gene Perret's

FUNNY BUSINESS:

Speaker's Treasury of Business Humor For All Occasions

Gene Perret's

FUNNY BUSINESS:

Speaker's Treasury of Business Humor For All Occasions

Gene Perret and Linda Perret

PRENTICE HALL
Englewood Cliffs, New Jersey 07632

Prentice-Hall International (UK) Limited, *London*
Prentice-Hall of Australia Pty. Limited, *Sydney*
Prentice-Hall Canada, Inc., *Toronto*
Prentice-Hall Hispanoamericana, S.A., *Mexico*
Prentice-Hall of India Private Limited, *New Delhi*
Prentice-Hall of Japan, Inc., *Tokyo*
Simon & Schuster Asia Pte. Ltd., *Singapore*
Editora Prentice-Hall do Brasil, Ltda., *Rio de Janeiro*

© 1990 *by*
PRENTICE-HALL, Inc.
Englewood Cliffs, NJ

10 9 8 7 6 5 4 3 2 1

Library of Congress Cataloging-in-Publication Data

Perret, Gene.
    [Funny business]
    Gene Perret's funny business : speaker's treasury of business
humor for all occasions / by Gene Perret and Linda Perret.
    p. cm.
    ISBN 0-13-352881-2
    ISBN 0-13-352535-X (paper)
    1. Business humor—Humor. 2. American wit and humor. 3. Public
speaking—Handbooks, manuals, etc. I. Perret, Linda. II. Title.
PN6231.B85P47 1990
818'.540208'035265—dc20   89-48143
                                                        CIP

ISBN   0-13-352881-2

ISBN   0-13-352535-X (PBK)

PRENTICE HALL
BUSINESS & PROFESSIONAL DIVISION
A division of Simon & Schuster
Englewood Cliffs, New Jersey 07632

To Bob
A tennis buddy
who always had
the latest joke

To
Gram and Grandpop
who I wish were here
today to see this

ABOUT THE AUTHORS

GENE PERRET has written comedy material for nightclub performers and television since 1959. His clients have included Bob Hope, Phyllis Diller, Slappy White, and Mickey Shaughnessy.

In television, Gene has written for *The Jim Nabors Hour, Laugh-In, The Bill Cosby Show, Mama's Family*, and has won three Emmies and a Writer's Guild Award during his five years on *The Carol Burnett Show*.

He has also written and produced *Welcome Back Kotter, The Tim Conway Show*, and the number one rated show at the time, *Three's Company*.

Gene has also been associated as staff writer with Bob Hope since 1969, has travelled to the war zones of Beirut and the Persian Gulf with the legendary comedian, and is presently the head writer on all Bob Hope television specials.

Gene has also written three books on humor:

Hit or Miss Management, (Houghton & Mifflin, 1980)

Comedy Writing Step-By-Step: How to Write and Sell (Your Sense of) Humor, (Samuel French, 1990)

How to Hold Your Audience With Humor, (Writer's Digest Books, 1984)

Using Humor For Effective Business Speaking, (Sterling, 1989)

He has also published essays and articles about humor for national magazines, such as *Reader's Digest, Mc Call's, Writer's Digest, Industry Week, The Toastmaster, Convention World*, and others.

In addition, Gene is in demand as a banquet humorist. In 1983, his first year on the lecture circuit, he was voted "The Top Discovery in the Field of Humor" by the International Platform Association.

LINDA PERRET, is the editor of *Round Table*, a monthly newsletter for humorous speakers and writers. In this capacity, she works with aspiring writers and performers in the comedy field, and also many executives who are interested in humor in their own communications.

Linda also organizes a *Round Table* convention each year. This is actually a workshop for aspiring humorists, featuring many top professional Hollywood writers. This convention is held in July of each year in Pasadena, California.

FROM THE AUTHORS

Comedy lines have a rhythm to them, a beat. They have a definite cadence not unlike a poem or a song lyric. Disrupting that tempo often destroys the overall effect.

That's why we have chosen not to use some of the newer devices of genderless writing. Using *he or she* or *a person* to replace one pronoun often ruins the flow of the sentence and the comedy impact.

We decided to use the masculine pronoun where there was a choice, rather than alternate. However, that decision was for consistency rather than any sort of sexist statement.

With few exceptions, all of the humor in this book applies to female and male business executives. Readers can use the pronoun of the appropriate gender, and the humor of the lines will be just as entertaining.

CONTENTS

PART ONE
THE PEOPLE OF BUSINESS
"If we could learn to get along in the business world without people, we'd
all be assured of our own parking space."

THE BIG MAHOFFS
"Don't get carried away with your own importance. Remember the pied
piper was a leader just because he knew how to play a flute."

THE LITTLE MAHOFFS
"Behind every genius in business is an assistant telling him which buttons
to push to get the telephone to work."

PART TWO
PARAPHERNALIA OF BUSINESS
*"Just think, if Moses were alive today, God could have faxed the ten
commandments to him."*

PART THREE
BUSINESS AND MONEY
*"The business world's greatest dilemma is trying to decide whether greed is
a virtue or a vice."*

THEIR MONEY
*"Every job description in the business world can be reduced to four words:
'Make money for us.' "*

YOUR MONEY
*"We pray each day for 'our daily bread;' but we have to negotiate with the
boss for 'a little jam and jelly on the side.' "*

PART FOUR
CONVENTIONS, COFFEE BREAKS AND OTHER OFFICE HIGH JINKS
"All work and no play makes Jack a dull boy, and also a real pigeon
on the golf course."

PART FIVE
EXECUTIVE PERKS & PEEVES
"Each position has its good and bad features. The good you keep; the bad
you delegate."

PERKS
"Happiness is the key to the executive washroom . . . whether you have to
go or not."

PEEVES FROM THE WORKERS
> *"To paraphrase Mom—'Just wait. Someday you'll have employees*
> *of your own.' "*

PEEVES FROM THE HIGHER-UPS
> *"Most people in business feel that the word 'Superior' is an honorary title."*

PEEVES FROM EACH OTHER
> *"It can be depressing to glance around at our co-workers and realize that*
> *technically they're considered our equals."*

PEEVES FROM OURSELVES
> *"We may be hard on ourselves, but we'll never be our own worst enemies*
> *as long as there are other people working in the company."*

PART SIX
BUSINESS PROTOCOL
"Just remember there are business ethics just as surely as there are rules in professional wrestling."

PART SEVEN
OFFICE SQUABBLES
"Put two people in an office and you have a feud. Put three people in an office and you have a feud with a clique."

PART EIGHT
BUSINESS ON THE MOVE
"Whoever said 'Getting there is half the fun,' has never had a connecting flight in Chicago."

PART NINE
OCCUPATIONS WE ALL DEAL WITH
"We are all brothers under our skin, and that's where most sub-contractors usually get."

PART TEN
HINTS ON USING HUMOR IN BUSINESS
"If you aren't having some fun, you might wonder just what you are doing in your business life . . . If employees, customers, and vendors don't laugh and have a good time at your company, something is wrong."
. . . PAUL HAWKEN

FOREWORD

I believe in humor. I have to. I'm still making payments on my last two faces.

But imagine what life would be like without humor. Milton Berle would have to go back to shopping in the men's department. Bob Hope would have a lot fewer memories. And I'd be just another great set of legs . . . for Colonel Sanders to bid on.

But humor does more than keep us comedians out of the unemployment line. A good joke makes you feel good, and some say it can actually prolong your life—two things that cannot be said about my cooking.

Humor is also a powerful tool which can be used by a speaker to get the audience on his side—which isn't a bad idea, especially if it's a long walk from the stage to the exit door.

Gene Perret, the co-author of this book with daughter Linda, also believes in humor. In fact, he's a humor enthusiast. He loves writing jokes, telling jokes, analyzing jokes, stealing jokes . . . (Actually, Gene doesn't have to steal jokes. He's written over 200,000 of them. If he steals one, chances are it was his anyway.)

Many of Gene's jokes are in my files. The rest are divided among such comedy greats as Bob Hope, Bill Cosby, Carol Burnett, and Tim Conway. (Of course, all 200,000 jokes can be found in Milton Berle's files as well.)

But beyond Gene's obvious writing talents, he is also a popular and gifted platform personality. (I had to say that. He's holding my hairdresser hostage.)

You see, Gene doesn't just sit on the sidelines and write books about performing humor. He's up there on the podium with the rest of us.

Gene knows first hand what it's like to try out that new joke or come up with a great adlib when the microphone falls to the floor. He's had to follow introductions where the master of ceremonies has mispronounced his name or misstated his credits. He's basked in the glory of that perfect performance, and he's had to sneak out the back door after that not-so-perfect presentation.

Gene has also had to deal with those "less than desirable" stage set-ups like when they put your lectern next to the kitchen and make you deliver orders between your points.

But he's learned, as you will, that humor can take the edge off almost any situation. And when used correctly, it can drive home a point like nothing else can.

So, learn from Gene's experiences, borrow his expertise, practice his proven techniques, but above all else, catch his enthusiasm. After all, in today's world, we need all the ambassadors of laughter we can get.

. . . PHYLLIS DILLER

HOW TO BEST USE THIS HUMOR COLLECTION

A comedian we heard at a comedy club recently said he had just finished reading a book called "Helium." He said, "I couldn't put it down."

This book is designed to be put down—many, many times. If you set it down often, it means you've picked it up often and used it. That's the purpose of a reference book.

We hope you enjoy a leisurely read-through. In fact, we recommend it. But read through the pages with a purpose.

This volume is mass produced. Each copy on the book store shelf is exactly the same as the next copy. It's not meant to stay that way, though. It's most effective when it becomes a personalized edition. Reader A will like and use certain parts of it; Reader B will prefer different parts. You have to make this *your* book.

We want the readers to use this book. In effect, it becomes your script. Some of the material in this book will be used in your speeches.

When performers in show business see a script for the first time, they read it with pencil in hand. Why? Because they make it a personalized script. It becomes a partner in the performance. The first thing they do is circle or highlight their speeches. This way their dialogue pops off the page at them. They don't want to miss a cue.

This also makes their study of the lines easier. They can skip right over those pages without highlighting, and concentrate on those scenes where they have lots to do.

The performers also change the dialogue to suit their own speech patterns and mark that on their scripts. We once had a young guest on a television variety show who felt embarrassed saying "You're a cool dude." She felt it wasn't what the young people were saying. It wasn't hip. She wanted the writers to change it. We said, "Say whatever you feel is natural for you." She crossed off "cool dude" and penciled in her own ad-lib.

Performers also pencil in questions about the dialogue. "Why am I so angry at this point?" "Doesn't my mood change too quickly here?" Later this will be a reminder to them to ask the writers or the director about this problem.

When they get the answer or the advice that helps them, they'll jot that onto the script, too. Then when they study, rehearse, read, or perform the scene, they'll know what the creative people expect from them.

Physical moves also go into each performer's script. They'll make a note on when they cross from one side of the stage to the other, when they stand, when they pick up a prop, and so on.

You can see, though, that the script for each performer begins to take on its own personality. Upon the first reading, all the sheets were identical; now they're unique. The performer needs his or her own copy because the notes in it are essential. This is how this book can become your personal script.

Musicians, too, will often add their own flair to sheet music. They'll change the voicing of a chord, or add a few notes of harmony, or do something to change the music as written.

We attended a rehearsal once where the director admonished the band to "play the ink." When we asked what he meant, he explained how the musicians will pencil in changes and additions to the sheet music. Normally, the band leader allows the improvisation, but sometimes the music must be played as written. Hence, "Play the ink."

In adding humor to your talks, you have the same creative liberties that performers and musicians have. In fact, humor demands that you bring your own style to the delivery. Your humor must reflect your personality, your preferences, your talents. Anything else would feel unnatural, and unnatural doesn't work in comedy.

So we want you to pick up a pencil when you read this book. Make notes, references, ask questions, jot down answers, cross out lines, write in new words—do whatever you want to make this book your functional script.

MARK THOSE ITEMS YOU LIKE OR CAN USE

This is a large collection of humor. Some of the jokes you will like; others you won't. Some you can use in your speaking; others you can't. Mark the ones that appeal to you. Jot down an "X," an arrow, a star, or highlight them with colored markers. Do something to harvest the wheat.

Obviously, you can't use all the material you like immediately. You can't predict when you'll need some of the material you would like to use. A strange thing about collections of humor is that the good references hide when you look for them. You know you read a quote or saw a joke that applies to "Leadership" in some book somewhere, but when you want it, you can't find it. By marking the book now, the lines will pop out at you later.

Most of the comedians that we've written comedy lines for do this. When material comes in, they immediately read through it and check off the lines they like. Those are retyped and the rest of the material is discarded.

Not all of the checked lines are used, but when the comedian wants a line, he or she doesn't have to read through the entire submission again to find a good one. The comic reads only through the selected lines.

It's a matter of efficiency. Your time is valuable so why waste it remaking decisions you've already made? Why read everything the next time through? Read only those lines you've marked.

MAKE NOTES ON THE JOKES YOU SELECT

Again, the comics that we've written for invariably see different applications for the material, and they'll note that. For instance, a joke that the writers submit on today's topic might tie in with a routine the comedian is already using. He or she will jot down, "Use this joke to open the Mother-in-Law routine," or some such remark.

In reading through this collection, you might realize that a particular quote might be useful in illustrating an idea of yours. Jot it down. Let the margin be your reminder.

Also, you might recognize some people in the lines you read. A joke about the man who never picked up a lunch check may remind you of "Good ol' Harry." Write Harry's name next to the joke.

CROSS REFERENCE

We tried to categorize the humor in this collection, but many of the subjects spill over. A joke about a cheap boss may also refer to a fellow worker who has high pockets. However, the joke is listed in only one area of the book. Some jokes that are listed under "Taxes" could also apply to "Cost Savings." If you recognize the connection, make a note of it.

Again, this is efficient. When you're looking for that great quote about "Cost Savings," you may not remember that it wasn't in that section at all. It was listed under "Taxes." However, if you have a note there, you'll find it.

All of the above hints help to make this mass produced book your personal script.

Remember, too, that none of the jokes in here are carved in stone. They can be used "as is" or they can be the raw material that helps you fashion your own humor. Any of the lines in here can be revised, changed, reworded to suit your particular tastes. Also, the jokes that are in here can be used as a springboard to other jokes. They may remind you of other gags that you've heard. They can be used as lead ins to that joke or in conjunction with other humor. Or the jokes may prompt you to write your own.

You might use the different categories simply to suggest areas that you can write about.

Later in this volume we have additional chapters to help you create your own humor.

This book is designed to help *you* with *your* humor. Make it *your* book. Make it *your* script.

PART ONE

THE PEOPLE OF BUSINESS

If we could learn to get along in the business world without
people, we'd all be assured of our own parking space.

THE BIG MAHOFFS

Don't get carried away with your own importance. Remember that the pied piper was a leader just because he knew how to play a flute.

MANAGEMENT VS. LABOR

Management and Labor get along like the shark and the sea bass. They always have and they always will. They just keep taking turns playing the shark.

■

God created the world in six days . . . with non-union help.

. . . with union help the task would have been impossible. Not only would the cost have been prohibitive, but God wouldn't have had the patience to deal with that many shop stewards.

. . . He would have said, "Let there be light," and an official from the local would have said, "Now just a doggone minute."

■

If God knew He had to deal with union labor He would have made each day just 8 hours long. That way there'd be no way anyone would ever get time-and-a-half for overtime.

■

Unions fight for what is fair. And if they get that, they'll ask for a little more.

Unions will always be at Management's throat, if for no other reason than it gets them away from the area management expects them to kiss.

■

Shop stewards are basically history teachers trying to inform management that slave labor went out years ago.

■

A union feels its job is to get a fair day's pay for a fair day's labor. However, they must argue with executives who don't understand either term—"fair" or "labor."

■

Unions are dedicated to fighting injustice and intimidation from materialistic management. They are like Robin Hoods with a credit union.

■

Labor feels like it is David fighting Goliath; Management feels like it is Goliath fighting 5000 or 6000 Davids.
. . . that the Teamsters invariably support.

■

To most executives, the Union is a chronic complainer with a contract.

■

The Unions have the grievance procedure to express their dislike for management policies. Management, though, has no such recourse . . . except, of course, the weekly paycheck.

■

Many people in business feel that the lowest form of life was the amoeba, until the unions introduced the shop steward.

■

Shop stewards are always discovering something wrong. In the business world, they're paid hypochondriacs.

■

The shop steward is an uncreative dimwit who can't think of anything to do with his hands except carry a picket sign.

■

Shop stewards are like letters that come in window envelopes–they seem to arrive every day and they rarely bring good news.

Shop stewards are the opposite of the old Town Crier. At least, when he shouted it meant all was well.

■

My Dad had a Solomon-like way of insuring justice and equality when my brother and I would argue about splitting the last piece of cake. One brother would slice the cake; the other would get to choose which piece he wanted.

■

"Good supervision is the art of getting average people to do superior work."— *Unknown*

■

"Good executives never put off until tomorrow what they can get someone else to do today."—*Unknown*

■

An executive is someone who talks to visitors while the employees get the work done.

■

Alabama's football coach, the legendary Bear Bryant, had a philosophy that made him a winning coach. It also might apply to good management-labor relationships. Coach Bryant said:

"I'm just a plowhand from Arkansas, but I have learned how to hold a team together. How to lift some men up, how to calm down others, until finally they've got one heartbeat together, a team. There's just three things I'd ever say:

"If anything goes bad, I did it.

"If anything goes semi-good, then we did it.

"If anything goes real good, then you did it.

"That's all it takes to get people to win football games for you."

■

Here's an historic clash between a worker and his boss:

Abraham Lincoln was walking along the hallway in the War Department building when an army officer, moving at double speed, barreled into him. When the young military man saw that he had crashed into none less than his Commander-in-Chief, he said, "Ten thousand pardons, Sir."

Lincoln said, "One is quite enough, but I wish our whole army would charge like that."

■

Frederich Engels was a German socialist leader and political philosopher who collaborated with Karl Marx on the Communist Manifesto in 1848. When he was a youngster, his father took him on a tour of the family textile factory–the factory that was to become young Frederich's inheritance.

The six-year old lad was bothered by the miserable working conditions there. He saw children about his own age working hard and for long hours.

He didn't have the courage to ask his stern father any questions about it, but he did question his mother when he got home.

"Will I soon have to go to work in the factory?" he asked.

His mother reassured him. "No Frederich, you won't. You can be glad that we own the factory."

That didn't quite satisfy him. He asked, "How about the children who do work there? Are they glad?"

His mother now put him off. She said, "Frederich, it's better that you don't worry your head about such things. You can't change things."

The problem bothered the boy. He thought about it as he went to sleep. The next day when his mother woke him, he said, "Mother, suppose I want to change things . . . then what . . . ?"

■

"Of course there's a different law for the rich and the poor; otherwise, who would go into business?"—*E. Ralph Stewart*

■

One shop steward had a good definition for an exchange of opinions. He said, "That's when you go to your boss with your opinion and leave with his."

■

A supervisor was berating one of his factory workers in front of several other employees. He scolded him non-stop. The worker was getting angrier and angrier, redder and redder. And the boss was running out of words.

He said, "You're the biggest bonehead in the world. You're the champion bonehead of all boneheads. If they had an Olympic event for boneheads, you'd win the silver medal."

The worker was now about to tear into the boss. Then he paused. He said, "Wait a minute. Why wouldn't I win the gold medal?"

The boss said, "Because you're such a bonehead, that's why."

■

The supervisor called one of his workers into his office and told him that he was being pink-slipped.

The employee got furious. He said, "You think you're a big shot because you're the lousy supervisor. Well, big deal. You know what supervisors do? They don't do nothing. They don't lift a finger to help production. They just stand around looking stupid and don't do one damn lick of work the whole entire day."

The boss said, "That's why you're being fired. Too many people are mistaking you for the supervisor."

CHEAP BOSSES

My boss is so cheap he not only has the first dollar he ever made, but also the arm of the man who handed it to him.

■

He hasn't picked up a check since he met this streetwalker in Prague.

■

They say that crime doesn't pay, but it will if it goes to lunch with him.

■

He squeezes a buck so hard, George Washington has to wear a truss under his leotards.

■

He'd be a happy man if the government could find a way to print its money on fly-paper.

■

Even at meetings when he puts in his two-cents worth, he gets a co-signer.

■

The only thing he's ever taken out of his wallet was the picture of Linda Darnell that came with it.
. . . he sold that.

■

You know he's frugal. Any man who owns a Zip-loc wallet . . .

■

He's a hoarder. He knows "you can't take it with you," but he's planning on coming back to get it.

■

He buys suits with 2 pairs of pants, then tries to run the jacket through the Xerox machine.

■

Handwriting experts say you can tell how cheap a person is by how small their margins are. This guy writes completely on both sides of the paper, and also around the four outside edges.

He knows money can't buy happiness, but that's alright with him. He likes money more than happiness anyway.

■

He's stingy with office supplies, too. To get a legal pad from him you have to pass the bar exam.
. . . each time.

■

At work, he only provides loose leaf books with two rings. He thinks that third hole is a waste of paper.

■

He demands that all official memos be written on a single sheet of paper. He's trying to save on paper clips.

■

He hates to spend from his own budget for office supplies. He's the only boss I've ever worked for who would go to the department down the hall and ask to borrow a cup of pencils.

■

Before he writes up a new supply requisition he first trims the form in black.

■

Here's a guy who may take the prize for cheapness: He wanted to hit the lottery. If he could just win a few million dollars, all his troubles would be solvable. So he prayed. And he didn't hit. He prayed harder. He still didn't win. He prayed harder and longer.
Finally as he prayed sincerely one night, the Lord appeared to him and said, "Do me a favor, will you– buy a ticket."

■

One salesman was bothered by a manager who was a stickler on going over each item of the expense account. Regardless of how meticulously this man listed every expense, the boss would find something to complain about. Legitimate, necessary expenses were questioned.
Once the boss complained about dinner and drinks that were listed as "entertaining a client." The salesman objected; the expenses were required. The boss said, "The client's expenses are justified, but I'm not paying for drinks for you."
When the boss went over the next expense account he complimented the employee. He said, "I'm pleased. I don't see any frivolous expenses listed here for you."
The salesman said, "That's right. You don't see them, but they're there."

There's a story told about the proprietor who may have been the world's champion stingiest boss. No matter how well business was going, he was constantly trying to cut back on expenses, to lay off help. He lived only to cut costs.

Then he died.

Many former workers showed up at his funeral. As the procession began one past employee noted that the casket was carried up the church aisle by four members of his staff.

The man asked the funeral director why there were only four pall bearers. The undertaker said, "At the start of the day there were six, but the deceased sat up and let two of them go."

■

Harold Ross began *The New Yorker* magazine in 1925, virtually on a shoestring. To keep the periodical in production during the early times, he had to keep a close eye on expenses.

He hired Dorothy Parker to do an article for the magazine, but she never showed up to do the assignment. He called and asked her why. She said, "Someone else was using the pencil."

■

King Louis XVIII was reviewing the budget with Talleyrand, the head of the provisional government. Talleyrand said, "Your majesty, there is an omission."

The King said, "What?"

Talleyrand said, "There's no budget allotted for payment of the deputies."

The King said, "The deputies? They should perform their duties without recompense. It should be purely an honorable position."

Talleyrand said, "Without payment? But Your Majesty, that would cost us too much!"

■

An engineer worked for a notoriously tight-fisted boss. He developed a patent that made a lot of money for the company, but when he asked to share in the income, the boss refused.

He said, "You came up with that idea on my time, time that I paid you for. That idea belongs to me and you have no right to share in the profits."

Later, the company engineers were working on a particularly perplexing problem. At a staff meeting, this man proudly announced that he had the solution.

The boss said, "Well, let's have it."

The man said, "I'm sorry, sir, but I can't do that. I thought of it this morning while shaving, and that's my time."

A woman lived with a man who was the world champion penny-pincher. He was rich and successful, but he guarded his money so carefully, that they lived near the poverty level.

This man was so cheap that he didn't even want to share his wealth after his passing. He insisted not only that he have a frugal funeral, but also that his wife make sure that he be buried with all of his wealth.

She went along with his wishes. She bought the cheapest casket she could find, laid him out in an inexpensive suit, wrote a check for his entire fortune and put in his breast pocket.

. . . She figured let him figure out how to cash it.

■

I went on a business trip with my boss who was really the cheapest man alive.

One night he was late getting back to the hotel and I asked where he'd been. He told me he met a young lady, they went out for a while, then he dropped her off at her hotel.

I said, "Was she pretty?"

He said, "Was she? The entire cab ride to her hotel I could hardly keep my eyes on the meter."

HARD-NOSED BOSSES

I have a boss who makes Simon Legree look like Mother Theresa.

This man has a black belt in Management.

He's like a "Dirty Harry" with an MBA.

He has an MBA after his name. We think that's because he's a member of "Mean Bastards Anonymous."

He's a bitter manager. He's never quite forgiven Ebenezer Scrooge for deserting.

His goal in life is to someday own and operate a Turkish prison.

■

Our boss likes each of his employees to keep his eye on the ball, his shoulder to the wheel, and his nose to the grindstone. The only problem is it's hard to find desk chairs for people in that position.

■

It's hard to tell whether he's managing with his heart or his head. They're both made of stone.

He has the personality only a mother could love—provided she didn't have to work for him.

■

He warns that his workers will miss target dates only over his dead body. He doesn't realize that's the way we would prefer to miss them.

■

He's so mean, though, he won't die like normal people. Legend has it that the only way to kill his kind is to affix a "Happy Face" sticker to his heart.

■

He wants production regardless of how people feel about it. He's the kind of guy that would introduce microwaves into crematoriums.

■

He's the kind of guy that Dale Carnegie would like to punch in the mouth.

■

He's so cold blooded he would give the Mafia a bad name.

■

He watches Jacques Cousteau specials and roots for the sharks.

■

He makes out work schedules that are so tough the union doesn't even fight them. They simply turn them over to the ACLU.

. . . and they turn them over to the ASPCA.

■

Everybody hates him. At the office picnic tug-o-war, he's always the only one on his side of the rope.

. . . still, he's won it for the past three years.

■

We had a guy come into the office an hour late. He was banged up, bruised, and bandaged. The boss says to him, "Where have you been? You're an hour late for work."

The guy says, "I fell down a flight of stairs."

The boss says, "And that took a whole hour?"

■

Here's a guy who was about as unyielding and hard-nosed a leader as you could want. He was a pioneer who married a young lady, and after the wedding celebration he and his wife loaded up all their belongings on a buckboard, hitched up the mule, and started out to their new log cabin.

On the way, the mule decided to stop. The man didn't get upset, didn't get angry. He just sat there calmly and said, "That's one."

When the mule was good and ready it started pulling the wagon again. After a little while, it stopped again for a rest. The pioneer sat there unperturbed and calmly said, "That's two."

The mule started up again, but then stopped again. The man said, "That's three." He got down from the buckboard, pulled his gun, and shot the mule dead.

Now the bride got all upset. She said, "What'd you do a dumb thing like that for? We now have to take time to bury this mule. We have no animals to pull our buckboard. We've got miles and miles to go yet and we're going to have to pull this buckboard all by ourselves. Why did you do a dumb thing like that?"

The man looked at her and said, "That's one."

■

Here's another example of tough leadership. John McKay coached the University of Southern California football team for many years before coaching the Tampa Bay Buccaneers of the NFL.

After one game where his USC team was beaten decisively, McKay probably felt this team didn't exert themselves the way they could have. He came into their locker room after the defeat and said simply, "The team bus leaves in half an hour. Those who need showers, take 'em."

■

"You can't help liking the managing director—if you don't, he fires you." —*Anonymous*

■

"I don't want any yes-men around me. I want everybody to tell me the truth even if it costs them their jobs."—*Samuel Goldwyn*

■

Otto Klemperer was a maestro who was a difficult task-master. He rarely handed out praise to his musicians.

After one brilliant performance, though, he applauded his orchestra with a loud and enthusiastic, "Good!"

The musicians were so delighted they applauded themselves.

Klemperer frowned at the outburst. He said, "Not *that* good."

■

Charles M. Schwab learned his executive and managerial skills under Andrew Carnegie. Carnegie may have been among the hardest-nosed of hard-nosed bosses. He demanded outstanding performance from all his associates all of the time.

Once Schwab was particularly pleased with some work he had done while on a business trip. He wired his boss, "All previous records broken yesterday."

Carnegie wired back, "What have you done today?"

■

One manager was not only a demanding boss but thought of himself as an inspiring motivator, too. He would call his workers together fairly regularly for his "Win one for the Gipper" type of productivity stimulating lectures. The workers tired of them quickly.

At one session, an employee sat near the back, away from the manager's gaze, and dozed off during the oration. He snuck in a good twenty-minute nap.

When he woke up he turned to the person next to him and said, "What's he been talking about?"

The fellow worker said, "We don't know. He hasn't told us yet."

■

I knew one boss who had a permanent sign on the wall behind his desk. It read: "Of course I want it today. If I wanted it tomorrow, I would have given it to you tomorrow."

■

Jack Benny may have been the toughest boss of all time when he was honorary manager of the Hollywood All-Stars when they played an exhibition game against the professional team in Los Angeles. Jack handed a bat to his first batter and said, "Go up to the plate and hit a home run."

The batter struck out, and Jack Benny quit. He said, "How can I manage them if they won't follow orders?"

■

There was a manager once who was a real SOB. He would tear into his staff at meetings; he'd raise hell with clients and customers; he'd strike terror into the hearts of the employees when he walked through the workplace; he was a demon with Board members, staff, employees, clients, customers, and passers-by.

When he died, though, his loyal staff showed up at his funeral. Just as they lowered the casket into the open grave, a bolt of lightning flashed across the sky followed by the loud crack of thunder. One executive turned to the other and said, "Well, I guess he's arrived."

■

There was one boss who was a real SOB. He alienated everybody, and was proud of it. He was, that is, until the day came when he was seriously ill.

The minister came to see him and said, "My good friend, I'm afraid things look bad. I'm here to comfort you in your last hours and help you to accept the Lord and denounce Satan."

The boss said, "Reverend, I appreciate your effort and your concern, and I'm willing to accept the Lord. As far as denouncing Satan, though, I may skip that. I've made so damn many enemies in this life, I'd rather not make any in the next."

HATED BOSSES

There was once a boss who was so hated by his employees that everyone in the office learned the Heimlich maneuver in reverse.

▪

When he was out sick, people from the office sent him a bouquet of Venus fly-traps.

... that hadn't been fed in weeks.

Before they sent it, they let it sniff some articles of his clothing.

▪

He'd get the same Christmas gift every year from his employees–a deer skin hunting jacket.

▪

He had a lot of enemies. People used to hide under their desks everytime he started his electric pencil sharpener.

▪

He had the only secretary whose job description included food tasting and starting his car for him.

▪

He worked straight through lunch every day. It was safer than eating food that had been near his employees.

▪

He was so despised that every time a new baby was born anywhere in the world, his popularity rating went down by one.

▪

Everybody despised this guy. He had the only staff meetings in the entire company that began with a strip search.

▪

Nobody liked the guy. When he was a kid he had an imaginary playmate who used to beat him up.

His rocking horse once kicked him in the head.

■

He finished last every year in a company popularity poll. And he only finished that high because he voted for himself.

■

No one wanted to work for him. Promotions into his department were handled on a volunteer basis only.

■

He once collapsed at work and they summoned the paramedics by letter.
. . . fourth class mail.

■

I've had bosses who couldn't stand me either. One gave me such a bad job evaluation, I not only didn't get a raise, I had to bring back money I'd made for the past three months.

■

My boss and I got along like brothers—Cain and Abel.

■

I once had a boss who hated my guts. He preferred absenteeism to me.

If I called in ill, he'd send me a "stay sick" card.

■

My boss and I had a personality clash. I had one, he didn't.

■

We had a disagreement over salary negotiations. I wanted a ten percent increase. He wanted to have me deported.

THE LITTLE MAHOFFS

Behind every genius in business is an assistant telling him which buttons to push to get the telephone to work.

RECEPTIONISTS

The receptionist is the first smiling face you see each workday. Depending on how business is going, it's often the last smiling face you see each workday, too.

■

Some receptionists are dedicated to putting a little fun into office life. They take all of our phone messages and turn them into an office scavenger hunt.

■

Some receptionists are people who take your phone messages while you're away, and distribute them to various other people in the office.

■

You must have received a message like this sometime: "A Mr. Somebody called–I didn't catch his name–and he didn't give me a chance to jot down the number. The message had something to do with life or death or something like that. Call him."

■

A receptionist is generally an entry level position. She's among the lowest paid in an office full of high-priced executives or professionals. Yet she's the only one there who knows how to operate the phones.

It's amazing that many people have four years of college, possibly six years of post-graduate study, and never learned how to place an outgoing call.

■

If the receptionist takes a day off, many executives have to call 911 to help them place a call.

■

Of course, any receptionist who knows how to operate some of those telephone consoles can probably also fly a 747.

■

The receptionist is the attractive, bright, charming, personable person who greets you when you first enter an office. She goes out of her way to be helpful to you. Unless you're a vendor. Then she becomes the bouncer.

■

The receptionist is the first person you see when you visit an office, and the last person you see when you leave. And if she does her job right, she's sometimes the only person you see while you're there.

■

I've been in offices where the receptionist was tough. Some may say she was only doing her job, but I personally feel the strip search has no place in business.

■

Some receptionists can ask "May I help you" in such a way that if you answer you feel like you've just accepted a challenge for a duel.

■

One receptionist didn't mince words about her intentions. She said, "Mr. Wilson is in a meeting. Would you care to have a seat or should I book a room for you in a nearby hotel?"

■

Some receptionists are tough to get past. Visitors get the impression they only accepted this job as training for their real goal–to become checkpoint guards at the Berlin Wall.

. . . outwardly they wear high heels, an elegant business suit, and a sensible blouse; but inside they're wearing hob-nailed boots, and carrying an automatic weapon.

■

Businesses expect their receptionists to be firm. They should be well-groomed, personable, intelligent, and trained in karate, if necessary.

You know you're in for a long wait when the receptionist says, "He's in a meeting, but you're welcome to have a seat and wait. May I bring you a cup of coffee and perhaps a pillow and blanket?"

■

Receptionists should remember: it doesn't cost anymore to be pleasant to visitors. And if it did, it wouldn't be reflected in your paycheck.

■

All receptionists should be friendly, courteous, kind, and validate parking.

■

Some receptionists are always pleasant simply because they don't know what the hell is going on in the office. Some other receptionists are always grumpy simply because they're the only ones who do know what the hell is going on in the office.

SECRETARIES

Though it may sound blasphemous, God is not all-seeing, all-knowing, and all-powerful. His secretary is.

God is like all bosses. He can do all things except make His own coffee in the morning.

Well, He can make it, but He just changes it from water.

God hands out all the blessings, but His secretary shops for them.

■

Secretaries are the training wheels of executives.

■

Two of the saddest sights in the business world are a briefcase without a handle and an executive without a secretary.

■

An executive without a secretary is like a turtle without a shell . . . except the turtle probably moves faster.

. . . and gets more done.

■

When the boss doesn't show up for work, the secretary can find plenty to do. When the secretary doesn't show up for work, the boss has trouble finding his desk.

Every executive needs an efficient secretary. It's either that or learn to dial the phone himself.

■

If all the secretaries walked out, business would not shut down. But nobody would get any coffee.
. . . Well, not any *decent* coffee.

And no one would have a lunch reservation.

■

There would be no communication without secretaries. Who would get on the phone first?

■

A good secretary can do more than type and take dictation. A good secretary can also create the illusion that the boss is in charge.

■

A good secretary can manipulate the boss without ever letting him see the strings.

■

Behind every great secretary is a boss saying, "Tell them I'm at a meeting."

■

One secretary finally refused to answer the phone for her boss. She said, "Nine out of ten times it's for you, anyway."

■

There's a fine line between good secretarial work and a dictatorship.

■

There are those who say Hitler was a nice guy; his secretary wanted to conquer the world.

■

Napoleon Bonaparte once said to his secretary, "You, too, will be immortal."
She said, "Why?"
He said, "Because you are Napoleon's secretary."
She said, "Really? Give me the name of Alexander the Great's secretary."

■

An executive was dictating a letter to his secretary. He said, "Take this letter to the firm of Simmons, Lasker, & Bolton. Dear Gentlemen..."
The secretary said, "Boss, I hate to contradict you, but I've dated all three of those jerks, and there's not a one of them who's a gentleman."

SUPERVISORS

Supervisors are low men on the management totem pole. It's amazing how they can manage to get so much done with so many wooden heads above them.

■

I had one supervisor whose hobby was gardening. He used to get up bright and early on Saturday morning and putter around on his hands and knees in the garden. At least, that was the story that he fed the neighbors.

. . . the truth was he was just getting home from Friday night.

■

Gardening is good training for supervisory positions. Upper management likes to hire men who are used to being on their knees a lot.

■

Management does like to make supervisors out of men who raise roses. They like to have a man in that job who's used to handling thorns.

■

Handling flowers helps a man when it comes to handling men. We had one worker who wasn't producing, so the supervisor came down the aisle and watered him.

This gentleman immediately improved his output considerably. He didn't mind the water too much, but he knew the next step was fertilizer.

■

Two of a supervisor's toughest tasks are dealing with management and dealing with people.

. . . believe me, they're not the same.

■

A supervisor is a man in charge. He tells shipping where the product should go; he tells manufacturing where parts should go; and occasionally, he tells management where it can go.

■

The supervisor is the leader of the herd. When he's happy, his employees are happy. When he's upset, his employees are upset. When he's on vacation...

■

The supervisor is a man who can bring gaiety, laughter, and joy into the workplace . . . just by being absent.

The supervisor brings good news to some of his workers and bad news to others, but whatever the news he brings, it's always the same as the rumor you heard two or three weeks ago.

■

The supervisor has to tell little white lies every once in a while. He has to say, "I hope you're feeling better soon" when you call in sick on opening day of the World Series.

■

The supervisor is the sounding board between the office and the factory. He's the liaison between his department and other departments. He's the mediator between management and labor. He's a matador with bull coming at him from both sides.

■

When the last quitting bell sounds and he goes to that Big Management Association Dinner in the sky, St. Peter will stop him, reach for the Golden Book, and ask for his name and occupation.

He'll give his name and say, "I was a supervisor. "

St. Peter will close the book and say, "Enter! You've already been through hell."

THE PEOPLE WHO KEEP US IN BUSINESS

*If the customer is always right, why don't we let him
run our business?*

THE CUSTOMER

Customer: In the business world that's short for "If you've got the money, honey; I've got the time."

■

Whoever said "The customer is always right" was probably a customer.
If he was, he wasn't right.

■

Anyone who thinks the customer is always right has never sold door-to-door.

■

It's not that the customer is always right. It's that we want our competitors to tell him he's wrong.
. . . that way we get his future business.

■

The customer may not always be right, but he's always the one with the money.

■

The customer is the goose that lays the golden egg. Our job is to get him to lay them in our direction.

Customers come in many different sizes and shapes—credit cards, cash, checks . . .

■

Some businesses are strictly out for the money. The customer is merely the courier.

■

Some business people consider the customer a wallet with a person attached.

■

A business without customers is like a rope with only one end.
Even if you could find one, what would you do with it?

■

As long as you have customers, you'll have complaints. Unless you're an undertaker.

Come to think of it, they do, too. Lazarus demanded a refund.

■

If they can have "Pain-free Dentistry," why can't we have "Customer-free Profits?"

■

Did you know when bulls mate with cows on the farm it's referred to as "servicing?" It makes one a little wary of the term "customer service," doesn't it?

■

Customer service means you're still polite to the buyer even after the check clears.

■

Of course, some companies consider their product "customer revenge."

■

Hookers have the right idea. All of their customers are illegal.

■

We absolutely need customers. Without them we'd be like the Rabbi, Minister, and Priest who were playing some high stakes poker one night when the police raided the game. The police asked the Rabbi if he was gambling. He bowed his head, prayed silently for forgiveness and said, "No, I wasn't gambling." They asked the Minister if he had been gambling. He bowed his head and silently asked for forgiveness and said, "No, Officer, I was not gambling." Then the police asked the Priest if he was gambling. The Priest said, "With whom?"

A woman went into the corner butcher shop and ordered some sliced salami.

The butcher said, "How much do you want?"

She said, "Just slice; I'll tell you when."

He started slicing, and slicing.

He said, "This enough?"

She said, "Keep slicing."

He sliced a few more and asked again. "Now?"

She said, "Keep slicing please. I'll tell you when."

He sliced some more.

She finally said, "OK, stop there."

He stopped slicing.

She said, "I'll take the next three slices."

■

A salesman was having a heated discussion with one customer. Finally, the manager of the store rushed out and chastised the salesman.

He said, "How many times do I have to tell you? Don't argue with the customer. Our store policy is that the customer is always right."

The salesman said, "But that's just the point, Boss. The customer was arguing that he was wrong."

■

Many times we face customers who aren't too smart, but many times, too, it's the employee who is not too clever.

A man went into a hardware store and bought some rat poison.

The clerk said, "Should I wrap it for you?"

The man said, "No, I'll send the rats over and you can feed it to them personally."

■

A man stopped in at a bar on his way home from work. He ordered a shot of whiskey, and the bartender poured it for him.

He drank it down quickly and ordered another. The bartender poured him another.

Finally, the customer said to the bartender, "Are you the owner?"

The bartender said he was.

The customer said, "I'm a pretty successful businessman. I've had two drinks in here and I've got an idea for you that can double the amount of alcohol you sell."

The owner said, "What is it?"

The guy said, "Will you pick up my tab if I tell you?"

The bartender tore up the man's bill and said, "Now how can I double the amount of alcohol I sell."

The man said, "Fill up the glasses."

And left.

Sometimes customers have to endure a lot of hype, truth-bending, or downright lying from the salespeople they deal with. Here's a story that might apply:

Two men were comparing their fishing vacations. Like most good fishermen, each was trying to top the other.

The first man said, "I'm telling you, I found the greatest fishing spot in the entire North American Continent. I pulled in a rainbow trout from this stream that was the biggest trout I've ever laid eyes on. It was a size. It weighed 125 pounds. I'm telling you, 125 pounds."

The other guy said, "That's great. I was fishing, too, but I was doing salt-water fishing. I was just a few miles offshore in a place where a lot of old ships are supposed to have gone down, and the fish live and grow in these old sunken ships, you know. So I feel something on my line, and I pull and I tug and this thing feels like it weighs 500 pounds. Finally I pull it up and it's not a fish at all. It's an old ship's lantern, you know. It's a brass lamp that must be 200 years old, with a glass cylinder, and inside the cylinder, the lamp is still burning. I'm telling you it's still burning."

The first guy looks at him for awhile then says, "OK, I'll tell you what—let's compromise. I'll take 115 pounds off the trout if you'll blow out the light."

■

One customer summed up a salesman's exaggerated pitch with these words: "All right, quit lying already. I believe you."

COLLECTING FROM CUSTOMERS

They say "A fool and his money are soon parted." Most of our customers aren't fools.

■

One customer wrote to a manufacturer, "Send me your product. If it's any good, I'll send you a check." The manufacturer wrote back, "Send me your check. If it's any good, we'll send you our product."

■

Getting some customers to part with money is like pulling teeth. You have to give them novocaine first.

■

Some customers are so tight-fisted with their cash that if George Washington could talk it would have to be in a high pitched voice.

When they finally do open their wallets, George Washington blinks at the light.

Many customers go with the lowest bid and then don't even want to pay that.

■

Good workmen never consider a job completed until the check clears.

■

The Indians only got $24 worth of beads for the entire island of Manhattan. I'll bet you anything you want that at least 3 of those beads were for late charges.

■

The whole world wants delivery to be on time and payment to be delayed.

■

The next time you're in a traffic jam, consider that only three of those cars are paid for.

■

The Bible decreed that we "earn our bread by the sweat of our brow." But we have to sweat in a lot of other places before we collect for it.

■

I like the people who claimed that they couldn't pay for the newly installed burglar alarm because they didn't have any money.
. . . It makes you wonder why they needed the burglar alarm in the first place.

■

So many people are reluctant to pay, you could almost sell your product at cost and make a good living just off the late charges.

■

Business is so bad now that even those people who don't intend to pay, aren't buying.

■

You can understand why people don't want to part with their money. But they have to understand, once they take delivery, it's no longer their money.
. . . It's your money.

■

Despite what they say, you *can* have your cake and eat it, too. Just ask any baker who hasn't been paid yet.

■

It's expensive to constantly notify delinquent accounts that their payments are overdue. One enterprising company had so many they cut costs by dunning them in the form of a chain letter.

We're all guilty. "Let him who is without dunning notices cast the first payment."

■

People are reluctant to pay because of the unwritten law: The appliance breaks the day after the final payment is mailed in.

■

One gentleman went to a new doctor and inquired about costs. The doctor told him the initial visit would be $50. The man was furious. "Fifty dollars just for a look-see in the office. There may not be anything wrong with me." The doctor said it would be $75 for all visits after that. Now the man was incensed. "If I'm a good customer, I should get preferred rates. That's too much to pay just for a visit to a doctor."

Finally, the doctor said, "Look, why did you come to me if you couldn't afford it?" The man said, "Because I heard you're the best, and when it comes to my health, money is no object."

■

There's a tale about a struggling young actor who was cold and hungry while trying to make it in New York. He went into a cafeteria and had a full meal. When the check came, he confessed that he couldn't pay it.

He told how things weren't working out for him now, but if the proprietor would just wait a little while, he'd pay everything in full.

The proprietor said, "I'll just write your name on the wall, and when you get the money, you pay me." The actor said, "Wait a minute, I don't want all the other professionals who come in here to see that I'm doing so poorly I can't even buy myself lunch." The owner said, "Don't worry. Nobody'll see it. Your hat and coat will be hanging over it."

■

Here's a dunning notice that shows some humor and inventiveness:
Dear Mr. Wilson:
Our records indicate that we have already done more for you than your own mother did. We carried you for 15 months.

■

One power and light company, in a show of graciousness, sent out 113,000 letters to customers thanking them for being good customers and for paying their bills on time.

The cost of sending the letters came to $45,000 and was added to the company costs the next time they applied for a rate increase.

■

One man was even held in contempt of court for paying his bill as previously ordered by the court. The man had refused to pay $35 because he was unhappy with the merchandise. The store took him to court and the judge ordered that he pay in full.

He was held in contempt of court when he paid the entire bill in change molded into a huge vat of Jell-O.

■

Certain mobsters have their own way of collecting delinquent debts. One guy had to collect from a friend who owed several thousand dollars. The gangster said, "Look, I didn't want to lend you the money in the first place, but now that I did, you have to pay up immediately or I kill you."

The victim pleaded: "Look, we've been friends all our lives. I've done things for you; you've done things for me. Give me a break. I can't raise this kind of money this fast. Let me pay it off a little each week."

The hood compromised. He said, "OK, but just because we're friends. Each week, you pay me as much as you can, and I'll only wound you."

■

Here's a dunning notice that got some attention:

Dear Customer:

We agree that money isn't everything; often it's not even enough.

However we also agree with Woody Allen who said, "Money is better than poverty, if only for financial reasons."

We agree with Joe E. Lewis who said, "I've been rich and I've been poor. Rich is better."

We agree that money can't buy friends, but it can get you to hang around with a better class of enemies.

We agree that money is the root of all evil, but we're in there rooting.

We know that money can't buy happiness. In fact, it can't buy anything for us until you send us the damn money you owe us.

■

One poor gentlemen who was overwhelmed with bills and collection threats was honestly trying to square his account with everyone. He was sitting at his kitchen table writing the last of several checks when his wife came in and announced that she had just bought a new fur coat.

He said, "Damn, everytime I just about make ends meet, you go out shopping and move the ends."

■

A man had borrowed money from a business associate with the clear understanding that he would pay it back in full after six months. When the due date arrived, though, the man couldn't repay. He begged for an extension, but the lender was furious with him. He said, "You either pay me back on the day we agreed, or I'll take you to court."

The night before the payment had to be made the debtor still had no money. He couldn't sleep worrying about it. He paced back and forth in his bedroom.

Finally, his wife said, "Come to sleep."

He said, "I can't sleep worrying about the money."

She said, "Then pay the money back."

He said, "I don't have the money to pay it back."

She said, "Then don't pay it back."

He said, "I have to pay it back. It's *his* money."

She said, "If it's *his* money, then come to bed. Let *him* walk the floor."

*What a bright world this would be if all new employees
were half as good as their resumes said they would be.*

RESUMES

There are two times when a person can be a hero–in daydreams and in a resume.

■

It's depressing to think that our professional lives can be reduced to one side of a single sheet of paper.

■

Resumes are a single sheet of fiction that we write and hope someone else will provide the happy ending.

■

Resumes tell only half the story, which is about four times the truth.

■

Resumes should be written on one side of a single sheet of paper, with margins large enough for the reader to add a few notes and a grain of salt.

■

About all one can tell from a resume is that the author either owns a typewriter or knows someone who does.

Hiring a worker from a resume is like trying to hire a ball player from his bubblegum card.

■

Workers should be hired the same way the Church canonizes saints—on the basis of a resume and two validated miracles.

■

In the business world, we call it a resume; in the crime world, they call it a 'rap sheet.'

■

It's sad when you reduce your entire professional life to one sheet of paper and discover the margins are more interesting than the typing.

■

Some people write creative resumes about themselves that are so enticing that they'd love to meet the person who could live up to them.

■

Whoever said "Honesty is the best policy" obviously never had to write a resume.

■

Resumes are hard to read. It's the combination of white lies on white paper.

■

Always leave plenty of margin space on your resume. That's where the people who read them jot in the truth.

■

Sometimes employers are so impressed by your resume that they want to hire you on the spot. Which puts pressure on you. Do you want to work for anyone that gullible?

■

A resume should list only the highlights of your professional career, if any.

■

Resumes are important. They are something you write about your past that could affect your future.

■

It's funny how self-centered we get when we write our resumes. Do you think anyone at IBM really cares what your hobbies are?

Some resumes are easy to see through. Like the twenty-five year old hopeful who listed 36 years of experience.

. . . He claimed he worked a lot of overtime.

■

Horace Greeley was a journalist, a politician, and the founder of the New York Tribune. He's also noted as the man who first wrote, "Go west, young man." He must have typed that epigram, though, because his handwriting was practically illegible.

Once he wrote a note to a lackluster employee dismissing him. The note supposedly accused the young man of gross neglect of duty.

The fired employee later met Greeley and thanked him for the note. He said that it had been most useful.

Greeley wondered how such a condemning note could be useful.

The man explained, "Nobody could read it, so I declared it a letter of recommendation, gave it my own interpretation, and obtained several first-class situations by it. I am really very much obliged to you."

■

President Lincoln realized that in government, as in the private sector, prize positions are often offered on the basis of "who you know" not "what you know."

A woman once pleaded with Lincoln. She said, "Mr. President, you must give me a colonel's commission for my son. I demand it of you, Sir, not as a favor but as a right. My grandfathers fought at Lexington; my uncle was the only man who did not run at Bladensburg; my father fought at New Orleans, and my husband was killed at Monterey."

Lincoln said, "Madam, I guess your family has done enough for our country. It's time to give somebody else a chance."

■

A church committee was having final discussions to decide who would become their new pastor. Only a few candidates remained.

One board member had a favorite and he tried to influence the other members of the committee with a little white lie.

He said, "I think I should mention about Reverend So-and-so that he is an extremely pious clergyman. He fasts every single day of the week, so that he will be well prepared for his preaching on Sunday."

Another board member said, "Wait a minute. I've just been in town a few days and I saw your Reverend at the local diner enjoying a very substantial lunch."

The guy said, "Oh. Well, that also shows you that on top of being very holy, he's also very modest. He just eats on weekdays to hide the fact that he's fasting."

One job applicant submitted a lengthy resume. It was almost 10 pages long. He used a device that authors have used in submitting manuscripts for years. He stuck two of the pages together with a bit of glue on the edges.

When the man was turned down for the job and his resume returned, he noticed that the pages were still stuck together.

He went to the man who was doing the hiring and complained bitterly. He said, "You never even got to pages three and four. How can you express an opinion of me when you only read one or two pages of my resume?"

The man said, "I would think that only reading page one, and then returning the rest, would be expressing my opinion."

•

A faithful employee was passed over for a promotion. An outsider got the job. This man went to the boss to express his dissatisfaction.

The boss was understanding, but firm. He tossed the other gentleman's resume to the employee and said, "Glance through that."

The man did. It was impressive.

The boss asked, "Now, do you think I hired the right man?"

The employee said, "Well if you're going to be swayed by ability..."

•

A gentleman applied for a job and the personnel manager told him that the resume he submitted was to be no longer than one side of a sheet of paper.

The man submitted several sheets and told the interviewer, "I'm sorry, Sir, but my list of accomplishments is so long that I can't reduce them to one page. Is there anything we can do about that?"

The interviewer said, "There certainly is. I can guarantee that after this interview, your resume won't be any longer."

THE JOB APPLICATION FORM

If Personnel Managers ran the military, prisoners of war would be required to give their name, rank, serial number, and the salary they expected.

... also, state their reasons for leaving their last prison.

•

It takes some courage to write in the real salary that you hope to get. For a long time, in the space after "salary," I used to write in, "If it's not too inconvenient."

One job application read:

Starting salary at previous employment . . . $22,400

Ending salary at previous employment . . . $22,400

Reason for leaving previous employment . . . $22,400

■

Why do we go to the trouble of calling them first and last names when every company wants "last name first, and first name last?"

. . . and God help any applicant who puts the middle initial in the middle.

. . . it should go at the end. Right after first name last.

■

The job application tells a lot about prospective employees. Like do they know how to use a ball point pen.

■

One person spent 48 minutes completing 8 different forms, all with triple carbons. She was applying for the position of "Efficiency Expert."

■

Some companies require psychological evaluation to insure that everyone that works there is sound. That may explain why so many upper management openings are filled from outside.

■

Some of the psychological tests are weird. They must be written by people who couldn't pass them.

■

Besides, no one really wants all normal people working in a company. It makes for terribly dull Christmas parties.

■

The sex question is the most misunderstood. Many think the "m" or "f" following it means "many" or "few."

■

I saw one application where the question said "Sex?" and the applicant wrote in "occasionally . . . but never during working hours."

■

Remember the good old days, when the sex question only had two possible spaces you could check?

■

Our world is getting so crazy today that after the job application form question "sex" there are three spaces marked "m," "f," and "other."

Job applications you shouldn't accept:
- Any where the applicant prefers crayon to ball point pen.
- Any where the answers are funnier than the questions
- Any where parole officers are listed under "references."
- Any where "witchcraft" is listed under "hobbies."

Job Applications you should always accept:
- Any where the last name first and the first name last followed by the middle initial (if any) are exactly the same as your boss's, except followed by "Jr."

■

A young job hopeful was taking an exam for employment. One of the questions was, "How far is the earth from sun?" The kid wrote, "I am unable to ascertain the exact distance with any acceptable accuracy, however, I do believe the sun is far enough away from the earth that it will not interfere with the proper performance of my duties should I get this job."

He got the job.

■

A test given to applicants asked, "How many British soldiers landed on American soil during the American Revolution?"

One hopeful wrote, "I don't know exactly, but I'm sure it was a lot more than went home again."

THE JOB INTERVIEW

A job interview is like meeting your girlfriend's parents for the first time. Except the parents ask you how much you make; the interviewer *tells* you.

■

The job interview is a religious experience. That's when you go into the office full of faith and hope on the chance that they might show a little charity.

It'd be nice to have a job without job interviews, but it's a little like wishing for marriage without mothers-in-law.

■

Your palms generally sweat when you interview for a new job. That's why most of the interviewers shakes hands with you at the beginning.

■

Always remember to clear two things before going in for your interview–your throat, and your police record.

The best answer to the question "How much money do you expect to earn?" is "All of it."

·

People expect you to be nervous for your job interview, but it is considered bad policy to bite your nails—or anybody else's.

·

The job interview is important. They say that doctors bury their mistakes; personnel managers send them to work in another department.

·

One man was asked during his interview if any of his relatives suffered from insanity. He said, "No. They all seem to enjoy it."

·

Personnel Managers should carefully screen young applicants because in today's business world, the only way to get rid of them after they're hired is retirement.

·

My boss used to tell the Personnel Manager to consider job applicants as carefully as if he were going to marry them. He used to tell him that until he met the Personnel Manager's wife.

·

You know it's going to be a tough interview when . . .

. . . the company representative invites you to have a chair and allows you one phone call before the interview starts.

. . . the company representative opens with: "Anything you say can and will be used against you."

. . . the executive who interviews you wears military boots, a monocle, and carries a swagger stick.

. . . you go into the interviewer's office and notice all the walls are padded.

. . .you notice that one of the plaques on the interviewer's wall says that he was the winner of last year's "Rubber Hose Award."

...the interviewer's first action is to make a paper airplane out of your resume.

. . . you don't know if it's real or your imagination running wild, but the interviewer looks—and dresses like—Mr. T.

. . . the interviewer offers you a cup of coffee? a cigarette? a blindfold?

. . . you're escorted into the interviewer's office by the company chaplain.

You know it *was* a tough interview when . . .

. . . the interviewer thanks you and invites you back in a week or two to take a make-up interview.

■

When James Joyce was a young man and badly in need of funds, he applied for a job at a bank.

"Do you smoke?" the interviewer asked

Joyce said, "No."

The bank employee asked, "Do you drink?"

Joyce told him he didn't.

The man asked, "Do you go with girls?"

Joyce said, "No."

The interviewer said, "Get outta here. You'd probably rob the bank."

■

President Lincoln once turned down a person recommended for a position because he didn't like his face.

One of his cabinet members argued with the President. He said that he didn't think not liking someone's face was a sufficient and satisfactory explanation for turning down an applicant.

Lincoln didn't agree. He said, "Every man over forty is responsible for his face."

■

Sometimes the wrong answer to a question is the right answer.

A youngster once had a reputation for being a dummy. People would give him the option of picking either a nickel or a dime and the child always picked the nickel.

One man didn't quite believe the story, so he tried the youngster. He presented a shiny new nickel and dime and asked which the youngster wanted.

The man cautioned the lad to think carefully before choosing.

The boy said, "Well, the nickel is so much bigger, and it has a big buffalo on it, and an Indian. I love Indians. Yes, I think I'll take the nickel."

The man said, "Son, don't you know that a dime is worth twice as much money as the nickel?"

The boy said, "Yes sir, I know that."

The man said, "Then why in the world would you choose the nickel?"

The boy said, "Because if I ever take the dime, people will stop playing this game with me."

■

An old sea captain was quizzing a young sailor who wanted work as a seaman on the captain's vessel.

The captain asked, "What would you do if you were on watch and a sudden storm came up from the starboard?"

The sailor said, "I'd immediately throw out an anchor, sir."

The captain said, "Suppose another storm started approaching aft?"

The sailor said, "I'd throw out another anchor, sir."

The captain said, "Well, now what if a third storm started brewing forward?"

The sailor said, "I'd throw out an anchor, sir."

The captain said, "Just a minute, young man. Where the hell are you getting all these anchors?"

The sailor said, "The same place you're getting all the damn storms."

■

A man was being interviewed by a company psychiatrist for employment. They wanted to test his integrity.

The doctor said, "If you found a million dollars, and you could find out who the owner was, but no one in the world would ever know that you found the money, what would you do?"

The job applicant said, "If it belonged to a poor family, I'd give it back."

■

An employer was interviewing a middle aged job applicant. The man had been a pro-football player, was now retired, and looking for regular employment.

The employer asked, "How were your grades in school?"

The man answered honestly. He said, "Well, Sir, they were good and bad. When I first went to college, I was at the bottom of my class. Then I started playing football and made All-American and I shot up to somewhere about the middle. Then about three years ago, there was a fire at the school. All the records were destroyed, and I decided then that I finished third in my graduating class."

■

This is not a job interview, but it reveals a lot about qualifications.

An All-American football player was being suspended from athletics because of poor scholastic ability. His coach pleaded his case eloquently before the board.

The coach said, "Ladies and gentlemen, we are supposed to be teachers. Each one of us knows the value of an adequate education. If this lad is banned from the football squad, he'll drop out of school. He'll never complete his college work. I beg of you, give this boy another examination. Yes, I'm asking because he's valuable to our football squad, but I'm also asking because a mind is a terrible thing to waste."

The board relented. They agreed to ask the young man one question. If he answered it correctly, he could play; if he answered wrong, he was out.

The school representative said to the player, "How much is 13 and 13?"

The kid thought. He agonized. He struggled. He counted on his fingers. He finally said, "Twenty-six."

The coach immediately jumped up and shouted, "Give him another chance."

HIRING

Hiring is a frightening task for an executive. Very few new employees come with a warranty.

■

Hiring is the most painstaking decision an executive has to make. Make a mistake with anything else, it can be fixed. Make a mistake in hiring and you may have to share an office with it.

■

Hiring is always a risk. There are many things the resume can't do. One of those is predict the future.

■

Hiring is an inexact science. To test that theory just look at some of the clowns who work with you.

. . . they're probably looking at you.

■

Hiring is exciting, though, because of it's unpredictability. It's like searching for the prize in a box of Cracker Jack.

. . . often with comparable results.

■

Hiring a new employee is like having a child except without the nine months to prepare for it.

■

New employees are like new puppies–you have to clean up after them until they get the hang of it.

■

There's a serious generation gap in business recruiting. People are hired at the entry level by people at the exit level.

PEOPLE ON THE WAY OUT

All good things must come to an end...hopefully with a comfortable serverance arrangement.

FIRING

Firing is an interesting part of an executive's duties. It can be one of the most trying; then again, it can be one of the most rewarding.

■

Firing a troublesome employee is a relief. It's like getting rid of a headache by using his head.

■

A termination notice is one time when it's definitely better to give than to receive.

■

There are no easy ways to fire anyone, but they're generally all easier than keeping him.

■

My boss once promised me a little something extra in my paycheck. It was my severance pay.

■

I've been kicked out of many companies. That's why now if I drop a pencil, I don't dare bend over to pick it up.

Whoever said, "Parting is such sweet sorrow," probably got a large severance settlement.

■

Firing is like a divorce except the alimony doesn't last as long.

■

Generally you know when you're about to be fired, but sometimes your head has a surprised look on it when it rolls to a stop.

■

There is a time when your own head-rolling is welcome. That's when it's the only part of your body the company hasn't yet cut off.

■

Harry S. Truman summed it up pretty well: "It's a recession when your neighbor loses his job; it's a depression when you lose your own."

■

Will Rogers spoke about unemployment, too. He said, "I can't figure whether we made any progress in the last hundred years or not. If a man wasn't working, he sat in front of the grocery store and whittled. Also, if a man was idle in one part of the country, you didn't hear about it in the other parts of the country.

■

It's important for executives to keep track of who they're hiring and firing. Sir Lew Grade, the legendary theatrical entrepreneur in England, when he was an agent saw an act called Winters and Fielding at the Old Metropolitan Theatre.

They impressed him so much that he rushed backstage, not only to compliment them, but also to woo them away from their present management and make them part of his stable.

"I can make you big stars," he said, "and also get you much bigger money. I know I can do better than your present agent."

The performers seemed impressed.

Lew Grade asked, "By the way, who are your agents?" They said, "Lew and Leslie Grade."

■

Some executives simply refuse to call it hiring and firing.

In 1985 one of the nation's top ten oil companies terminated 40 of the 550 people who worked at its corporate headquarters. The people had no job and received no salary, but the company insisted that they weren't "laid off."

Instead a company spokesperson said, "We're managing our staff's resources. Sometimes you manage them up, and sometimes you manage them down."

Another large corporation in 1979 euphemistically referred to some firings as "headcount reductions."

■

Another large corporation in 1986 used this sort of double talk to mask their head-rolling binge. Instead of simply saying "Sorry, Charlie, but your services are no longer needed," they said there were "surpluses" in several of their divisions. To correct that situation, a new "force management plan" would be introduced and implemented. The new plan was to correct "force imbalance."

(It doesn't sound like anyone's been fired yet, does it?)

They went on to say that once "surplus managers" were identified, (uh-oh) "they would be given a separation payment to leave."

(That might be called firing somebody.)

Many of these separations, the company confessed, would be the "involuntary" kind.

■

Sometimes firing a person is not easy. General Ulysses S. Grant, during the height of the Civil War, argued vehemently and repeatedly with the War Department to have one incompetent General removed from his assignment, but to no avail.

Finally, in desperation, he sent a telegram to them saying: "I beg that you relieve General (so-and-so), at least until all danger is over."

■

One jazz musician cut through all the red tape of head-chopping.

He had a small combo and wanted to get rid of one guy who was not only a bad musician, but troublesome on the tour. He wanted him gone *immediately*.

He told the guy, but the musician pleaded. "Let me finish the tour." No.

"You gotta keep me on, man. I need the money." The answer was still no.

Now the musician leaned on legalities. "You can't just dump me cold, man. I got a contract that says you gotta give me two weeks notice."

The band leader said, "Let's just say that two weeks from now you will have known about this for four."

■

One poor race horse tried and tried but just couldn't quite run fast enough to land in the money. The owner was spending quite a bit of money on his care and feeding and naturally had to expect some return.

The jockey, too, liked the horse and tried to help, but nothing seemed to work.

Finally, the owner came to the stables before an important race and said to the jockey, "Either that nag wins some money today or tomorrow he's going to be pulling a milk wagon."

The horse panted and sweated, stretched and strained, but just couldn't keep up with the other thoroughbreds. The jockey wouldn't give up, though. He egged the horse on. He shouted encouragement to the animal. He started to give it the whip, doing everything he could to get the horse to go faster.

Finally the horse turned and said, "Hey, man, take it easy on that whip. I got to get up and go to work in the morning."

■

There was once a hard-nosed boss who was famous for firing workers he didn't care for.

Once he called a worker into his office and asked, "Are you happy working here."

The terrified man said, "Yes, sir. Very happy."

The boss said, "Then you're fired. I don't want anyone here who's content with the kind of money I pay."

RETIREMENT

There's no justice. Youth is wasted on the young, and retirement is wasted on the old.

■

Retirement means you can do nothing all day, and you don't even have to show up at the office to do it anymore.

■

Retirement is when you can sit back leisurely and think of all those things you should've said to the boss.

■

Retirement is doing absolutely nothing. It's a lot like work only you get paid less for it.

■

Some people wonder what they're going to do when they retire, which is a heluva lot more than they ever did when they were working.

■

Some wives don't like retirement. They say, "I married him for better or for worse, but I had no idea that would include lunch every day."

■

Retirement is a time when we sit around doing nothing all day. That's because whatever we do want to do hurts too much.

Retirement is when you can get out of bed anytime of the day you want to . . . and as many times during the day as you want to.

■

Race horses are retired to stud. That would be a good idea for us, but they'd have to do it before age 65.

■

Some workers hit 65. Our guest of honor beat the hell out of it.

■

My friend says he can do the same things at 65 that he did when he was 18. It kind of gives you an idea of what a rotten youth he must have had.

■

Our guest of honor has reached the age of 65—the hard way . . . with the same body he started with.

■

Retirement is when your favorite indoor activity becomes prune juice.

■

My friend says when he gets up in the morning now he doesn't feel 65. In fact, he doesn't feel anything until noon.
. . . by then, it's time for his nap.

■

My friend says he does the same things at 65 that he did when he was 40. He just takes a nap after each one now.

■

For some people retirement is when it takes you longer to rest up after doing something than it took you to do it.

■

Our guest of honor says that for his retirement he just wants to lie back and do absolutely nothing. He'll just pretend he's a politician.

■

He's going to enjoy doing nothing during his retirement. He left word for his fanny not to move at all unless it's on fire.

■

He left word with his family and neighbors, if they see anything moving at all, they're to call a doctor. It's a convulsion.

He may even give up sex. He says it's still fun, but it's such a waste of lying-in-bed time.

■

Our guest of honor doesn't want any excitement to interfere with his retirement. If Dolly Parton comes on TV, he'll look at her face.

■

He won't even watch daytime soap operas during his retirement. He gets jealous of people who spend more time in bed than he does.

■

Our retiree told me: "I used to sow some wild oats, but not anymore. Not when your plow horse is dragging like mine is."

■

Our retiree says that his golf game keeps him young, and it's true. You have to be in pretty good shape to get to some of the places where he hits his drives.

He doesn't swing like an old man. An old woman, maybe . . .

■

Our retiree is like good wine. He gets better with age. Of course, you have to let him breathe a little longer.
    . . . and it's a lot more effort popping his cork.

■

Our friend may be retiring, but he still grabs for all the gusto he can . . . even if it's just for something to hold onto.

■

65 is such a nice round age, and our guest of honor hasn't had anything nice and round for quite some time.

■

You know you're getting up in years when:
    . . . prune juice makes you light headed.
    . . . you go in for a transplant only to find out they don't make those parts anymore.
    . . . you try to recapture your youth only to find out your memory isn't that good.
    . . . when Boy Scouts *don't help you across the street. They figure if you don't make it all the way across, they won't get credit for a good deed.*
    . . . when your life flashes before your eyes and you fall asleep during it.
    . . . when your life flashes before your eyes and it's so long it has an intermission.

. . . when your doctor starts calling you into the office first.

. . . when someone tells you that sex is like riding a bike—you never forget how. Then it dawns on you—you have no desire to ride a bike, either.

. . . when the spirit is willing, but the flesh is weak.

■

Retirement means twice as much husband on half as much money.—*Anonymous*

■

Stephen Leacock offers these words to young fellows looking forward to retirement: Have nothing to do with it. Listen: it's like this, Have you ever been out for a late autumn walk in the closing part of the afternoon, and suddenly looked up to realize that the leaves have practically all gone? And the sun had set and the day gone before you knew it—and with that a cold wind blows across the landscape? That's retirement.

■

After Calvin Coolidge left the White House, he had to fill out a form to confirm his membership in the National Press Club. In the space marked "Occupation," the former President simply wrote "retired." The next space said, "Remarks." Coolidge wrote, "and glad of it."

■

Bernard Baruch had a press conference on his 95th birthday. He announced to the journalists that during the coming year he planned to learn to speak Greek fluently. One of the reporters asked, "Mr. Baruch, you're 95 years old. Why would you want to learn to speak Greek now?" Baruch said, "I am 95 years old. It's now or never."

■

W. Somerset Maugham spoke at a party honoring him on his 80th birthday. Maugham said, "There are many virtues in growing old." Then he paused. It didn't seem as if he would continue. People shuffled and coughed nervously. The audience was embarrassed and didn't know what to do to help the guest of honor. Maugham put his hand up to show that everything was all right, then continued: ". . . I'm just trying to think what they are."

■

George Burns enjoys his non-retirement and takes his age in stride. Burns says, "When I get up in the morning the first thing I do is read the obituaries. If my name's not in there, I shave."

The father of basketball great, Bill Russell, had a clever response when someone asked him why he hadn't retired yet.

Mr. Russell said, "I gave them thirty good years of my life. Now I want to give them a few of the bad ones."

■

One gentleman's wife summed up her thoughts on her husband's retirement. She said, "I know I promised to love, honor, and obey, in sickness and in health until death do us part; but I didn't know it didn't know it would include having him around the house everyday for lunch."

■

One older employee decided that the company hadn't done enough for his retirement, so before leaving the company he embezzled a few bucks to help see him through his golden years.

He got caught, prosecuted, convicted, and sentenced to 45 years in prison.

The gentleman said, "Your honor, I'm 65 years old now. I'll never live long enough to serve that severe a sentence."

The judge was very considerate and said, "Just do the best you can."

MANDATORY RETIREMENT

Mandatory retirement . . . the kitchen disposal unit of Industry.

■

The company doesn't want you when you're old and useless. They prefer people who are young and useless.

■

Mandatory retirement is when management stuffs you into a paper bag and puts you on the doorstep to be picked up by the Goodwill Industries people.

■

They call it "putting you out to pasture," which is a fitting name for it because grass is usually about all you can afford to eat.

■

A wise man prepares financially for his leisure years. Take pictures over the years of some key executives at the office Christmas parties.

. . . it's called the "Polaroid Pension Plan."

Remember, blackmail is better than no mail at all.

It's a time when you don't have to get up in the morning, you have no scheduled meetings to attend, you can do whatever you want whenever you want to. So what does management give you? A watch.

■

One retiree summed it up nicely. He said, "It's not that I feel so useless. It's that I'm not getting paid as much for it."

■

With some employees you wonder how you'll ever get along without them; with some you wonder what to get them as a going away gift; with others you wonder how they or you will know when they've retired.

■

One manager made the following presentation to a retiring employee: "We wanted to give you something you've had your eye on since you began working here." Then he gave him the clock on the wall.

■

A few parting comments from managers to retiring employees:

. . . We don't know how we'll ever replace you. That's because we haven't yet been able to figure out what you do.

. . . As of today, Charlie becomes a gentleman of leisure, only now, Thank God, he does it on his own time.

. . . May God speed your way. Lord knows, nothing we did around here could.

. . . We feel we're not losing a worker; we're gaining a parking space.

. . . We feel the same way about you as we do about all workers who leave us. We're not losing a friend; we're gaining a desk to rifle.

. . . We want you to go home and do absolutely nothing. And don't worry in the least about us. We have plenty of people who do absolutely nothing right here.

. . . We know you'll enjoy your leisure time at home. You always did around here.

. . . It's going to be hard to replace you, quite frankly because upper management doesn't think it's necessary.

. . . You'll be gone but not forgotten. No, we'll be fixing some of the things you've done for years to come.

. . . You'll always have a place in our hearts, which, as you know, is more than you ever had in our parking lot.

George Burns had this to say about madatory retirment: "Retirement at sixty-five is ridiculous. When I was sixty-five, I still had pimples.

Someone once asked George Burns when he was going to retire. He said, "To what?"

■

Thomas Edison stayed eternally young by continuing to work. He was still inventing when he was in his eighties.

When he and Henry Ford visited the home of their mutual friend, Luther Burbank, in California, they were asked to sign a guest book. Beside the space for the name and address was a space marked "interests." Edison wrote in that space, "Everything."

■

One man was very unhappy when he finally retired and discovered that his pension was not anywhere near what he had hoped it would be.

He said at his retirement party, "Working for this company is like an expensive violin. Once the music has ended, the strings are still attached."

■

A retiree went to his doctor complaining about a pain in his left knee.

The doctor said, "I think it's old age."

The man said, "Baloney. My right knee is the same age and it feels fine."

■

A man was retired early from his company. He didn't like it. He fought it. But they retired him anyway. At his farewell party, his boss spoke. During his speech, the guest of honor dozed off.

The boss seized that opportunity to editorialize. He said, "Charlie here just dozed off. I think that says something about his age."

Charlie's eyes opened wide at that. He stood up and said, "When I fell asleep during your speech I wasn't showing my age, I was expressing an opinion."

■

Some men still stay active after retirement.

Two women were doing some back-fence gossiping one afternoon. One woman said, "I probably shouldn't be telling you this, but I think it's my duty as a friend. The men at the local bar are all talking about it—that your husband is chasing after women.

The other one said, "My husband is chasing after women?"

Her friend said, "That's right, and that's dangerous, at his age. What is he? Seventy?"

The other woman said, "He's seventy-two, and I say it's all right if he chases women. Dogs chase cars, too, but when they catch one, can they drive it?"

One hard working employee found it hard to fill time after his mandatory retirement. For the first time in his life he went to see a football game.

When he returned, his wife asked what it was like.

He said, "It was a lot like my retirment party. A big crowd of people come to see you kick off."

■

One ornery old gentleman was not pleased about having to retire from the work he loved. He didn't know what to do with all the leisure time he would have. He tried to find loopholes in the retirement regulations, but he couldn't. He pleaded with the company but they were inflexible.

Everyone knew he was unhappy about retiring and they feared that he would make a bitter speech at his farewell party.

He seemed to begin that way. He said, "I feel energetic and I feel healthy, but the company says I can't work. What am I to do? Now race horses retire to stud. Hey! there's an idea."

PENSION

Pension is when you get paid for a service you don't even perform anymore. It's like alimony.

■

A pension is nice. It's a going away gift to yourself.

■

When you're on pension, the money may not be much, but the working conditions are fabulous.

■

A pension is the ideal way to get a check–without having a boss hand it to you.

■

A pension gives a retiree independence. It affords one the option of either becoming a senior citizen or an old fart.

■

One problem with a pension, though–who do you go to to ask for a raise?

■

One nice thing about retiring to a pension–you're always assured of a parking place.

A pension used to be money you received long after you became non-productive. Today's workers consider money they receive after becoming non-productive their weekly paycheck.

■

A pension is money you receive for doing absolutely nothing. The trouble is, it's hard to earn overtime.

■

A pension is money you get for doing absolutely nothing. The only other person who gets that is a professional eunuch.

■

A pension enables one to enjoy the Golden Years with dignity . . . not much money, but dignity.

■

The company should contribute to your income when you're old and feeble. They're the ones who made you that way.

■

I knew one worker whose income actually went up when he retired. Apparently, he was better at doing nothing than he was at doing something.

■

All your life you learn that money can't buy happiness. When you go on pension you learn that it often doesn't buy groceries.

■

Wise workers prepare for their pension years. They begin to taper off on food, clothing, and shelter.

■

To all retirees I say, "Take your pension check and run with it. You certainly can't afford to take a plane or a bus."

■

Some people travel in their golden years. They see things, do things, buy things. These people are either happy pensioners or suspected embezzlers.

■

Pretty soon you'll be living on a pension. You may find that harder than anything you ever did in this office.

All pensioners should remember the words of some anonymous comedian who said, "I now have enough money to last me the rest of my life . . . unless I want to buy something."

■

Most pensions become effective around age 65, which is just the opposite of most pensioners.

■

One old pensioner went to his golf club to resign. The pro there asked him why.

He said, "I'm getting too old for golf. No one wants to play with me anymore and besides my eyes are so bad I can never see where the ball goes."

The pro said, "Nonsense. I'll team you up with old Pops. He's older than you are, he loves to play golf, and he's got eyes like a hawk. He'll spot the ball for you."

So they tried a round together. Our pensioner hit his first drive, turned to Pops and said, "Did you see the ball?"

Pops said, "Yep."

The pensioner said, "Where'd it go?"

Pops said, "I forget."

PEOPLE ON THE WAY UP AND DOWN

Few things are more disheartening than the realization that somehow "your career" has become "a job."

THE CORPORATE LADDER

The worst thing about being low man on the corporate totem pole is that you have so many wooden heads above you.

■

You meet the same people on the way down the corporate ladder as you meet on the way up. Except when you're on your way down, they're happier to see you.

■

The corporate ladder may be the only ladder in the world that you climb with your head and not your feet.

■

The corporate hierarchy is like watching a parade. No matter where you are someone else wants to be there.

■

The ladder is a fitting metaphor for the corporate hierarchy because as you look above you, you see mostly asses.

The ladder is a fitting metaphor for the corporate hierarchy, also because you climb it with your hands and feet. That leaves your teeth free to snarl and bite.

■

You climb the corporate ladder by stepping on just one rung at a time . . . or whoever happens to be on that rung at the time.

■

If the corporate ladder is just symbolic, how come most of my business suits have footprints on the back?

■

You should never climb the corporate ladder so quickly that you forget about those behind you. Take time to grease the rung you just left.

■

The trouble with executive competition is that when you get to the top of the ladder, management just brings in another ladder.
. . . Either that or they merge with another ladder company.
. . . Also, you'll notice very few ladders are built with rest stops.

■

Management always has you. No matter how high you climb, they still own the ladder.

■

Some ambitious executives are ruthless. It's amazing the depths they'll sink to to rise to new heights.

■

Remember, your mobility must always be upwards. ON the corporate ladder, "lateral" is a four-letter word.

■

As soon as you hit that corporate ladder you begin climbing, and you continue climbing until you either finish or are finished.
Sometimes you wonder if it is a ladder. It seems more like you're climbing a down escalator.

■

Executives can be ruthless, but nice. They push you off the ladder, then take up an office collection for a going away party.

■

If someone falls off the corporate ladder, it's not considered a tragedy. It's considered a job opening.

To me, it's kind of like dancing. No matter where I go on the dance floor, someone else seems to have gotten there first.

■

"The only things that evolve by themselves in an organization are disorder, friction, and malperformance." —*Peter Drucker*

■

Sometimes we overestimate our executives at the top of the ladder.

President Coolidge once invited several guests to sail with him along the Potomac in the Presidential Yacht.

A few of the guests noticed that the President stood alone at the rail gazing over the waters. They wondered what momentous thoughts were racing through his mind, what weighty problems he might be meditating on. They left him alone to his private contemplation.

Later Coolidge turned and motioned him for others to join. When they did, he pointed out over the sea and said, "That gull over there hasn't moved in twenty minutes. I think it's dead."

■

Not all people at the top of the executive ladder are geniuses. One CEO was on an outing with a dozen of his top executives. During their walk he said, "Look! There's a dead bird."

Eight of the executives looked up.

POSITIVE ATTITUDE

There are hundreds of books written every year that tell you that you can be anything you want and do anything you want. I guess none of those authors wanted the book to be a best seller.

■

Some companies encourage their employees to use a positive attitude to get what they want; other companies simply assign parking spaces.

■

You show me an employee who can't wait to get out of bed in the morning to go to work and I'll show you an employee whose company better have a good psychiatric medical plan.

■

If you can't wait to get out of bed in the morning to go to work, you're either in the right job or on the wrong mattress.

For many executives the toughest part of the day is around three o'clock. That's when they have to decide whether they're tired or lazy.

■

One executive said he liked employees who could think for themselves. It made it easier on them when they began looking for new employment.

He encouraged employees to think for themselves as long as they thought what he told them.

■

One manager said to his staff, "I'm sometimes right and I'm sometimes wrong. A positive attitude on your part is to agree with me in both cases."

He went on to say that he encouraged disagreement among his executives, even if they disagreed with him. He said, "All of you are entitled to your own stupid opinions."

■

This executive had the right mental attitude. He said, "I may have my faults, but being wrong has never been one of them."

That's a little better than the boss who may be wrong, but is never in doubt.

■

Working people are required many times each day to force themselves to use a positive mental attitude to overcome adversity on the job–especially if they work in a place that has a coin-operated coffee machine.

■

In the business world there is no substitute for enthusiasm. Although, kissing up to the boss works pretty well.

■

In the business world, a positive attitude is the fastest way to success–unless the boss happens to have a single daughter.

■

Psychiatrists say if you think about something long enough and hard enough, you will become that. I figure in about four weeks I will become Bo Derek.

■

The prime example of a positive attitude was General Custer when he first saw the Indians riding over the ridge toward them. He turned to his men and shouted, "Take no prisoners."

A company executive came out to a worksite one day to inspect the workmanship on the job. He came up to one carpenter and asked what he was doing. The guy said, "What does it look like I'm doing? I'm nailing this piece of cheap plywood to the floor and I don't have time to chew the fat with you, because this cheap company pays me on a piece work basis. So the sooner I get this piece of crap nailed down, I can move onto the next piece of crap and maybe make a few bucks today."

The executive moved on to a man who was laying bricks. He asked what he was doing. The man said, "I'm mixing mortar that is going to tenderly and devotedly hold each of these bricks in place. And one by one I'm going to set these bricks until they begin to take shape. They will rise row by row towards the heavens and eventually form a tall tower, the bell tower of a church. It will stand for years and years and summon the faithful to their prayers. This edifice I'm building will shelter them from the cold and the rain as they kneel and give their thanks to the God who created them. That's what I'm doing."

The bricklayer was fired because they were supposed to be building a garage.

■

Sometimes you have to have a positive attitude despite overwhelming odds.

A young college graduate wanted to work for this one firm. It was prestigious, it was high-paying, and it was also difficult to crack.

He presented himself for an interview and unabashedly extolled all of his virtues. He said, "I'm ambitious; I'm industrious; I'm a quick-learner; I've got excellent college grades and recommendations; and I'm willing to start at the bottom and work my way up."

The personnel manager said, "That's fine, but we have no entry level openings now. Why don't you come back in about ten years."

The youngster said, "Would morning or afternoon be better for you?"

■

A preacher once had a good definition between fact and faith. He said to his Sunday Congregation, "It is a fact that you are sitting there, and it is a fact that I am standing in this pulpit preaching to you. But it is faith that makes me believe you are listening to what I say."

■

One manager explained the difference between belief and faith to his employees. He said, "When I was a kid I used to go to the circus every year. And every year they had this great act where a man would push a wheel barrow across a high wire. He had to balance himself and the wheel barrow and there was no net beneath him if he fell. Now I went to the circus every year and I believed that he would push the wheel barrow from one end of the high wire to the other. That's belief. If I was willing to sit in the wheel barrow, that would be faith."

One executive kept this sign on his desk: "Either lead, follow, or get out of the way."

■

Sometimes a positive attitude depends entirely on how you look at things.

A youngster once got a new bat and ball for his birthday. He was so eager to try it out that he pestered his Dad to take him to the park. Finally, the father gave in.

When they got there, the kid said, "Watch this, Dad." He tossed the ball up in the air, swung at it real hard with the bat, and missed.

He picked the ball up again, and said, "Watch, Dad." He tossed it up, swung and missed again.

This went on and on many more times, but each time the kid was just as enthused when he hollered "Watch this one, Dad."

Finally, the kid picked the bat and ball up, walked over to his father and said, "What do you think, Dad. Have you ever seen such great pitching?"

■

Someone once said: "An optimist is a father who will let his son take the new car on a date. A pessimist is one who won't. A cynic is one who did."

PROMOTIONS

A promotion is a sign that either you've been doing something right, or your boss just did something wrong.

■

Any worker who gets a promotion is twice blessed. He or she got the upgrade, and fellow workers didn't.

■

Some feel that a promotion is even better than a raise, until they realize that the Super Market charges a Vice-President the same for a pound of butter as they charge an Assistant Vice-President.

■

There's only one thing better than having the boss call you into his office and say, "Pack your things; you're moving up." That is having him call you into his office and say, "Pack your things; you're moving in."

■

A promotion is the company's way of saying, "Congratulations. Now let's see if you can get work out of people like you."

It's nice to reach what the Peter Principle calls "your level of incompetence." At last, you can relax and blend in with the other executives.

■

Don't be ashamed to admit that you have risen to your level of incompetence. Maybe incompetence is what you do best.

■

Some may say that you've risen to your level of incompetence. That's all right. It's better to rise to it than be demoted to it.

■

Call it a promotion, call it an upgrade, call it an advancement, call it a step upwards, call it a career move, call it whatever you want; it's still a carrot on a stick.

■

Some promotions come with a pay raise; some don't. "With" is better.

■

A promotion usually entails more work. You don't get your name painted on the door just for being cute, you know.

■

A good rule of thumb, too, is: the longer the title, the longer the hours.

■

A promotion generally changes who you report to, until eventually you report to the cashier and pick up your severance pay.

■

Some promotions elevate you above your working companions. It makes you their boss, and them your ex-friends.

■

One worker to a co-worker who was just elevated to head of the department: "Congratulations. I never liked you anyway."

■

Remember, you meet the same people on the way down the ladder as you meet on the way up. Which is great. You get to step over them in two directions.

■

One gentleman who was bypassed for a promotion, asked the boss, "What about my qualifications?" The boss said, "I don't want to talk about your qualifications. What's past is past."

Getting a promotion over one's fellow workers is a sweet feeling. It's like sitting in the first class section of a plane and watching the others trudge back to coach.

■

I admire the honesty of one gentleman who was promoted to the head of a department over all of his co-workers. After the announcement he spoke to his employees and said, "My friends, I'm not going to change—but all of you had better."

■

Everything I am today I owe to the company. And despite that my lawyer insists I have no case.

■

Some wise man once said, "I want to be what I was when I wanted to be what I am now."

■

Don't be discouraged if you don't get the promotion you wanted. Keep in mind that when King Tut was your age, he had already been dead several years.

■

Jean Cocteau, the French artist, writer, and film director, was once asked if he believed in luck.

He said, "Of course. How else can you explain the success of those you don't like?"

■

President Coolidge, at the end of his elected term in office, announced that he did not "choose to run" for re-election. Reporters wanted to know more details. One asked him point blank: "Mr. President, exactly why don't you want to be President again?"

Coolidge said, "There's no chance for advancement."

■

Sometimes our ambition plays tricks on us, and sometimes our superiors know that. King Louis XIV did.

He once asked one of his courtiers, "Do you know Spanish?"

The man said, "No, Sire. I don't."

The King said, "Pity."

Now the courtier thought that Louis XIV had some phenomenal ambassadorship ready for anyone who spoke Spanish. The man devoted himself to a study of the language. After many hours of work, he presented himself before the King and proudly announced that he was fluent in Spanish.

The King said, "Do you know it well enough to speak with Spaniards conversationally?"

The courtier said, "Yes, Sire."

The King said, "Congratulations. You can now read *Don Quixote* in the original."

King Louis XIV said this years ago about promotions: "Every time I fill a vacant place I make 100 malcontents and one ingrate."

PASSED OVER FOR A PROMOTION

Being passed over for a promotion is always a painful experience. It's like having a stake driven through your wallet.

■

It's like having a guy ask you to hold his clothes while he makes love to your girl.

■

It's always sad to learn that someone got the promotion you were expecting. It's like a corporate "Dear John" letter.

■

It's like saddling up a horse for someone else to ride.

■

My boss said, "Well, you didn't get the promotion this time, but I guess this will inspire you to work even harder." I said, "Guess again."

■

My manager said, "I'm sorry you didn't get that promotion. I already had your new name plate made up." I said, "You think you've got troubles. I already have the money spent."

■

I told my manager, "I dreamed about getting that job night and day." The boss said, "That's the problem. During the day you were supposed to be working for us."

■

How come most companies promote early retirement but late promotions?

■

I once worked diligently, competently, and faithfully to get a promotion and then was passed over. My boss said, "Your time will come." I said, "Well, come to my desk and wake me when it gets here."

Sometimes so many people pass you by you feel like a road sign on the highway to success.

One boss told me, "You didn't get the promotion because you were over-qualified." I said, "From now on I'll pattern myself more after you."

■

One manager said to me, "I'm saving you till the right promotion comes along." I said, "I'm not Shirley MacLaine. I'd prefer to get it in *this* lifetime."

■

One boss said, "You didn't get the promotion because you're not right for the job." I said, "That's never hurt your career."

■

The boss says he likes me but I'm always passed over for promotions. I feel like the "Miss Congeniality" of the corporate world.

■

My boss said, "Promotions aren't everything." I said, "I know, but they're ten percent more each week than I've got now."

■

I complained to my boss, "All my friends are being promoted and I'm not." My boss said, "That's simply not true. They're no longer your friends."

■

It seems whenever you get passed over for a promotion, it always goes to someone you can't stand. I don't know how companies can do that—stab you in the back and kick you in the crotch all at the same time.

■

They give the job to the biggest nincompoop in the office. You know if you're less qualified than he is, you should be in remedial executive school.

The only thing in the office less qualified than him is the electric stapling machine. . . . and then only when it's out of staples.

OFFICE POLITICS

You know what a politician is—that's a person who is dedicated to the service of others in order to get what he wants.

An office politician is a person who is dedicated to the principles of life, liberty, and the pursuit of your job.

■

An office politician is someone who considers himself on the ladder of success and you one of the rungs.

■

An office politician is one who has the attitude: "What's mine is mine; what's yours is ours."

■

An office politician is a person who will kiss the boss's ring . . . even if he keeps it in his back pocket.

■

The office politician is always behind somebody—either kissing or stabbing.

■

Office politics—that's the art of getting ahead while kissing another part of the boss's body.

■

Office politicians are the ones who wear 5-piece suits to the office. That's a three-piece suit with 2 knee pads.

■

Most office politicians aren't "Yes-men." It's too hard to pucker and talk at the same time.

■

Politicians are good for one thing in an office—they help the indoor plants grow.
Some of them are so full of b.s., their resumes draw flies.

■

Office politics is just like a horse race where everyone jockeys for position, except in a horse race they use complete horses.

■

One worker was resigned to it. He wore a sign on his chest that said, "In case of office politics, stab other side."

■

Be wary of office politicians. There's a fine line between back slapping and back stabbing.

Office politicians will step over anyone to get ahead. Many of them wear special shoes to give them better footing on gabardine.

■

They'll step over anybody to get a promotion. So when they get friendly with you, beware. They're just looking you over closely, trying to find footholds.

■

Office politician is an impossible position. It's trying to stand head and shoulders above your peers while bowing down to your superiors.

■

Remember, when you spend so much time bowing down to the boss, you present an excellent target to your fellow workers.

■

I hate office politics. I just happen to enjoy mowing my boss's lawn on weekends. . . . And shining his shoes during the week.

■

Pinkus was worried about business. Conditions were terrible and getting worse. So his friend, in order to get his mind off business, invited him to his first baseball game.

A batter came up, swung at the ball and the umpire yelled, "Strike!" The batter swung at the ball again and the umpire yelled, "Strike!" The batter swung again and missed and the umpire yelled, "Strike three, you're out!"

"What a difference," smiled Pinkus. "In my store they holler 'strike' only once and everybody's out!"

■

One office politician had finally managed a dinner invitation to the boss's house. He was delighted to be included, but also a bit concerned about how to act. He certainly didn't want to make any dumb mistakes because a good impression this evening could mean a promotion.

So this gentleman devised a foolproof system for preventing gauche blunders. He would simply do whatever his boss, the host did.

During dinner the boss took a little bit of his coffee and poured it into his saucer. The office politician poured some coffee into his saucer. Then the boss took the cream pitcher and poured lots of cream into his saucer. The politician asked for the cream pitcher and poured lots of it into his saucer, too.

Then the boss took his saucer and set it on the floor for his cat.

THE JOB EVALUATION

An Indian tribe had a test of manhood ritual that consisted of a three day fast, a 26-mile run through the forest, a fight to the death, unarmed, against a starving grizzly bear, and a climb to a mountaintop to gather feathers from a ferocious eagle. It's considered easier than sitting through a job evaluation review.

■

The modern job evaluation is a periodic business ritual where the boss calls you into his office, says "How are you doing," and then proceeds to tell you.

■

A job review is an annual or semi-annual ritual where your boss tells you you're good for nothing, but you insist on a salary anyway.

■

A job review is an annual or semi-annual ritual where your boss tells you not only that you're good for nothing, but you're not so good for what they're paying you.

■

A job evaluation is when the company compares what you're worth to what they pay you. All ties go to the company.

■

It's a one-sided sort of affair. It's like betting with the umpire on whether he's going to call you out or safe.

■

One employee responded after his review: "If you say I'm doing that badly, why do you get so upset when I don't show up for work?"

■

It's demoralizing to sit there quietly while someone tells you what you're worth. It's even more demoralizing when they start telling you what you're not worth.

■

There's only one thing more irritating than the boss telling you that you're not performing up to par, and that is when he proves it.

■

Job reviews serve a financial function in business. They make the employees think twice before asking for the next raise.

The job review is the company's way of keeping you humble–whether you deserve to be or not.

■

Job evaluations are a throwback to savage rituals where a warrior would survive a test of bravery and endurance and be rewarded with another feather or a tiny bauble. We're rewarded with pretty much the same thing after taxes.

■

One extraordinary worker scored a perfect 5 on every area of his job review, and the company rewarded him commensurately–with a $5 a week raise.

■

You show me a worker who enjoys his job review and I'll show you a worker who can look his boss in the eye and call him "Dad."

■

Some feel the periodic job review is futile. It's like buying a new car and then meeting with the dealer every year to complain about the price.

Others feel it's beneficial. It's turning down a request for a raise before it's asked.

■

Sometimes the job review is an employee who thinks he's an asset to the company being lectured on effectiveness by a person he considers worthless. It's like Hulk Hogan getting self-defense lessons from Pee Wee Herman.

■

Most job evaluations boil down to: "You're doing all right, but you could do much better." Ironically, that's the same evaluation most employees have of their weekly salary.

■

Some managers get right to the meat of the job review. Like the one I had who called me into his office and said, "Have a seat even though you don't deserve one."

■

I once signed a job evaluation form with a pseudonym. I figured, "If you're going to make up things about me, I'm going to make up a new name."

■

Once I refused to sign the job evaluation form. I said, "I'll come back and sign the non-fiction version."

■

Of course, some reviews are superb—or so I'm told.

After an across the board evaluation of all workers, one company speaker began his emceeing chores with: "I'm happy to be here. Of course, after last week's evaluations, I'm happy to be anywhere."

■

There was once a musician who received an extemporaneous job evaluation by the band leader. It came at a rehearsal session and was in front of the entire orchestra. The leader yelled, "You're the worst musician I've ever had in this band. You play lousy, with no emotion, no soul. You can't stay on beat, and half the time you're out of tune."

The musician said calmly, "How's my posture?"

Some job reviews are subject to change.

A manager of a nightclub once asked one of his employees about a new young singer who was appearing in Las Vegas.

"Did you catch her act?"

The employee said, "Yes, I did."

"What'd you think?"

He said, "I think she's the worst singer I ever saw in my life. First of all, she don't look good. She's not attractive. Has no sex appeal. Her voice is weak, you know. It's like a squeaky little voice that actually irritates you to listen to it. She has no beat, no rhythm. She picks lousy songs to sing, and she has no personality on stage. She stinks."

The manager said, "Well, the owner likes her and wants to sign her."

The employee said, "Wait a minute. You didn't let me finish."

PART TWO

PARAPHERNALIA OF BUSINESS

Just think, if Moses were alive today, God could have faxed
the ten commandments to him.

STATUS OFFICE

The status office is in nowadays. One executive's office was so ornate he didn't even have a secretary. In keeping with his office decor, he had a handmaiden.

■

The status office should be large, it should be secure, and it should be apart from the other executive offices. The ultimate, if possible, is an office with a moat.

...Preferably a moat with an alligator, although a reasonably aggressive secretary will do.

■

An executive's goal should be to have an office that is larger than any other room in the building—including the underground parking lot.

■

Your office should be so large that even after visitors are admitted to it, they still have to ask directions to your desk.

■

The really top level executive is able to play a game of raquetball during lunch without having to leave his office.

... or move any of the furniture.

■

One executive had an office so large it could sleep ten, which made it perfect for staff meetings.

■

The status office should always have a window—preferably of stained glass.

■

Status offices are usually on the uppermost floor of the building. Top executives want no one above them except God—and that's only because He has seniority.

■

And the desk should be large. What you want is a desk that has its own zip code.

■

What you want is a desk large enough so you can put pictures of your family in one corner of it—lifesize pictures.

You want a desk so large that when you have to pass documents from one side of it to the other, you have to call Federal Express.

■

Every executive should long for a desk that is so huge that confused airline pilots mistake it for a runway.

■

And of course, you want a chair that befits your station in life. That would be a high-backed, over-stuffed, leather upholstered model that you order from "Thrones-R-Us."

■

And it should be large. It seems that as one's head gets bigger, so do other parts of the anatomy.

■

There should be a phone on the desk that has more buttons on it than a 747 control panel. And the executive should know how to use at least one of those buttons.

■

Everything in the status office should be expensive. Even the picture of your family on the corner of your desk should be posed for by professional models.

■

I've seen executive offices where the wastebasket was bigger and made of better materials than my office.

■

And you should have carpeting that is much more plush than the rest of the office. When visitors walk into your office, anyone under 5'1" should disappear.

■

One businessman was travelling first class as befitted his station in life—so he thought. He had the power briefcase with him, suitably stuffed with all sorts of seemingly important papers, the Official Airline Travel Guide, a copy of the Wall Street Journal, and other whatnot.

However, when the plane took off, he felt a little inferior. All the other executives in first class found some reason to use the new phone that airlines provide.

One by one, each of them used his or her credit card to make an important call.

He tried to think of a reason to call, but couldn't. However, he also couldn't just sit there and be a nobody. So he finally found a reason to use the airline phone.

He called out for a pizza.

Charles Townsend Copeland was an English professor at Harvard for many years. He occupied tiny, inconvenient office space at the top floors of Harvard's Hollis Hall.

It wasn't that he was sentenced to those offices. In fact, many times the administration offered to relocate him in more prestigious quarters, but Copeland refused.

He liked his tiny rooms on the top floor. He said, "It's the only place in Cambridge where God alone is above me. He's busy, but he's quiet."

∎

All of us are guilty of wanting to enjoy whatever stature we might have. There's a story of a diocesan Archbishop who enjoyed the pomp and circumstance–and many of the perks of his office.

He attended a charity dinner with many other clergymen one night and was annoyed by a draft from behind. Finally, he called over one of the waiters and said, "Please close that window behind me and open one behind one of the monsignors."

∎

Another example of religious snobbery was the man who wore a medal that read, "I am an important Catholic. In case of accident, please call a Bishop."

∎

A lowly immigrant came to America to prosper. Though he couldn't read or write, he was a determined worker and a shrewd businessman. He opened a tiny tailor shop.

When he saved enough to begin a savings account he went to the bank and simply made two x's for his signature.

His tailor shop prospered and his bank account grew. His tiny shop grew into a chain of shops, and then into a well known custom-tailoring house. After that he began a company to manufacture ready made clothing. Then he sold the company to a large conglomerate for millions of dollars.

When he went to deposit the money into his account he endorsed it with *three* x's instead of the customary two. One bank official asked why the extra x?

This gentleman said, "I think I'm doing well enough now to have a middle initial."

∎

One hard-working, ambitious young executive was thrilled when the manager called him into his office and said, "Here's the key to the executive washroom."

The young man said, "Thank you, sir."

The manager said, "Have it cleaned before the Regional Manager gets here."

DREARY OFFICES

Lower level executives get the offices with no decorations on the wall, no windows, and on their next promotion, the promise of a door.

■

You know the kind of offices they give to lower level executives. The Supreme Court would consider them cruel and unusual workspace.

■

Some offices are so dank and dreary, maintenance people have to come in twice a week and scrape mushrooms.

■

The prime concern among top executives is burnout. Among lower executives it's mildew.

■

These offices are so dreary, the new occupant doesn't know whether to sit at the desk or hang upside down from the ceiling.

■

Mediocre executives are kept the same way fine wine is.

■

The hard part sometimes is finding a comfortable office chair that will roll smoothly on mud floors.

■

The desks are usually warped. You've heard of Chippendale furniture? This is hill and dale.

■

Lower executives' offices are often so dismal that you feel you should be led to them by six pall bearers.

■

They're crypt-like. Along with your name on the door you're allowed two lines of epitaph.

■

They're so crypt-like that sometimes it takes new occupants several hours to work up the courage to sit up in them and unfold their hands from across their chests.

Lower executives often have no connection to the outside world. Top executives do; they just chose to ignore it.

■

Lower executives' offices are ones where you have to press the elevator's "up" button to get to the parking garage.

■

You know you're in a lower executive office when you have to share office space with the emergency food and water supplies.

■

Of course, when an executive leaves this office, he usually misses all the heavy traffic. All the other drivers are generally home by the time he's finished blinking at the light.

■

These offices are usually small. The executive must move around in them very gingerly so that he doesn't lose anything to the electric pencil sharpener.

■

Only lower level executives can occupy these small offices because any document over 12 pages long doesn't fit.

■

You know you're a low level executive when they measure your waist, chest, and inseam before assigning you an office.

■

I once had one office that was so small the silverfish in my old files were hunchbacked.

■

One uninitiated executive buzzed his secretary and said, "Please come in here with your stenography pad and pencil." She said, "Your office is too small. You can pick any two of the three."

■

You'll never get a swelled head sitting in these offices. It won't fit.

■

One executive had to fire his secretary because she was too buxom. Every time she came into his office she erased his chalkboard.

DESKS—NEAT AND MESSY

Some workers keep their desks so neat they always look like they're for sale.

■

I know one guy who keeps his desk so neat, if you leave a phone message on it, you have to wrap it in Saran Wrap.
   . . . In fact, he won't accept a phone message unless it's been scotchguarded.

■

This guy keeps his desktop spotless. He takes ten percent of his salary in Lemon Pledge.

■

This guy can make coffee cup stains disappear by staring at them.

■

This guy even throws his trash away in alphabetical order.

■

This guy is fanatical about neatness. He's the kind who could stay a week at a motel and when he checked out the little strip of paper would still be around the toilet seat.

■

He's really a fanatic about neatness. He hates his hands because they have fingerprints on them.

■

I stopped by to see him one time and there was no desk–it was at the dry cleaners.

■

This executive keeps his desktop so clean you could eat off it. In fact, his desk set converts to place mats for six.

■

One guy I know has such a messy desk, he has to wear a hard hat to look for a pencil.

■

This guy once cleaned off his desktop and we found an old employee we thought had been laid off.

■

This guy has papers on his desk so old the top of his desk has been declared a national landmark by the Silverfish Society of America.

The top of his desk looks like a compost pile.

■

If the top of his desk were a neighborhood, they would tear it down and put up a slum.

■

He keeps every document he's ever worked on. If you ever got to the bottom layer of his desktop, you just might find the Magna Carta.

■

One guy's desk is so bad they're taking bets in the office about which will come first–this guy's retirement or death by avalanche.

■

It's good job security, though, because if they ever fire him and give him just enough time to clean out his desk, he knows he's got at least two more years of work.

■

Junk is piled up so high, this guy has the only desk in the place with a retaining wall.

... and liability insurance.

NEW TECHNOLOGY

Every device in the office is now high-tech. And to think so many of us moved into management because we could never quite master punching the time clock.

■

We have machines in the office that do things today that yesterday weren't even worth doing.

■

Have you ever seen the control panel in the cockpit of a 747? Well that's what the front of our new Xerox machine looks like.

■

It has color reproduction, size reduction, half-tone capability, sorting, collating, and much more. All that just to get the material ready for our new high-tech paper shredding machine.

Remember the old days when the only thing that had that many buttons on it was the front of a sailor's trousers?

■

That new machine is so elaborate our office has trouble generating a document that is important enough to feed into it.

■

My manager tried to operate the Xerox machine himself the other day. He followed all the instructions, pushed all the buttons, waited patiently, and sure enough . . . out came a cup of coffee with two sugars and extra cream.

■

My boss read an article the other day that said with proper management the photocopying machine could become unnecessary. He had copies run off for everybody.

■

Pretty soon even paper clips will become useless once their batteries run down.

■

Someday all these high-tech electronic machines are going to break down in your office and you're going to have to be prepared to sit around all day and think.

■

Everything is electronic today. The modern office measures productivity in BPS–beeps per second.

■

Every different beep has a different meaning. The modern executive's career could be over today if he's tone deaf.

■

In today's office anything that doesn't beep is turned into a planter.

■

My boss wanted me to wear an electronic pager. I refused. I don't want anything else on my body that might fall off.

■

Even dial-a-prayer now has a fax number.

■

How do these machines do all the things they do? I'm still trying to figure out how those old scales in the drug stores could tell your fortune.

If some of these office machines were at Disneyland, they would be an E ticket, at least.

■

At this point in office technology aren't you glad you're not a "Carbon Paper Czar?"

■

They even have machines that are user-friendly. They give you instructions as you go. Now if they could just invent one that could teach the boss how to make his own coffee in the morning.

■

They have machines now that dial the telephone for you. And some executives were just beginning to get the hang of that on their own.

■

Whoever invented paging devices should be tied to a tree and beeped to death.

■

Everybody has a beeper nowadays. Ma Bell used to reach out and touch someone; now she hooks herself onto your belt.

■

A beeper used to be a status symbol. Nowadays even people who can't afford a belt are wearing beepers.

■

It used to be a status symbol to have the maitre'd page you in a restaurant. Now it's an insult. It means you're not important enough to wear a beeper.

■

At my age, I refuse to wear a beeper. I don't want that to be the only thing on my body that works right.

■

Beepers can't be trusted anyway. You may rush into the office for a supposed crisis only to find out it was just the guy next door opening his automatic garage door.

COMPUTERS

A gentleman came home from the office and complained to his wife, "What a terrible day. The computer broke down and we had to sit around all afternoon and think."

Computers aren't smart; they're stupid. They must be. They actually do what we tell them.

■

Computers are versatile, too. At the end of the day, we can now list all of our mistakes in alphabetical order.

■

Computers have changed the way we do business. Rather than fabricate an excuse nowadays, we just say, "The computer's down."

■

The computer is a wondrous instrument. It can perform complex mathematical evaluations in a fraction of a milli-second, it can analyze and interpret information it gathers from all over the world, it can communicate with other computers. It can do everything, apparently, except get my gas bill right.

■

If the computer is so damned smart, how come it gets blamed for all the errors?

■

Computers aren't intelligent, but they do have their own form of common sense. You never see a computer make an ass of itself at the office Christmas party.

■

Computers are supposed to be a tool of the executive. Then how come we have to take classes to learn to do things their way?

■

The executive world is intimidating. After four years of college and some post-graduate work, they sit you behind an impressive desk, face to face with a tiny little machine that's smarter than you are.

■

The computer is a poor substitute for human intelligence, but then so are a lot of executives.

■

Computer experts are working feverishly to develop artificial intelligence. Some of the people in my office have perfected it without the help of a computer.

■

The computer will never fully replace humans. It may someday be capable of artificial intelligence, but it will never master real stupidity like we have.

We've become too dependent on computers. I know one office where the computers went down and they handed out pacifiers to get the workers through the day.

■

We're almost totally dependent on computers. I know of one despondent executive who jumped off the ledge of his building, but Norton Utilities kept bringing him back.

■

The big difference between humans and computers is that computers can't think . . . but they know it.

■

Computers can't think. That may be why so many of us have adapted to them so readily.

■

Computers are fast. In a fraction of a milli-second we can now make the same dumb mistake that used to take hours before.

■

In the business world, computers have replaced the slide rule . . . and possibly a few slide rule owners.

■

With a computer we can now do a full eight hours of work in just one hour. Of course, it takes seven hours to figure out what we did.

■

This is the computer age in the business world. There are now more computers on desks than there are coffee cup rings.

■

The computer now brings a world of information into the workplace. Remember when that task was handled by the office gossip?

■

I have a friend who bought two home computers just to help him with his financial situation. And it works. Now when bill collectors call he just says, "I'd like to send a check today, but unfortunately, all my computers are down."

■

The problem with computers is that they do exactly what we tell them. It's like the general who issued an order to all the sentries on base that no vehicle was to be permitted to enter or leave the premises without an official identification seal.

One young soldier was on guard duty when the General's car pulled up to the gate. It didn't have an identification seal, so the youngster followed orders and refused to let it pass.

The General naturally was furious. He said, "Young man, I'm the highest ranking officer on this base, let this vehicle pass." The soldier refused.

The General said, "I'm the General who issued this order. Now let us drive on through." The kid said, "No." Finally the General said, "I'm in charge on this base, and I'm giving my driver an order to go right on through. Do you understand that? Do you have any questions?" The kid said, "Yes sir, just one. Who do I shoot first, you or your driver?"

■

A woman was confiding to a friend that she was still a virgin. Her friend couldn't believe it.

She asked, "How can that be? You've been married three times."

The woman said, "Oh, it's quite easy to explain. You see the first time I got married it was for pure love. My husband was in the military and right after the wedding, he shipped out. He never came back to me. I never saw him again.

"My second marriage was simply for convenience. My husband was wealthy, he was up in years, and he was lonely. He married for companionship and I married for money. However, the marriage was never consummated."

But her girlfriend asked, "How about your third husband, though. He's young, healthy, good-looking, and you've been married for several months now. How can you still be a virgin?"

The woman said, "Oh, my present husband works with computers. He just sits on the edge of the bed and tells me how good it's going to be."

■

"Computers can figure out all kinds of problems, except the things in the world that just don't add up."— *James Magary*

■

"In a few minutes a computer can make a mistake so great that it would take many men many months to equal it."—*Merle L. Meacham*

■

Computers and their word processing software may totally eliminate the typewriter as we know it today from the market place.

However, the typewriter has had a comfortable place in the business world, even though it had a shaky start.

In 1897, the Wagner Typewriting Machine Company tried to sell its patent to the typewriter to the Remington Arms Company. But Remington's president said, "No mere machine can replace a reliable and honest clerk." They didn't buy the invention.

Underwood acquired Wagner and the patent and went on to sell more than 12 million typewriters during the next fifty years.

ANSWERING MACHINES

I know why people are living longer today. Because when the Angel of Death calls, all he gets is an answering machine.

■

We spend one-third of our lives sleeping, one-third working, and one-third waiting for the beep.

■

If we wanted to listen to beeps, we could call the Road-Runner.

■

All we get today are answering machines. It's getting so people can't think of anything to say until they first hear the sound of the beep.

■

I don't know why people can't answer their phones. Where is everybody? Probably at the factory making more answering machines.

■

I called one guy 100 times and kept getting his answering machine. I finally went to his house. He also had a door answering machine.

■

We have machines now talking to other machines. The end of the world could come tomorrow and AT & T wouldn't find out about it for two months.

■

You can run up a $1000 phone bill nowadays and never talk to a human being.

■

They have computers, vending machines, answering machines, dialing machines. Do you know something? Human beings are becoming obsolete.

■

They have machines that can do whatever needs to be done on the telephone. That's so that three or four months after the last man on earth dies, the telephone company will still be making money.

Everything you do is through a machine. For all you know, you could be the last man on earth.

■

If people really wanted to talk to machines, "My Mother The Car" would still be on television.

■

Just for fun I called the Suicide Prevention number last week and got a recording.
. . . They said, "We can't come to the phone right now, but at the sound of the beep please leave your name and what ledge you're calling from."

■

I tried to call one executive 26 times and all I got was his machine. I finally wrote him a letter. I got back a letter written by a computer.

■

That's the way executives set up lunch dates nowadays. They say, "Have your machine call my machine."

■

Sometimes I get hungry for the sound of the human voice. I call the operator and say, "I want to place a call to Arizona; I'll talk to anyone."

■

I did talk to a human being the other day. It was a wrong number.

■

Some executives get disoriented when they place a call and a human answers. They put *their* machine on.

■

I tried to say my goodnight prayers last evening and got a message from God "I'm not in right now, please wait for the beep."

OFFICE FURNITURE

Some of today's modern office furniture looks great, but is terribly uncomfortable. It was designed by asses but not for them.

■

These designers must have spent many years studying art. You think they could have thrown in at least one semester studying the human anatomy.

They remind me of the guy at the ball park who shouted "Down in front." The guy in front shouted back, "I don't bend that way."

■

Some of today's modern chairs don't even look like furniture; they look like medical apparatus.

■

Anyone can sit in today's modern chairs, but you need a technician to help you out of them.

■

Some of these modern office chairs look beautiful, but then I imagine a Venus Fly Trap looks attractive to a house fly, too.

■

Some of these modern art-deco chairs look dangerous. Put a little piece of cheese in them, and they look like someone finally built a better mouse trap.

■

Some of this modern office furniture is so avant-garde it's hard to tell whether it's a chair, a coffee table, or a Rubik's cube.

■

A lot of waiting rooms are furnished with the ultra-modern chairs. They eat harmful salesmen.

■

The decor in some modern offices is weird. It looks like beach furniture that got a job.

■

Some of the modern stuff is nothing more than chrome tubing and canvas. It resembles plumbing work in traction.

■

Shoddy office furniture is responsible for holding down unemployment. When furniture gets shabby enough, rather than throw it out, most companies would rather hire someone lowly enough to sit in it.

■

Have you ever seen that tag that reads "Do not remove under penalty of law?" I've been given office furniture where that was the only thing on it that didn't need repair.

■

I've had office furniture that the company had put on the Goodwill truck, but the truck threw it back.

Wheels won't roll, drawers won't open, doors won't latch. Yes, I've been in offices where neither the employees nor the furniture worked.

■

Upper management always gets more elegant furniture. The bigger the brain, the better the seat you get to put it in.

■

Here's a poem about faulty office furniture. It's called . . .

THE BIG BOSS

I came to work an ambitious young man.
I dispatch my duties as best I can.
That's why to me it was no joke
When I learned one wheel on my desk chair was broke.

For one broken wheel could be sufficient
To make a worker less efficient.
And that was unacceptable to me
Because you see some day I hope to be

The Big Boss.

So I mentioned it to my supervisor,
That workman's number one advisor,
I thought he should be the first to know
That one of my wheels refused to go.

He said, "I'm glad you came to me
That's one of the reasons I'm here, you see.
To help you any way I can,
But this must go to a bigger man,

The Big Boss.

So I saw my manager and in all good will
He sent me even higher still.
And the next, with proper etiquette,
Sent me even higher yet.

I met the company's highest nobility,
But all declined responsibility.

I travelled here and I travelled there,
Searching for the one man who could fix my chair—

The Big Boss.

Then I gave up bobbing like a cork
And financed myself a trip to New York.
This problem was too big to be ignored,
So I appeared before the Chairman of the Board.

I said, "Sir, to you this may not be a big deal,
But I'm a worker with a broken wheel."
But he paid no attention to what I said.
He just pulled out a gun and shot me dead.

But he was The Big Boss.

Next thing I know I was in the sky
And a man named St. Peter came along and said "Hi"
He checked my name and dossier
And motioned for me to "Come this way."

He lead me through the Pearly Gate
And told me to have a seat and wait
It would only be a minute or two
And then he'd introduce me to...

The Big Boss.

And then I stood before Him...and He spoke to me

"You've been a good worker so I've saved you space
Come I'll show you to your place.
From now on you're working only for Me
And this is your desk for Eternity."

And the desk was all gold with a silver desk set
And the chair . . . the chair was covered with red velvet.
He said, "This is your desk for time without end.
It's your reward for being a friend

...of The Big Boss."

Then I sat at my desk just as proud as could be
And tried out the chair He'd reserved just for me.
But He heard not my words as He vanished to smoke:
"Good Lord, one of the wheels is broke."

■

Sometimes workers can't win for losing.

One enterprising and industrious young clerk was working so hard on so many projects that he hardly had time to clean one undertaking off his desk before beginning the next or making room for the one to follow. His desk was a montage of papers, blueprints, open and closed folders, and various utensils.

The boss wandered through the office one morning and seeing the chaotic state of the worker's desk top said, in a voice loud enough for others to hear, "I hope your mind isn't as cluttered as that desk."

Now the young man worked even harder. He not only completed his assigned tasks, but also found the time to organize his desk top, too.

The boss roamed through the office a few days later, saw the young worker's neat desk and said, loud enough for others to hear, "I hope your mind isn't as empty as that desk top."

PAPER CLIPS

Albert Einstein and an assistant finished a draft of a paper they were working on and searched through the desk for a paper clip. The only one either man could find was bent so horribly out of shape that it was no longer functional.

Now they both searched around the room for some sort of tool that would rebend the clip into usable shape.

During the search, the assistant found a full box of unused paper clips. Einstein immediately molded one of them into a tool that would rebend the original clip into shape.

The assistant was baffled. He asked Einstein why he would repair the paper clip when there were so many perfectly good ones available.

Einstein said, "Once I become set on a goal, it's hard to deflect me from it."

■

Paper clips have only two intended functions—to hold papers together and to serve as playthings for bored employees.

They're fascinating, fun to bend and unbend, easily linked together into amusing chains, and so simple that even an executive can operate them.

■

Paper clips are the tinker toys of the business world.

■

They're also the saboteurs of the Xerox and fax machines.

Paper clips are always going where they're not wanted, jamming machinery, and slowing down office productivity. They're like tiny, inanimate shop stewards.

■

The two things that cause the most work stoppages to complex office machinery are the stray paper clip and executives who think they can operate the equipment while their secretaries are away.

The stray paper clip is more easily remediable. You can reason with a paper clip.

■

Paper clips can sometimes be valuable in the office and at other times totally useless. They're like employees.

■

Paper clips can be more necessary than the workers. In a pinch, you can't use an employee as a pipe cleaner.

■

Papers clips do remind you of employees. They're totally worthless until they're bent into the proper shape.

■

Also, like employees, they're relatively inexpensive.
. . . and disposable.

■

Most paper clips are like most employees. They're found in various places around the office not doing what they were intended to do.

■

Paper clips have only one useful attribute–their shape. Some employees don't even have that.

■

No matter where you look in a business office, you'll find stray paper clips lying around. They're like jelly beans during the Reagan administration.

One manager on a cost savings kick gave a scathing speech to his charges about wasting paper clips. He said, "Too many of you are disposing of paper clips while they're still useful. They are not designed to be cast away after one use. They should be saved and reused. Everything in this office should be considered valuable until it is proven to be of no further usefulness to the company. Do you understand that?"

One employee said, "I understand it, sir. And I hope you'll remember those words nine months from now when I reach the age of 65."

■

Many paper clips are used just once and then discarded while they still have some usefulness. They're just the opposite of consultants.

■

Paper clips are like company policy, too. They're frequently redesigned but rarely improved.

■

Paper clips should be pure metal. Paper clips coated with plastic are like Harley-Davidsons with training wheels.

FILING

The way my secretary does it, filing is a lost art.

■

My secretary tells me that organization means a place for everything and everything in its place. She just won't tell me where that place is.

■

She's proud of her filing system. In fact, right now she's writing a dictionary where the words are listed in chronological order.

■

She also owns a calendar where the days are listed in the order of their importance.

■

She's writing a book explaining her filing system. It's titled "Office Filing–From A to M."

■

Filing is the art of putting something away and being able to get your hands on it again. If not, then to be able to get your hands on whoever it was who put it away.

We have a filing system in our office that could be sold to Parker Brothers as a game.

■

The rule of thumb in our office is: If you ever want to see it again, don't let it out of your sight now.

■

Our office invented the IITS filing system—"It's In There Somewhere."

The three F system isn't bad either: Finish it; File it; Forget it.

■

I have a filing system that is totally useless. Shirley MacLaine comes back more often than folders I've filed.

■

My system works fine until you want to find something.

■

My mother always used to say she'd find things in the last place she'd look, so that's where I file them.

■

I only have two letters in my filing system–M and N. M is for "Miscellaneous;" N is for "Non-miscellaneous."

■

I may improve it by reducing the two letters to just one–L for "Lost."

■

My filing system operates on a 'non-demand' basis. I can only find things I'm not looking for.

■

Folders in my filing system are like your kids who go off to college. Once they get in there, they're rarely heard from again.

■

I finally had to hire an assistant just to do my filing. Now there are two of us who can't find anything.

...but each of us has someone to blame.

■

Some office-wise worker once observed:

"If your office is typical, three quarters of the things in your files should have been placed in your wastebasket."

One executive used to end each work day by taking papers out of his "In" tray and placing them in his "Out" tray. Another employee questioned him about it.

He said, "I do it every night. You'd be surprised how little of it ever comes back."

■

Samuel Goldwyn's secretary once asked if she could get rid of the material in his files that had been there for over ten years. Goldwyn said, "Yes, but make copies."

PART THREE

BUSINESS
AND MONEY

The business world's greatest dilemma is trying to decide whether greed is a virtue or a vice.

THEIR MONEY

Every job description in the business world can be reduced to four words: "Make money for us."

BUDGET

The ironic thing about budgets is that they're a pain in the ass even though you're spending someone else's money.

■

A departmental budget is trying to get blood from rocks while management keeps telling you to use less rocks.

■

The budget drives industry like a V-8 engine drives your car. The bosses keep asking, "Can't you get by on 7 cylinders?"

■

The budget is the heart of your office. And upper management's job is to clog your arteries.

■

The difference between a "budget proposal" and an "approved budget" is the difference between "millionaire" and "air."

■

Most budget proposals come back with more slashes in them than the guy who first told Zorro he dressed like a sissy.

Anyone who believes the whole is equal to the sum of its parts has never had to submit a budget to upper management.

Upper management wants you to prepare a budget where the total is equal to *some* of its parts.

■

Budget time in corporate life is when your boss becomes a giant red pencil.

■

Budget time is almost impossible. Picture Dolly Parton trying to slip into Phyllis Diller's bra.

■

Budget time is when you say, "Here's what I want"; they say, "Here's what you'll get"; and "Here's what you need" is somewhere between the two.

■

You go into a budget meeting with your hat in your hand. When you come out, you discover you probably could have gotten more by just passing the hat around the room.

■

It's fun playing golf with executives who are reviewing budgets. Instead of shouting "fore," they shout "3.95."

■

Of course, any executive who doesn't want to justify what he spends should get out of business and into politics where he belongs.

■

In the business world, you can't spend what you don't have. Unlike government where you can just raise taxes to get it.

■

I like the housewife who had a simple reply to budgeting. She told the bank official who called, "I can't be overdrawn. I still have blank checks left."

■

The first budget proposal submitted is usually just poorly disguised departmental embezzlement.

The first budget approved is usually just poorly disguised managerial welfare.

■

The first budget proposal is usually excessive. We all enjoy spending money that isn't ours.

Never threaten management by saying, "This is what I need to run my office." They might counter with "Here's who we can get to run your office."

■

You have a budget like you have a limit in a poker game. You're not supposed to go beyond it till at least an hour after the game started. —*Will Rogers*

■

Funny thing showed up in the papers. Something we hadn't heard of in so long that it seemed like reviving an article from King Tut's tomb. It was the Budget! They are even talking about balancing him. Of course, they won't be able to do that–you take a rope walker that's laid off for years, and they never come back— but it's good to hear the old boy's name mentioned again. Budget is the name, spelled B-U-D-G-E-T, pronounced bud-jet.—*Will Rogers*

■

The budget is a mythical beanbag. Congress votes mythical beans into it, and then tries to reach in and pull real beans out. —*Will Rogers*

■

The noted humorist and cartoonist, James Thurber, was not the most meticulous accountant of his own budget. An executive at his bank called him in for a meeting, and Thurber readily confessed that he never kept records of any of the checks he wrote.

The bank official asked, "How do you know how much money is in your account?"

Thurber said, "I thought that was *your* business."

■

A school kid solved his budget problem with some innovation, and many businesses today use the same type of inventiveness.

The teacher told the kid, "You have 3 apples, and 10 people to divide them up amongst. How do you do it?"

The kid said, "I make applesauce."

■

When it comes to finances we all feel compelled to bend the truth a little bit. Hollywood especially is noted for its "creative bookkeeping." This story about a writer sums it up:

This writer had just had one of his movies released. It was playing on a theatre on Wilshire Boulevard. He happened to pass by it one day and stopped in to talk to the theatre manager. He asked how the box office was doing.

The manager said, "This is the worst film we've had in years. We're doing terrible business."

The writer said, "Really?"

The manager said, "This picture's been here for three days. We did $9 worth of business. Can you imagine that? In three days we did $9."

Now the writer was depressed. He went to "Nate and Al's Deli" in Beverly Hills for lunch, figuring he'd run into a few other writers who might cheer him up.

The first writer who came in said, "Hey, I see your movie is playing on Wilshire. How's it doing?"

The author said, "I don't want to talk about it."

The other writer said, "C'mon. You can tell me."

The author said, "I don't want to talk about the movie."

His friend said, "C'mon, I'm a writer, too. I know the business. How's it doing at the box office?"

The guy said, "I don't want to talk about it."

His friend said, "Tell me."

The writer said, "All right. It did $18."

■

Here's a classic solution to a common budgetary disagreement:

A gentlemen said, "My wife wanted a new fur coat and I wanted a new car. We couldn't afford both of them so we compromised. We bought the fur coat, but we keep it in the garage."

■

Sometimes the skills of the workplace don't translate to home life.

A man was eager to go to sleep. He asked his wife to turn out the light.

She said, "I'm reading a mystery book. "

He looked at her and said, "That looks like our household budget."

She said, "It is."

■

One woman told her friends over lunch that she and her husband saved money by going over their household budget every single night.

Someone asked, "How does that save you money?"

She said, "By the time we make any sense of it, it's too late to go out and spend anything."

PROFIT AND LOSS

You all know what a dollar sign is. That's the corporate version of the happy face symbol.

In the executive world you either make a profit or you make a fool of yourself.

∎

In the executive world you either make a profit or you make room for your replacement.

∎

Love may make the world go 'round, but money makes it worth the trip.

∎

In the management world, the opposite of "profit" is "unemployment."

∎

A manager who shows a profit is a good manager. A manager who shows a loss is an ex-manager.

∎

No one in business says "good-bye" to a dollar. They say "See you later."

∎

Every company is in business to make money. The entire business world can be considered a "human claw machine."

∎

If you show a big profit, you're a big success; if you show a small profit, you're a failure. If you show no profit, you'll soon be working for the guy who showed a big profit.
. . . for a salary so small he'll be able to show a *bigger* profit.

∎

Business people know it's no accident that "loss" is a 4-letter word.

∎

"Loss" is to the business world what "who forgot to fill the pool up with water" is to the world of high diving.

∎

My boss used to say, "If you show a loss once, you've done something wrong. If you show a loss twice, I've done something wrong."

∎

To paraphrase comedian Joe E. Lewis: "As a business person, I've made money and I've lost money. Making it is better."

∎

Making money can't buy happiness. Losing it can't buy anything.

There's a difference between spending money and losing money. Spending money is an investment in your business; losing money is investing in a chain of Joan Crawford Day Care Centers.

■

Spending company money to make money is good business. Spending company money for any other reason is good-bye.

■

Remember, the bible said, "If you cast your bread upon the water it will return to you a hundredfold." What your company is going to do with 100 loaves of wet bread is your problem.

■

Keep in mind the business axiom: "If you ask a fair price for services rendered, you're going to be outbid every time."

■

Jackie Mason tells a joke that applies to profit and loss. He says, "My grandfather always told me, 'Never watch your money; watch your health.' So one day I was watching my health; somebody stole my money. It was my grandfather."

■

"It is no secret that organized crime in America takes in over forty billion dollars a year. This is quite a profitable sum, especially when one considers that the Mafia spends very little for office supplies." — *Woody Allen*

■

What was the only business failure ever suffered by the late Charles Engelhard, gold tycoon and president of Engelhard Minerals & Chemical Corp.?

Engelhard invested in an African timber estate on the banks of the Zambesi River. Not until too late did he learn that in the dry season the river reverses direction and flows inland, making it impossible to float timber to port. He tried to recoup his losses by planting crops on the estate. It would have worked—if only the Zambesi's hippopotamuses hadn't lumbered out of the river and eaten all of Engelhard's crops.

■

After creating Corfam, a substitute for leather, Du Pont couldn't market it successfully in the 1960's. Corfam was put on expensive shoes to enhance its image, but sales remained sluggish—even after cheaper shoes were made of the product. Du Pont was convinced the artifical material was all but useless and sold it to Poland at a multimillion dollar loss in 1974. Only then did the price of leather on the world market soar, making Corfam an extremely profitable material.

Will Rogers admitted: "I would never make a good economist. You know, an economist is a man that can tell you anything about . . . well, he will tell you what can happen under any given condition, and his guess is liable to be as good as anybody else's, too."

■

Woody Allen explained the teaching of economics about as well as anybody. He wrote this description of a course in economics theory:

ECONOMIC THEORY: a systematic application and critical evaluation of the basic analytic concepts of economic theory, with an emphasis on money and why it's good. Fixed coefficient production functions cost and supply curves, and nonconvexity comprise the first semester, with the second semester concentrating on spending, making change, and keeping a neat wallet. The Federal Reserve System is analyzed, and advanced students are coached in the proper method of filing out a deposit slip. Other topics include: Inflation and Depression—how to dress for each. Loans, interest, welching.

■

A man went into a bar and asked how much it cost for a ham sandwich. The bartender said it was $3.00. He said, "OK, give me a ham sandwich."

The bartender served him the sandwich and said, "That'll be three bucks."

The man asked, "How much is a beer?"

The bartender said, "$1.50." The customer said, "Give me two beers."

The bartender served up two beers and said, "That's another three bucks."

The customer said, "Here, I'll pay for the beers with the sandwich."

The bartender said, "What are you talking about?"

The customer said, "The sandwich is three bucks and the beers are three bucks. I'm paying for the beers with the sandwich."

The bartender said, "You never paid for the sandwich."

The customer gulped down the beers and said, "Why should I? I'm not going to eat it."

■

Around the turn of the century a young man asked a question of Bernard Baruch, an established financial tycoon. He said, "Mr. Baruch, is there any sure way to earn a million dollars?"

Baruch said, "All you have to do is buy a million bags of flour at $1 a bag, then sell them for $2 a bag."

Baruch was joking, but the man took him seriously. That's how August Hecker started Hecker's Flour Mills, at one time the largest company of its kind in the world.

"Takeovers are for the public good, but that's not why I do it. I do it to make money."—*corporate raider, James Goldsmith*

·

Here's a story of a hard-nosed businessman who was determined that no one would get the best of him.

Chris Von Der Ahe was the president of the St. Louis Browns way back in the 1880's. He went to visit his team one day and discovered that someone was damaging the equipment in the locker room. Naturally, this would cost him money so he demanded to know who the vandal was. No one answered.

He said, "I'll give one hundred dollars to find out who did this."

A long silence followed then Arlie Latham, the third baseman, said, "I know who did it."

Chris said, "Who?"

Latham said, "Give me the money first." The executive counted off one hundred dollars and handed it to the third baseman.

Latham said, "I did it."

Now the President of the club was furious, but remained a strict disciplinarian. He said, "For that little trick, Latham, I'm fining you fifty dollars," and stormed out of the locker room.

·

We're all interested in the profits.

A young man was courting a pretty young girl. The girl told him, "My father is a very successful businessman. When he was quite young he amassed a large fortune. Would you like to know how he did it?"

The man said, "Not really. I'd just like to know . . . does he still have it?"

·

In 1986, a discount store ran a television commercial for a stereo set. They said it cost only "299 bananas." Sure enough, people took the ad literally and showed up at the store with 11,000 bananas.

The store chain accepted the "currency," and lost $10,465 on stereos.

COST SAVINGS

Costs are to a business what in-laws are to a marriage. You know you'll always have them, but you try to get rid of as many of them as you can.

Remember that God made the world in seven days, but labor and supplies were cheaper then.

■

We formed a cost savings team at our company and their first official act was to schedule their meetings at noon so the company would have to pay for lunch.

■

It would seem like the ideal in the business world would be to reduce costs completely, until you remember that your salary is part of it.

■

The secret, of course, is to reduce unnecessary costs completely and then make sure that you're not one of those.

■

Cost saving is a wonderful thing. It's what separates private industry from the government.

■

Cost saving in a company is commendable—unless your job becomes part of it.

■

A good employee will try to reduce costs so he can ask for a raise.

■

Controlling costs is essential in business . . . unless you're working for the government.

■

That's why very few businesses are set up in lighthouses. There are no corners to cut.

■

Family run businesses are ideal. If your relatives keep costs down, fine. If they don't, cut them out of your will.

■

Unnecessary costs are like a virus on your business, and when they hit, the treatment is the same–everybody gets a shot in the ass.

■

Some cost savings teams use generous "fudge factors." When I was a kid and wanted a baseball glove, I told my mother I'd save her $1.25 a week by running to school behind the bus. My brother said he'd save her $25.00 a week by running to school behind a taxi cab.

■

I was put on a cost savings team at my company that had a quota of $450,000 a year. I was supposed to save the company almost 1/2 a million dollars—the same company that just refused me a $5 a week raise.

So I didn't work very hard on cost savings. I simply went in to my manager and asked for a $500,000 a year raise. Naturally, he turned me down, so I figured I was now $50,000 over my cost savings quota.

We had such a stiff cost savings quota that our team used to bring back stationery supplies we stole from the company last year.

Once the president of our company was kidnapped and a $10 million dollar ransom was demanded. Every cost savings team in the company wanted to take credit for not paying it.

■

A woman went into her corner butcher shop and asked if they had lamb chops.
The butcher said, "Yeah, we got fine lamb chops."
She said, "How much?"
He said, "The lamb chops are $1.85 a pound."
She said, "$1.85 a pound? In the butcher shop down the street they're only $1.60 a pound."
So the butcher said, "Then why don't you buy them there?"
She said, "They're all out of lamb chops."
He said, "Oh. When I'm all out of them, they're only $1.29 a pound."

■

I knew a young entrepreneur who set up a business where he lost 10 cents on every item he sold. He said, "It wasn't too bad when we were first starting, but once we got successful, it drove us out of business."

■

I knew an executive who complained that his department would be the most successful in the company if it weren't for his costs. His boss said, "Yeah, and Germany would have won World War II if it weren't for their injuries."

■

One company carried cost savings to extremes. When they elected a new chairman, they prepared attractive press releases and sent them to newspapers and business publications across the country.

A year later, they mailed out the same release. They had discovered many unused press releases in their files, so they mailed them out again rather than trash them.

The company spokesman said, "We wanted to remind people of the appointment."

■

One company discovered that it was costly to have mass firings. So to save money they initiated "requested departures" from twenty-six people.

■

Here's the ultimate in cost savings:

A farmer resented the money he had to spend to feed his plowhorse. He told his wife, "That lazy, good-for-nothing animal eats up precious oats and hay every single day. Tomorrow I'm going to eliminate the oats and see how that affects him."

A few weeks later he was satisfied that the horse was just as productive on a diet of pure hay. However, he decided to gradually cut down on the amount of hay he offered the horse.

The poor animal survived on less and less hay, still doing it's work. The farmer was delighted and was going to try to cut out the feeding altogether.

He did. The horse lasted for a short while but finally succumbed.

The farmer was heartbroken. He said, "What lousy luck. Just when I'd gotten that beast to learn to live without food, it ups and dies."

PRODUCTIVITY

My manager once wrote a book called "Up Your Output."

It not only described his managerial goals, but how he intended to accomplish them.

■

Productivity is the bottom line in business. If you're not producing, you'd better be related to the boss or one of his children.

■

God said, "Go forth, produce and multiply." He sounds like the world's first sales manager.

■

Business is like a game show. Produce and you can come back next week; don't produce and the company has some nice parting gifts for you.

It doesn't matter what grades you got in school. Your grades in business all have to have a $ in front of them.

■

Money can't buy happiness, but it can buy a new employee to replace the one who's not producing any.

■

Productivity is another word for efficiency, and both of them are another word for profits.

■

Everyone knows you can't get blood from a stone. Productivity is the art of convincing the stone that it's not only possible, but not that unusual.

■

Productivity is not only getting blood from a stone, but the following month, raising the stone's quota.

■

Too many executives get confused. They think raising the blood pressure helps raise productivity.
    . . . *anybody's* blood pressure.
    . . . *everybody's* blood pressure.

■

A good executive can remain calm and unruffled and still raise productivity—provided his employees are going bonkers.

■

"Put up or shut up" used to be our business creed–until shop stewards arrived and eliminated the "shut up" part.

■

The business world expects a return for every dollar it pays out. You may consider it a salary, but they consider it a loan.

■

God judges your behavior once a lifetime, Santa Claus checks your performance once a year; but management checks up on you once a week.
    That's probably fair. God and Santa Claus don't pay your salary.

■

Just to show you how the company feels about you, they check your health maybe once a year, but they check your productivity week to week.

Productivity studies have shown that millions of Americans aren't working, but they have jobs.

■

PRODUCTIVITY: Doing things wrong faster than ever before.

■

PRODUCTIVITY GAIN: Being able to use the time you saved to do work that doesn't need to be done in the first place.

■

A patrolman picked up a vagrant. He asked the man, "Do you ever work?"
The man said, "Now and then."
The officer asked, "What do you do?"
The man said, "This and that."
The policeman said, "Where do you do it?"
The man said, "Here and there."
So the cop took him into the police station.
The vagrant said, "When am I getting out of here?"
The cop said, "Sooner or later."

■

Studio head, Louis B. Mayer, measured everything in terms of productivity. Even when he relaxed, he relaxed with productivity in mind.

He took up golf but didn't play like other golfers did. He brought two caddies along with him. One would be stationed far down the fairway to locate the ball instantly. He'd prepare the shot for Mayer while the other one ran on ahead to be ready to locate the next shot.

When the game was over, Mayer didn't care about the score. He'd simply check his watch and say, "We made it in two hours and 8 minutes. Six minutes better than yesterday."

■

When John Kennedy was running for President in 1960, he visited a West Virginia coal mine. One of the workers there confronted him and said, "I hear you're the son of one of the wealthiest men in the country. Is that right?"

Kennedy said it was.

The miner said, "I heard you got everything you ever wanted. Is that true?"

Kennedy said, "Pretty much so."

The miner asked, "Is it true you've never done a day's work with your hands in your entire life?"

Kennedy said it was true.

The miner said, "Let me tell you this, you haven't missed a thing."

Here's a gentleman who really knew how to get work done. And he was an uneducated farmer who never had any formal management training. He was picked up by the Federal agents and jailed for making moonshine.

The revenue people suspected that he still had a lot of moonshine buried around the farm, so they cautioned the warden to screen his mail.

Sure enough, in his first letter to his wife he scribbled this cryptic note at the bottom of the page: "The you-know-what is buried in the field behind the barn."

The Federal agents turned up that whole field and found nothing.

In another letter to his wife, the man confessed, "I must be getting old and forgetful. I told you the you-know-what was behind the barn. I was wrong. It's buried in the field west of the creek."

The agents plowed all of that field up, too. Still they found no illegal moonshine.

In the gentleman's next letter he told his wife, "Honey, now that the government has done our spring plowing for us, go ahead and plant the corn."

■

Sometimes you find that when you have a good product–something that people want–productivity just automatically increases.

A travelling salesman stopped in a small town and after a tough day on the road, wanted a drink. He went to the local restaurant but discovered that this town was dry. No alcohol could be sold. However, the clerk there told him that he might be able to persuade the town pharmacist to sell him some alcohol strictly for medicinal purposes.

He tried, but the pharmacist had strict ethics. He said, "I can't sell you drinking alcohol for recreational purposes. I can only let you have it if there is a bonafide medical emergency."

The salesman asked what would constitute a bonafide medical emergency.

The pharmacist said, "Well, a snake bite would qualify."

The salesman said, "Where can I find a snake?"

The pharmacist said, "There's one generally hanging out behind the livery stable. He's a local snake. Very cooperative, and won't say a word of this to anybody."

The salesman left and came back later. He was shaking his head and said to the pharmacist, "It didn't work. That snake's so busy biting local drunks, he don't have time to bite a stranger."

YOUR MONEY

We pray each day for "our daily bread"; but we have to ne-gotiate with the boss for "a little jam and jelly on the side."

PAYDAY

Payday is the only day of the week when you leave the office without the company owing you something.

■

Payday is beautiful. It's the only morning you wake up *knowing* things are going to get better.

■

Payday is the day when you and the company settle all debts.

■

Payday is what we used to call in the schoolyard, "Put up or shut up."

■

Payday is when you open your envelope and find out what a pound of flesh is selling for these days.
. . . minus taxes, of course.

■

It's funny, but the ride home from work seems softer when the pockets are full.

■

Payday is the day that makes it all worthwhile . . . at least to you, if not the company.

Payday used to be a reward for a job well-done. Nowadays, thanks to union contracts, it's a reward for a job no matter how it's done.

■

The paycheck is the company's way of saying "Thank you." Most of us, of course, wish they would say it a little louder.

■

It's strange that the company says "Thank you" just once a week, and we say "You're welcome" for at least 40 hours.

■

Researchers say that people don't really go to work each day for the money. I wonder if these people do all that research for a pat on the head and an occasional lump of sugar?

■

Payday is the day when we stand up and shout, "Pay me what I'm worth;" and the bastards do.

■

Money is supposed to be the root of all evil, and come payday we're all in there rooting.

■

We all work hard for our money, and come payday it's nice to be able to take home about 70 percent of it to the family.

■

Four days a week our family greets our homecoming with open arms. On payday, they greet us with open palms.

■

Payday is somewhat like Judgment Day, except better. On Judgment day you get rewarded for how good you've been; on payday it's just for how many hours you worked.

■

"A fair day's wage for a fair day's work" seems to work in theory, but somehow both sides feel they're getting a bum deal.

■

The money seems to go from the company to the bank to your debtors. You put in 40 hours of hard work just to act as the middle man.

"Another day, another dollar" to you is just a cliche. To the company accounting department, though, it's a fond memory of a bygone era.

■

"Money won't buy happiness, but it will pay the salaries of a large research staff to study the problem."—*Bill Vaughan*

■

"Wealth–any income that is at least one hundred dollars more a year than the income of one's wife's sister's husband." —*H.L. Mencken*

■

An author once wrote to George Bernard Shaw asking permission to include one of Shaw's pieces in an anthology. The man explained that he was very young and couldn't pay Shaw his usual fee. George Bernard Shaw wrote back and said, "I'll wait till you grow up."

TAKE-HOME PAY

The difference between "pay" and "take-home pay" is the difference between "all" and "nothing at all."

■

Do you know why they call it "take-home pay?" Where else can you go with it?

■

It's discouraging to pick up your paycheck and find out it's been pre-spent.

■

Take a good look at your paycheck stub sometime. There's one area there for what you get and eight different areas for what somebody else gets.

■

You've got all these partners at work, but none of them help you shovel the car out on snowy mornings.

■

If you have all these partners on your payroll check, how come you're the only one who has to get up at 6 to get to the office on time?

■

They shouldn't even call it "pay;" they should call it "leftovers."

They shouldn't even make it "take-home pay." They should give you a choice—"Do you want to take it home, or do you want to spend it here?"

■

My Dad used to say that his paycheck each Friday would burn a hole in his pocket. What they leave you nowadays hardly gets your pockets warm.

■

Payroll deductions—they're the moths in your financial closet.

■

It's terrible to see all that money is gone from your paycheck, and your wife hasn't even gotten to it yet.

■

"Take-home pay" is what you have left after you pay Uncle Sam his weekly allowance.

■

Personal income can be a joke. Salary is the set-up; and "take-home pay" is the punchline.

■

You know what "take-home pay" is. In boxing they call it "the loser's share."

■

"Take-home pay" is your consolation prize for a job well done.

■

Look at all the deductions on your paycheck. Wouldn't it be nice if we could lose weight that easily?

■

PeeWee Herman looks like Arnold Schwarzenegger after deductions.

■

I make sure I never bring work home from the office and my payroll deductions make sure I never bring my salary home from the office, either.

■

Payroll deductions—they're also known as "salary piranhas."

■

The payroll deductions seem to grow every year. Soon you may just open your pay envelope and find an I.O.U.

One accountant admonished his client: "You have to learn to live within your means. Who do you think you are–the government?"

∎

You have to love the worker who complained to his boss, "I've been underpaid for so long, if I ever do make ends meet, they won't recognize one another."

∎

One worker summed up his inadequate take-home salary. He said, "At the end of the money, I always seem to have a little bit of month left over."

∎

One executive tried to encourage a worker who complained of being underpaid. He said, "Don't worry. If you keep working hard and being faithful to the company, your ship will come in." The worker said, "Too late, boss. I think my pier is collapsing."

∎

One worker said that his take-home pay didn't even keep up with the rate of inflation: "All last year I had no money in my wallet. This year I still got no money and the wallet's not even paid for."

∎

Some executives literally don't realize that the employees need money for luxuries like food, clothing, and shelter.

Kingsley Martin was editor of *The New Statesman*. One day he went out of his way to compliment a new, young editor that had just been hired. His work was exceptional and Martin told him so.

The editor was naturally pleased with the praise and tried to capitalize on it. He said, "Mr. Martin, I thank you, and I'm happy that you're pleased with my work. However, I'm recently married and we're finding it hard to get by on the salary you're paying."

Martin was dumbfounded. He said, "Good God. You mean you haven't got a private income?"

∎

Somebody said it, and it makes sense: "You know, the more they knock New York, the bigger it gets. They don't have any tax money, so the city is just like a modern human being–it has to exist on borrowed money."

∎

Lefty Gomez was a great pitcher for the New York Yankees in the 1930's. However, after a losing season, management asked him to take a cut. It was a considerable cut, too—from $20,000 to $7,500.

Gomez said, "I'll tell you what. You keep the salary and pay me the cut."

Here's a guy who turned down a considerable raise, but didn't realize it at the time.

Sir Arthur Conan Doyle was attending rehearsals for a play he had written. A kid named Charlie, one of the actors in the play, wasn't happy with the three pounds a week he received as salary.

The actor kidded the author and suggested that they pool their incomes and each take half for the rest of their natural born lives.

Doyle chuckled and said, "I don't think so, Mr. Chaplin."

■

One youngster who's Dad had taken ill and missed work said a prayer. He showed the signs of a good future executive because he decided to put the prayer in writing. He wrote a letter to God saying, "Dear God, Mom has been complaining about how tough is it since Daddy got sick. Could you please send us a couple hundred dollars to help out until my Dad can get back to work. Thank you, Johnny."

Some of the his father's workers found out about the letter and took up an office collection. They raised $100 and sent it to the family.

Johnny sent off another letter to God. It said, "Dear God, thanks for the cash, but I was talking about a couple hundred dollars *after* deductions."

■

Sometimes it doesn't pay to get too much money at once.

A company discovered through a bookkeeping error that they owed thirty thousand dollars to a former employee's widow. Many years had passed and the widow was quite old and sickly. The executives were afraid to notify her directly. Someone suggested that they call her parish priest for advice.

He conferred with them and decided that he would tell the woman. He would break the news to her gently. On one of his visits to the widow he tactfully asked, "What would you do if, say, someone were to give you . . . oh . . . thirty thousand dollars?"

She said, "Why, I'd give it to the church."

The priest is expected to recover shortly.

■

A wealthy businessman was lecturing one of his employees on the wise use of his money. The man said, "When I arrived in this city, I only had fifty cents in my pocket. Did I go around crying, and whining, and moaning the blues? Certainly not. Not me."

The employee said, "You mean, you invested the fifty cents wisely?"

The rich man said, "I sure did. I used it to call my Dad to send more cash."

■

One worker said, "Einstein was smart, and Galileo was pretty good. Thomas Edison wasn't bad either. But the smartest guy I know is Charlie over in welding."

Another worker said, "What makes him so brilliant?"

The guy said, "He got his salary raised six months ago, and his wife hasn't found out about it yet."

■

A worker asked his accountant for a dependable rule-of-thumb for estimating the cost of living.

The accountant said, "Take your income—whatever it is—and add 25 percent."

OVERTIME

I appreciate my take-home pay, but without overtime I couldn't afford a home to take it to.

■

Philosophers believe time is man's most priceless commodity. Non-exempt employees think time-and-a-half is.

■

The workers credo is: If at first you don't succeed, do it later and get paid time-and-a-half for it.

■

Overtime pay is the Mae West of the non-exempt employees. It helps keep their heads above water.

■

Overtime pay is like the snake who accidentally gets caught in two electric pencil sharpeners at the same time. It makes both ends meat.

■

I'm not complaining, but overtime makes me feel like a hooker. I'm worth more when the sun goes down.

■

Overtime keeps a lot of us honest. If you're going to tell your spouse you're working late at the office, it better show up in your paycheck.

■

All work and no play makes Jack time-and-a-half.

■

Overtime fattens the paycheck. If you're going to work for a living, you might as well do it for high-caloric wages.

Upper management believes time-and-a-half is a crock-and-a-half.

■

My manager's philosophy is: Anything worth doing is worth doing on straight time.

■

Why should we give them 50 percent more for not getting the work done when we're paying them 33 1/3 percent less?

■

Management looks on time-and-a-half as a bonus for loafing during straight time.

■

Management hates to pay more than straight salary for any work, overtime or not. They consider it "slave management."

■

They consider overtime as "highway labor."

■

Our boss makes it known how he feels about paying extra for overtime work. He wants all the non-exempt people who work evenings or Saturdays to wear ski-masks.

And on payday he prefers that they back up to the window.

■

My boss pays the overtime bonus grudgingly. He puts the extra money in a gelatin mold.

■

My boss will be happy paying extra for overtime work only when the workers put in a man-and-a-half hour of work.

■

Young Robert Bernstein worked at New York's radio station WNEW. However, something about him impressed Albert Leventhal, the head of sales at Simon & Schuster. Leventhal hired Bernstein to come to work in the publishing house.

It turned out to be a wise selection. Bernstein was enthusiastic and energetic. Once Leventhal came to the office early, around 7:30 in the morning. Bernstein was already at his desk working hard.

When Bernstein saw his boss enter the office, he said, "I'm ambitious. What's your excuse for being here at this unearthly hour?"

Averell Harriman was a workaholic and expected his staff to be the same. One day he left his office at an unusually early hour for him. It was 5:30 P.M.

He told his staff when he left, "I'm not coming back this evening, so all of you can take a half-holiday."

■

Napoleon often worked 12 to 16 hours a day. He wanted his Council of State to match him hour for hour. At one late night session, several members nodded off. Napoleon chided them.

He said, "Let's keep awake, citizens. It's only two o'clock. We must earn our salaries."

Some members admired Napoleon's intensity; others hated it.

One supporter said, "God made Bonaparte and then rested."

A complainer said, "God should have rested earlier...while He had the chance."

■

Here's one theory offered by Mike Burstein and Ray Bruman for estimating completion time on projects:

> To bring a project in on time, take a well-researched guess at how long it will take and add time for gremlins and hidden variables. Then double your guess and move to the next unit of time. A job that should take an hour will take about two days. A three-day task will take about six weeks. A two-week task takes about four months. And a job that should take two quarters will take about four years.

ASKING FOR A RAISE

Most people work up the courage to ask for a raise by remembering that it takes less nerve to ask for the increase than it does to go home and tell your spouse that you couldn't work up the nerve.

■

When asking for a raise, don't be afraid to shoot for the stars. Give it a shot—ask for what you're worth.

■

Asking for a raise is easy. Proving you're worth it is the hard part.

■

You can always ask for a raise; you can always demand what you're worth. Of course, it helps if both of these things are the same.

By asking for a raise, you'll at least find out what you're worth–sometimes on the open market.

■

I knew one guy who asked for a raise and the boss promised to pay him what he was worth. The guy turned it down. He said, "Hell, I'm making more than that now."

■

In business, everybody gets paid what they're worth. The discrepancy is whether you get what you think you're worth or what they think you're worth.

■

Some people get excited about a raise. Others just consider it an apology for last year's salary.

■

If a raise is a reward for past performance, how come it's never retroactive?

■

I get a lump in my throat each time I ask for a raise. It's probably because the boss immediately starts strangling me.

■

I once admitted to my boss that I was very nervous about asking him for a raise. He comforted me. He told me I had good reason to be nervous.

■

Tell your boss that you want the raise for patriotic reasons. You owe it to your country to pay more taxes.

■

Ask for a raise anytime you're dumb enough to think you deserve it. Chances are you'll get one when the company is dumb enough to think you deserve it, too.

■

My boss likes me to ask for a raise. He enjoys a good laugh in the middle of the workday.

■

My boss agreed that I was worth more money and that I deserved more money. He was even willing to help me look for a company that would be willing to pay me more money.

■

I asked the boss for a raise once because I said I was doing the work of two men. He fired all three of us.

My boss and I are very far apart on contract renegotiations. I'm demanding a 30 percent increase and he's refusing to see me.

■

Once I told my superior, "I think I'm worth more. What will you give me?" She gave me just enough time to clean out my desk.

■

Avoid ultimatums. Few companies can resist the chance of losing you and saving money at the same time.

■

I left one company because of an ultimatum. I demanded to be paid what I was worth and they agreed. They studied it and discovered I wasn't worth keeping.

■

Once I demanded a major increase or I would resign and the boss refused to budge. We compromised. I pretended I never said it and he pretended he didn't hear it.

■

Negotiations between Fernando Valenzuela and the Dodgers got off to a bad start when his agent began by saying, "Stick 'em up."

■

It's always frightening when the agent who is going to negotiate shows up at the first meeting with a briefcase and a rake.

■

NEGOTIATING: If you are negotiating for money, pay careful attention to the increments of change in your opponent's demands. When the increments begin to decrease in size, your opponent is reaching his or her bargaining limit.—*Jeff Furman, Business Consultant*

■

Mrs. William Howells, wife of the novelist, hired a young lady to do her housework. Each day when she arrived for work, Mr. Howells would of course be there since his office was at home.

One day the young domestic approached Mrs. Howells and was a little embarrassed. She said, "Mrs. Howells, you pay me four dollars a week . . ."

Mrs. Howells quickly interrupted, "And I'm afraid that's all we can afford to pay you right now."

But the girl went on. She said, "Well, I'd be willing to work for three dollars a week . . . just until Mr. Howells finds a job."

I like the ballplayer (and management liked him, too) who had a good season and was offered a one-third increase in salary. This was before the age of agents, so the player held out for and got one-fourth.

■

A writer once worked for a nightclub comedian. The comedian was generous and willing to pay for the gags, but not in any regular schedule. The writer had to chase the performer all over the country and plead through the mails for the checks that were long overdue.

Then after writing a particularly good piece of material, the comic said, "You're really getting good. I'm going to raise your salary 75 bucks a week."

The comedy writer said, "Please don't pay me any more money. I work hard enough just getting the amount you're giving me now."

■

A nightclub comic tells this story about two of the cheapest bosses in the world:

I used to work in a small nightclub that was owned by a father and son team. Two of the cheapest men in the world. I'll give you an idea how cheap they were.

I'd be up on the stage telling my jokes to the crowd and the father would come out of this little office they had in the back. He'd be wearing an expensive Italian suit, snake skin shoes, and puffing a big cigar.

He'd walk around the club to see if the patrons were enjoying my jokes. He'd come and stand by the stage, puff on the big cigar, and go back into his little office.

About ten minutes later, the son would come out. He'd be wearing a shiny silk suit, puffing a big cigar. He'd walk around to see if the folks were enjoying my jokes. He'd come up by the stage and puff on that big cigar for awhile, then he'd go into that office in the back.

To show you how cheap these guys were . . . it was the *same* cigar.

■

There's a story told about Louis B. Mayer, the head of MGM studios. Robert Taylor had worked for the studio for some time without a pay increase, so he asked for and got an appointment to see Mayer.

Taylor said, "Mr. Mayer, I've been with this studio some time now. I've been doing bigger parts in better movies, but I've never received any more money."

Mayer looked hurt. He said, "My boy, you know I'm crazy about you and your talent. I think of you as my very own son. The Good Lord never saw fit to give me a son. He gave me two beautiful and devoted daughters, but if He had given me a son, I would want him to be just like you. We have big plans for you at the studio, you know. Things that you can't even begin to imagine."

Mayer was almost in tears. "It hurts me very deeply that you would come and ask for more money at a time like this."

Taylor apologized for the sorrow he caused and left Mayer's office.

A fellow actor asked when he came out of the office, "Did you get the raise?"

Taylor said, "No, but I gained a father."

STOCKS

Some executives make a lot of money from stock deals. I have bad luck in the stock market. I can always spot my stocks on the financial page. They're the ones trimmed in black.

■

I don't read the front page of the paper anymore. I just read the comics and the financial page. For me, that's the "funnies" and the "saddies."

■

I try to look up my stocks every morning in the newspapers, but it takes time. I have to keep flipping from the financial page to the obituaries.

■

It's amazing how fast I can lose money on my stocks. I reached into my pocket yesterday and my credit cards had turned to dust.

■

I lose money so fast, the inside of my wallet has skid marks.

■

My stocks drop so fast the newspapers don't even print them. They just pencil them in.

■

I called my broker yesterday and he put me on hold. By the time he got back on the phone, I had nothing left to talk to him about.

■

I really have bad luck in the stock market. My broker sends a calendar each year to most of his clients. He sends me a crying towel.

■

I should get out of the stock market and be more like Johnny Carson. He has all his money tied up in ex-wives.

I tried to call my broker yesterday, but his ledge was busy.

■

Of course, I worry about my broker. Every time I go to shake hands with him, his hand is stuck in a cookie jar.

■

My broker's letterhead has a Latin inscription on it. I finally found out it means, "I got mine; you get yours."

■

I can't win in the stock market. I started burying money in my back yard. The last earthquake moved it to someone else's property.

■

I lost so much money in the market this year I can afford to tell the truth on my tax return.

■

I lost so much in the market this year, we may have to trade my wife's fur coat in for the meat that used to be in it.

■

I did so bad this year, I had to switch brokers–from stock to pawn.

■

To me the stock market means a fool and his money are soon parted, except you pay a broker's fee.

■

All that insider trading has given the market a bad name. But it kept brokers from jumping off ledges. They were too embarrassed to be seen in public.

■

My broker thought about jumping off a ledge, but he didn't. He wanted to be the only thing in his office that didn't go down last year.

■

My broker promised me a modest return of 8 percent, and he was right. I've now got 8 percent of the money I used to have a year ago.

■

The American Association of Individual Investors gives this advice on purchasing stocks: Don't buy stocks for a year after a presidential inauguration. For some reason, the market almost always goes down in that period.

Edwin C. Bliss, a time management expert, says, "If your office is typical, three quarters of the things in your files should have been placed in your wastebasket.

■

Someone once described the stock market this way:

Three hundred thousand dollars for a seat on the Stock Exchange! You pay that for a seat where nobody sits down. They stand and yell and sell something they haven't got, and buy something they will never get.

That's not a seat; that's a license to hold a sucker up when he buys, and blackjack him when he sells; to commit petty larceny when he buys, and grand larceny when he sells.

■

Will Rogers had some pithy comments on stocks, too.

"There's a proverb on Wall Street: What goes up–must have been sent up by somebody."

"Don't gamble; take all your savings and buy some good stock, and hold it till it goes up, then sell it. If it don't go up, don't buy it."

"All the big financiers and stock-market writers are saying: good values are worth as much as they ever were. But that's the trouble, nobody knows what they ever were worth."

■

The President of the United States called an influential broker on Wall Street to tell him personally, "The economy is in good shape again. The outlook is fantastic. In fact, if I weren't the President of the United States I'd be investing in the stock market."

The man replied, "Sir, if you weren't the President of the United States, everyone would be investing in the stock market."

■

Three stockbrokers were enjoying some pleasant conversation along with their third martini.

One said, "This martini tastes good, and I don't care what people say, it's relaxing."

The second said, "I agree. Our profession is very hectic and we earn these few drinks we enjoy."

The first said, "That's right. It's not like we're alcoholics or anything." He turned to the third broker and asked, "What do you think."

The third said, "I think we'd better drink up and get the hell out of here. The market opens in ten minutes."

A stockbroker was working at his desk, when his secretary burst in. She was frantic.

"Sir . . . sir . . . there's an IRS agent outside. He's got a SEC official with him and another gentleman who says he's a Federal Marshall. They have a subpoena for you and I just don't know what to do. What should I tell them?"

The broker said, "You're a sweet lady, and a fine secretary, and I appreciate what you're doing, but my hiccups are already gone. Thank you."

■

Two down-and-outers sat on a park bench discussing better days.

"I had a glorious future at one time, Man. I know that may be hard to believe, but it's true. I was a college graduate, doing pretty good, but my wife wanted to be rich. So I got on Wall Street and started making even more money. I'd work ten, twelve, fifteen hours a day, but it was never enough. My wife would spent more than I ever made. It was driving me into the ground. Then finally she ran off with somebody who was doing even better than I was. I just fell apart. Now I'm here in the park, drinking cheap wine, and trying to drown my sorrows. How about you."

The other guy said, "I think I'm the guy she ran off with."

■

The stock market is very simple to figure out.

Someone once stopped J. P. Morgan as he was leaving his Wall Street office. They asked for a tip on what the stock market was going to do.

Morgan said, "It will fluctuate," and walked away.

TAXES

It's tax time again . . . that time of year when crime doesn't pay, but every citizen does.

■

It's tax time . . . that's the time of year when the government hollers to your money, "Abandon wallet."

■

Tax time is very much like election time. You have to send something to Washington whether you want to or not.

■

364 days a year it pays to be an American. On April 15th you pay to be an American.

Tax day . . . that's the government's way of telling you, "If you haven't spent it yet, you ain't going to."

■

This is the time of year when the American Eagle becomes a vulture.

■

You realize every April 15th that the dollar bill is the world's most cleverly designed boomerang.

■

This is the day that the government proves once again that you can't get blood from a stone, but you can from a wallet.

■

It's terrible to have tax time in the spring when everything turns green except your wallet.

■

Tax time . . . that's when all your pictures of George Washington give their farewell address.

■

This is when the government of the people, for the people, and by the people, does it to the people.

■

It's easy to tell when it's tax time. The statue on top of the Capitol Building is wearing a stocking over its face.

■

It's that time of year when they try to get crime off the streets and back on the tax forms where it belongs.

■

At tax time we all realize the fiddler must be paid, whether we like violin music or not.

■

April 15th is the day when you get to pay for the government you've been complaining about all year long.

■

Just because America is a free country doesn't mean it's inexpensive.

That funny feeling you get in your stomach before April 15th is fear; after April 15th it's hunger.

■

The theme song for April 15th is "Rags to Riches" played backwards.

■

I always send my tax money in with a smile. I have an accountant who uses sodium pentothal.

■

I used to feel bad about paying taxes until I looked at the national deficit. The government's broker than we are.

■

Science has finally discovered how to get blood from a stone–make it fill out a tax return.

■

It's kind of barbarian to have to fill out a tax return every year. It's kind of like being kidnapped and then being forced to write your own ransom note.

■

There are many ways to go about filing your tax returns. I always use the ultra-short form–unconditional surrender.

■

The government has three tax return forms now-the long form, the short form, and shaking you upside down by the ankles.

■

I just sent the government a blank check this year and told them to fill in the amount. Let them wrestle with their conscience for a change.

■

I don't know why we have to pay taxes anyway. Just reading the instruction booklet should be punishment enough.

■

Income taxes are getting simpler every year. All you do is take the money you made, subtract what you spent, and write a check for the difference.

■

I think eventually the government will come out with a real simplified tax form. They'll just issue a statement that says, "It's April 15th. You can keep any money that has your picture on it instead of George Washington's."

Someday they may come out with a real simplified tax form: "Send us everything you've got. You can owe us the rest."

■

If the government really wants to simplify tax returns, why don't they just print our money with a return address on it?

■

I pay my taxes every year with a smile. They keep writing back and asking for money.

■

I know a great way to reduce taxes. You pay only what you can understand in the instruction booklet.

■

If they make taxes simple, I can lay off four of my attorneys. If they make them fair, I have to hire six new ones.

■

Making taxes fair is like trying to give birth to one twin.

■

Taxes will never be fair—not so long as I have to pay them.

■

There used to be an old saying that a fool and his money are soon parted. Well, the government took that and wrote it into law.

■

"Income tax returns are the most imaginative fiction being written today."
—*Herman Wouk*

■

One hillbilly was talking to his friend and said, "My Uncle Jim wants me to help him with his taxes."

His friend said, "That's silly. How can you help him with his taxes? You can't even read or write."

The other guy said, "He don't want me to read or write. He wants me to pay 'em."

■

One poor businessman was called in for an audit on his tax return. When he got to the IRS offices, he took out an old box and dumped all of its contents on the official's desk.

There were bits of paper with handwritten notes on them, old half-torn credit card receipts, pages torn off a desk calendar with memos on them. Very little of it was readable, and practically none of it was acceptable.

The IRS executive said, "This is not going to work."

The businessman said, "This is the way I keep my records. This reminds me of all the deductions that I took on my tax returns."

The executive pushed everything back into the box and said, "If you want these deductions to be allowed I want to see receipts, invoice notices, inventory lists, and verified expense records."

The businessman slammed his fist on the desk and said, "You're getting me as mad as my partner."

The IRS official said, "What does your partner have to do with this?"

The businessman said, "He's starting to want to see those things, too."

■

A businessman was fighting a tax case in court, acting as his own lawyer and not doing very well. In frustration he slammed his fist on the desk and said, "As God is my judge, I don't owe these taxes."

The judge hearing the case said, "He's not. I am. You do."

■

My Dad always used to fill out his yearly returns on the dining room table at home. I was 12 years old before I found out that "damn" and "taxes" were two different words.

PART FOUR

CONVENTIONS, COFFEE BREAKS AND OTHER OFFICE HIGH JINKS

All work and no play makes Jack a dull boy, and also a real
pigeon on the golf course.

CONVENTIONS

You all know what conventions are: They're official hangovers with a golf tournament and coffee breaks thrown in.

■

I've never been to one convention where they've run out of notepads and pencils; but I've been to many where they've run out of swizzle sticks.

■

I went to one convention where I woke up in the hotel room the next morning, and my clothes were strewn all around the room. And I was still in them.

■

Some conventions set the tone for the entire year–hangovers.

■

Three guys I worked with used to play the same drinking game at every annual convention. They'd sit in the hotel bar drinking until early in the morning, then one of them would leave. The other two would try and guess which one left.

■

Conventions are yearly events where people of the same interests or from the same corporation get together to exchange pertinent information, discuss past activities, evaluate performances, formulate new and improved policies, set short and long range goals, meet important people, and appoint committee members who will be effective in carrying out directives. That's why everybody brings their golf clubs.

■

Conventions are what make corporations stronger each year. If they can survive the annual convention, they can withstand anything.

■

Conventions are very democratic. At those company get-togethers even people who don't have anything to say insist on standing up and saying it.

■

Conventions can be very educational, too. It gives civilians a chance to learn what army cooking tastes like.

■

I attended one convention where the main speaker rode into the auditorium on a huge white stallion. It was very unique, because it was the first time this particular convention ever featured a complete horse.

Most conventions feature excellent speakers, but unfortunately, very few listeners.

■

I've spoken at some conventions with fantastic speakers who were very knowledgeable about a lot of different things. I felt like Phyllis Diller in a roomful of Dolly Partons.

■

My message is lighthearted. I told my wife before going to one convention, "I'm going to travel a long distance, I'm going to work very hard, and no one is going to learn anything from me. I don't know if I can do it." She said, "Sure you can. Just remember our honeymoon."

■

Conventions are designed to give the attendees something they can take back home with them. Hopefully, they won't get it from someone they meet at the bar.

■

I always come home from a convention with a lot more than I started with . . . usually about 372 business cards.

■

If it weren't for conventions and trade shows, many of you would never get rid of your business cards.

■

The most unique convention I ever attended was at a nudist colony. It was fun up until the end; then it was very painful tearing the name tag off.

■

Name tags are the greatest things that ever happened to conventions. They allow you to remember who you are when you wake up in the morning.
. . . Provided, of course, you went to sleep in your own clothes.

■

I attended one management convention where the featured activity was a barbecue and rodeo at a nearby ranch. At the rodeo, the cowboys showed how they get the horses to buck. They wrap a rope around their . . . well . . . in the area of their hind quarters and they pull real tight. It gets the critters to perform pretty good.
    It showed that sooner or later, everything reverts back to effective management.

■

One gentlemen used to go to a convention each year, but his wife was never invited. He always said there was too much work to be done there for spouses to be invited. Instead her job was to pick out and rent a costume for him for the masquerade ball that was the highlight of the convention activities each year.

So one year she rented him a bunny costume, and just for the hell of it, she rented one for herself, too. She was going to find out just how much work and how much play was done at this convention.

Without his knowing it, she snuck off to the convention, got dressed in the bunny outfit, and went to the masquerade ball.

She spotted the other bunny costume, struck up a conversation, got a little flirtatious, and finally the "other bunny" propositioned her. She agreed to go to his room provided they both agreed not to take their masks off.

She stayed the night and they made passionate love many times over.

When her husband returned from the convention, she asked how it went. He said, "Fine. We got a lot of work done." She said, "Did you have a good time in your bunny outfit at the masquerade ball?" He said, "Oh, I was much too busy to go to that, so I lent the costume to Charlie. He said he had the greatest time of his life."

■

I once attended a convention awards banquet in Washington, D.C. A good friend of mine and a very funny speaker, Bob Murphey, was the featured speaker. There were about 1000 people at the dinner and the hotel wasn't prepared for that kind of a crowd.

The dinner went on forever with about a half-hour wait between the soup and the salad, and another half hour wait for the main course. Everyone there was talking about how slow the service was.

When the meal was finally completed, the first part of the program, since we were in the nation's capital, was a 7-minute film that showed the entire history of America. It was quick, almost instantaneous flashes of still pictures. They went by so fast that you could hardly make out what they were.

Then Bob Murphey spoke. He began: "Before I commence to say anything humorous, I'd just like to make one comment. I wish whoever had made that movie, had served the dinner."

■

A convention keynote speaker spoke for over two hours. Then he apologized to the assemblage for going over his allotted time. He said, "I'm sorry I spoke so long, but you see, I never wear a watch."

Someone from the audience said, "But there is a calendar on the wall behind you."

■

A motivational speaker spoke at a national convention on the subject of "Mind Over Matter." His premise was that the body feels only what the mind permits it to feel. Pain is in the mind. Illnesses are in the mind.

After his speech, he joined the conventioneers at their luncheon. One attendee came over to talk to him. He said, "Sir, do you really believe all of that? Are you really convinced that the body feels nothing at all? That it's only in the mind."

The speaker said, "Yes sir, I do."

The conventioneer then said, "Well, would you mind changing seats with me. I'm sitting in a draft."

■

Most conventioneers find a little time for fun during the busy convention workday. They play a little golf, maybe some poker, and often even go out for dinner and a show.

There were several out of town conventioneers at a show one night when the entertainer was doing her act. She noticed that the couple right in front were drinking quite a bit. In fact, they stayed for two shows and drank just as heavily for the second show.

Finally, during one number the singer noticed that the gentleman just silently slid right off his chair, and disappeared under the table.

The entertainer stopped her number and went to that table. She said to the attractive young lady, "Excuse me, Miss, but your husband just slid under the table."

The lady said, "Mind your own business. My husband just walked through that door."

SEMINARS

Most seminars are a wasted day with an evaluation form to fill out at the end.

■

Important things are learned at seminars. Usually, though, by the seminar leader.

■

Seminars are well intentioned, but generally there's more information in the brochure than at the event itself.

■

I spoke to an attendee after one seminar. He said "I know just as little as I knew before, but now all my ignorance is organized."

"In other words," he said, "I still don't know anything, but I have a notebook to keep it in."

■

To paraphrase, "Those who can, do: those who can't, start giving seminars on it."

I knew one executive who avoided them totally. He said, "I'm much too busy learning to attend seminars."

■

Some executives love them. They attend seminars four days a week and try to learn why they're only getting one day's work done.

■

One gentleman said, "If I just get one good idea from this seminar, it'll be more than I had all day yesterday."

■

There are seminar addicts in the business world. They can't get through a full work week without having a name tag stuck to their breast.

■

It could be a disease. They may be physically addicted to the adhesive that's on the back of those tags that say, "Hello! My name is . . . "

■

Some people love seminars. It's not that they learn anything. It's just that they enjoy introducing themselves to the rest of the room in one minute or less.

■

They're very diligent, too. Some people can go to a three hour seminar and come home with seven hours of notes.

■

One executive has become so hooked on seminars that he can't begin his work day until he's shaken hands with at least 27 strangers.

■

One executive claims the world record for sitting in on seminars. He has 732 certificates of completion and 3 hemorrhoid operations to prove it.

■

Training seminars are the business world's version of "Sesame Street."

■

They also have motivational seminars that tell you "You are Superman." I don't know what inspiration Superman is to executives except that he's allowed to go to work without wearing a shirt and tie.

■

They figure everyone can identify with Superman. The men because he's powerful; and the women because he wears panty hose.

Motivational seminars tell you you can be better than you are, which is a fair trade off because you're probably paying them more than they're worth.

■

One mediocre motivational seminar leader advised us all to plan our goals. He said, "Write down where you'll be five years from now." One of the attendees said, "Could you first tell us where you plan to be five years from now, because I don't want to be anywhere near that."

THE OFFICE PARTY

The office party is where some people make merry and others make fools of themselves.

■

The office party has ended more careers than mandatory retirement.

■

If you must drink at the office party, drink fast. The object is to pass out before you say anything stupid.

■

Speak well of everybody at the office party. It's hard to tell the important people from the unimportant people when all their faces are blurry.

■

Some fools hang around the punch bowl speaking indiscriminately. It's an office party game called, "bobbing for a new job."

■

The office party is when you say, "I'm going to tell the boss exactly what I think of him if it's the last thing I do"... and it is.

■

At the office, don't drink and party. The job you save may be your own.

■

The office party is when some people put their foot in their mouth and don't take it out until they start kicking themselves with it the following day.

■

It's a good rule of thumb never to come home from an office party with more clothes than you went with.

You know you got carried away at the office party when:

. . . they have xerographic proof of your indiscretions.

. . . your company parking place is sealed off with police tape the next day.

. . . you're driving to work in the morning and you pass your desk on a pick-up truck going the other way.

. . . there's a memo from the boss on your desk giving you the time and the location of the upcoming duel.

. . . instead of people showing you pictures of the party, they offer to sell them to you for a price.

. . . the next time you walk into your office, you notice there's a firing squad where your desk used to be.

. . . instead of your secretary greeting you the next day at work, her husband and three of her older brothers do.

. . . you walk into your office and find that your desk has been hung in effigy.

. . . the boss says he wants to see you and they send a priest to walk with you to his office.

. . . you get to work the next day and find that your company has relocated and left no forwarding address.

■

Dylan Thomas tells a tale on himself that epitomizes many people at company parties. He tells about a time he was drinking and talking freely at a gathering. Then he stopped. "Somebody's boring me," he said, "and I think it's me."

COMPANY PICNICS

Company picnics are fun. They're a pleasant mixture of management and mayonnaise.

■

The company picnic is that one day a year when the Tug-O-War replaces the grievance procedure.

■

People get a little high-spirited at the office picnic. Sometimes not only the sandwiches go bad, but entire careers.

Company picnics are good. Somehow it's good for morale to have everybody see the boss in Bermuda shorts.

... everyone realizes his management style has got to be in better shape than his knees.

■

Of course, some office workers can't relax. Even when they get together for a day in the park, they complain about the air conditioning.

■

Some office workers can't break old habits. Even at the company picnic they steal plastic forks.

■

One guy was the star of the softball game last year. He kept stealing bases like they were office supplies.

■

The softball game is always dramatic. There's nothing more exciting than a shop steward with a bat in his hand.

■

Management likes the company picnic. The workers relax, enjoy themselves, play games, and have fun. It's just like the office, but now they're on their own time.

■

Management rarely speaks officially at the company picnic. No experienced executive is ever going to give a lecture when there's that much unused food nearby.

■

Sometimes the food is pretty bad at company picnics. You wonder where are your Quality Control people when you really need them most?

■

The company picnic is a morale booster. It's an attempt to pick up productivity with potato salad.

■

It's a day to eat, drink, and be merry because tomorrow you may have to apologize for what you did today.

■

The office picnic is a day of fun, merriment, and laughter. Of course, every day could be like that if the boss wore short pants to the office.

Of course, I've been to company picnics where management thought that labor sabotaged it. They noticed all the ants were wearing little union buttons.

■

Of course, some workers don't trust management even at the company picnic. They bring along an OSHA official as a food taster.

■

The company picnic is a day for management to mingle with labor—although they do bring along a federal mediator to call balls and strikes at the softball game.

■

At the company picnic you can always spot the folks who do a lot of airline travel for the firm. They actually like the food.

■

Sometimes the best way to keep ants away from the company picnic is to let them taste the food beforehand.

COFFEE BREAKS

"Science may never come up with a better office communications system than the coffee break."—*Earl Wilson*

■

The coffee break has become an American tradition. It's like the siesta in Mexico–except the siesta doesn't leave ring stains on your desk.

■

The coffee break is important. There are offices where the Mr. Coffee machine has been named employee of the month.

■

The coffee break is like the seven-year itch, except it hits every hour and a half.

■

If you've constantly got your shoulder to the wheel, your nose to the grindstone, and your best foot forward, you have to break for coffee. There's no way you can swallow in that position.

■

The coffee break, even for those who realize that caffeine may not be good for them, still beats staying at the desk and working.

What puzzles me is where do the people who work at the Lipton Tea factory go for their coffee break.

... And are those employees who take one punished?

■

Executives feel comfortable when they're together and each one is holding a coffee mug in one hand and cradling the mug, feeling the warmth, with the other. It keeps their hands up where they all can see them.

■

Coffee breaks are different. It seems the more coffee the employees drink, the more tense management gets.

■

I had one worker who steadfastly refused to take a morning coffee break. He claimed it kept him awake all afternoon.

■

What's ironic is that people get away from their desk to relieve momentarily the stress of the workday. Then they go and face a vending machine.

■

The coffee vending machine of today is like the old cracker barrel of yesteryear, except that no one stood around in the general store kicking the hell out of the cracker barrel because it didn't give the right change.

■

You can't tell me those machines don't cheat. Where I used to work, the coffee machine on the third floor owned its own home.

■

If most vending machines were people they would wear ski masks.

■

The newer vending machines make change. They don't give it to you; they just make it.

■

Half the time the vending machines take your money and don't give you any coffee. They're coin operated Robin Hoods.

■

We had one machine that took so much money it didn't deserve, the union put it in charge of their negotiating committee.

I once put a quarter in a coffee vending machine, selected regular coffee, one sugar, light cream. It heated the water, brewed the coffee, mixed the ingredients, and poured it right down the drain because it didn't dispense a cup. It was the ultimate in automation. It not only brewed the coffee, it also drank it for me.

■

Some offices brew their own coffee, which is nice. Throughout the day you have the aroma of either freshly brewed coffee or of an empty pot baking itself to dust.

■

The trouble with home brewed-coffee in the office is that you're at the mercy of whoever brews the coffee. That could explain how Don King's hair got that way.

■

Coffee is as much a part of the office as ink pads, rubber bands, scotch tape . . . and many times it tastes about the same.

■

Novelty coffee mugs are the rage in offices today. Many of them are almost as funny as inter-office memos.

■

Coffee breaks seem to be essential even for those who don't have time to take them.

Peter Sellers was working diligently one day in his flat in London. His wife, Anne, was just as industrious in the kitchen.

When the doorbell rang, Anne answered it. It was a telegram. She paid the deliveryman, tipped him, and opened the wire. It read: "Bring me a cup of coffee. Peter."

■

The coffee break is a fairly well established and universally accepted practice in today's business world. In fact, many companies include it as part of the basic agreement.

The coffee break is a time for relaxing chatter and friendly banter. Workers gather around with warm coffee and cold comments about their fellow workers.

It's a common occurrence several times during the normal work day. However, one coffee break was uncommon and happened during a not so normal day. It was during the Civil War.

The Union troops had just crossed Antietam Creek and faced heavy Confederate resistance in their effort to reach Sharpsburg.

A 19-year-old sergeant in the Ohio regiment carried a bucket of hot coffee and some hot rations to the men of his regiment at the front line. He voluntarily ladled hot coffee into tin cups and served the fresh cooked food until all the men had their fill.

That was September 17, 1862. A monument to the first coffee break still stands on the site of that battlefield in western Maryland. The sergeant who served the refreshments was named William McKinley. He later became the 25th President of the United States.

VACATIONS

Vacation is that time of year when you get away from the trials and tribulations of the office and enjoy some trials and tribulations with your own family.

■

Vacation is a time to get away and forget about everything. I know my kids always forget to go to the bathroom before we leave.

■

After travelling with your family you begin to appreciate your co-workers more. At least your co-workers remember to go to the bathroom before leaving the house.

■

I find after most of my vacations that the boss is glad to have me back—almost as glad as the family is to send me back.

■

Vacation is two weeks where you get away from it all. Then you come back to find that "it all" just waited patiently on your desk for your return.

■

It's amazing how you can come back from a two week vacation and find six weeks of work piled up on your desk.

... The only way to prevent that from happening is to take the desk with you on your vacation.

... It's a little bit of extra luggage to carry, but it's worth it.

■

It can take some of the fun out of your vacation when you discover that neither last year's budget nor last year's bathing suit fits.

■

Wouldn't it be nice if they paid you during your 50 weeks of work the way they charge you during your two weeks of vacation?

It's amazing after 50 weeks of work to realize how little we can afford for our two weeks vacation.

■

Workers need a vacation to refresh their minds, renew their spirits, remind them that they need a job to be able to pay for next year's vacation.

■

Experts recommend that people do something totally different on their vacations. For a lot of us that would be work.

■

When you do nothing for two weeks and get paid for it, that's the perfect vacation. When you do nothing for 50 weeks and get paid for it, that's the perfect job.

■

The question is do we need two weeks of vacation to recover from 50 weeks of work, or 50 weeks of work to recover from a two-week vacation?

■

The best vacation is one where you want to get back to work because you're in no condition to continue relaxing.

■

Some workers claim their real vacation is when the boss takes his.

■

Some workers worry that they'll be hurting business by taking their vacation. Believe me, if the company got along with you, they'll get along without you.

■

You needn't worry about taking a vacation. You can get a little concerned when you come back and discover that no one noticed you were gone.

■

If it weren't for summer vacations think how many mosquitoes would starve to death.

■

A cocktail waitress went to her boss and demanded an immediate vacation.
He said, "Why?"
She said, "I need time off. I'm not looking my best."
He said, "You look fine to me. What makes you think you don't look good?"
She said, "The businessmen who come in here are starting to count their change."

One man came back from vacation and a fellow worker said, "Did you go on your usual camping trip with the family."

The guy said, "No. We just opened all the doors, removed the window screens, ate off dirty dishes, and got the same effect."

■

One worker saves money by only going away on vacation every third year.

Someone asked what he does during the other two years. He said, "The first we talk about how much last year's vacation cost, and the second we talk about how we're going to pay for next year's."

■

Thomas Edison was a voracious worker. He came home one night and his wife scolded him. She said, "Thomas, you're working much too hard, and I insist you take a rest. You must take a vacation."

Edison said, "Where would I go?"

His wife said, "Just sit back, relax, and think about the one place on this earth you would like to be more than any other place in the world."

Edison said, "I'll do it, and go tomorrow."

The next day he was back to work in his laboratory.

■

Two workers vacationed by roughing it in the woods. It was kind of a hunting, fishing, do-nothing-but-manly-things-in-the-woods kind of a trip. Neither one of them was a great outdoorsman, but they both enjoyed the adventure in the great outdoors.

Until a bear showed up.

The bear looked fierce. He was certainly huge. He also looked mean and hungry. He roared and both men shook.

Then one gentleman sat down and started unlacing his heavy hunting boots. His friend said, "What are you doing?" The guy said, "I'm taking off these heavy shoes and slipping into my running shoes."

The bear kept coming closer.

His companion said, "That won't do you any good. You'll never outrace that bear."

The man said, "I don't have to outrace the bear. I just have to outrace you."

■

A gentleman and his wife enjoyed a pleasant vacation at a very swank hotel–until they checked out. Then they found their bill was padded with extras.

The man said, "You charged me for the tennis court, and I don't even play tennis."

The clerk said, "But the courts are there for your use. They're lighted and kept clean. Someone has to pay."

The man said, "$15 a day for the spa. We never went to the spa. We didn't even know you had a spa."

The clerk said, "But it was there for your use."

"How about this continental breakfast from 7 till 10? We never even got up till noon."

The clerk said, "That's your privilege, Sir, but the breakfast was available for you."

Finally the guy paid his bill in full, got his receipt and then punched the clerk in the nose. The guy was holding his bleeding nose, and said, "What the hell did you do that for?"

The man said, "That's for sleeping with my wife."

The clerk said, "Sleeping with your wife? I never touched your wife."

The man said, "Well, she was available for you."

GAMBLING IN THE OFFICE

Gambling goes on in most business offices. I mean, even besides the stock option plan.

■

Gambling is condoned in most offices. It's the only acceptable form of office gambling where if you lose, you're not entitled to severance pay.

■

Some places of business have gambling going on every single day. Others have assigned parking places.

■

Minor gambling is a part of business life–especially if you work in a place that has a coin-operated coffee machine.

■

Most business offices operate what they call betting pools. They call them that because sooner or later you're going to take a bath.

Technically, they're illegal, but somehow that doesn't seem out of place in a business office.

■

Football pools are very big. They're like Lotto with Gatorade.

They're very simple to play. You pay your money and you pick the teams you like, and after they lose, you don't like them anymore.

There are always a few private bets going on in the office, too. Working is like golf. If you're not good at it, you have to do something to make it interesting.

■

"Paycheck Poker" is a popular game in many offices. People chip in and whoever can make the best poker hand out of their paycheck number wins. It's an attempt by underpaid employees to find something on their paychecks that they like.

It's a way of having a little fun with your paycheck before your spouse and the IRS get to it.

It's an unabashed attempt to make some money off your paycheck.

Since the company refuses to give you any more, you try to get your fellow employees to.

■

You know the IRS allows you to deduct your gambling losses. That's nice of them, isn't it? What do they care? They're going to get it from whoever wins anyway.

Of course, on the tax form you have to swear to tell the truth, the whole truth, and never to bet on the Toronto Blue Jays.

Of course, some people never worry about the technicalities. They just list their bookie as a dependent.

■

You can deduct legitimate gambling losses. Isn't that nice of the politicians–to let us gamble with their money for a change?

■

It's nice to be able to declare gambling losses. Now when you lose the football pool, you just think of it as a tax write-off.

■

It's nice that the government lets us deduct gambling losses. You can now think of the government as a partner in each week's football pool.
    . . . unless you win.

■

Of course, gambling is losing popularity nowadays anyway. That's why they have condom ads on TV.

GOLF

I like Bob Hope's answer when someone asks "How's your golf game?" He says, "If it was a boxing match, they'd stop it."

■

For those of you who lost at today's tournament, just remember there's always next year. That's the same thing they tell the best man at Liz Taylor weddings.

■

Everybody at this convention is a golfer. The other night we had spaghetti dinner and nobody ate anything. They all just sat around and talked about what a great lie their meatballs had.

■

There are a lot of golfers at this banquet. I handed one guy the cream and sugar and he corrected my grip.

But I really knew he was a golfer when he took three lumps of sugar and wrote down two.

■

There are so many golfers at this banquet that they changed the menu. They were going to serve broccoli, but to this group it would look too much like a divot.

My boss today told me he admired my golf swing. That's like having PeeWee Herman admire your muscles.

My boss thinks an expert golf swing is one where after you make contact with the ball, you know in which direction to look.

My boss drinks a little bit when he plays golf. He's the only guy I know who can take a divot with his breath.

He gets mad when he plays. This year the rules committee was thinking of declaring his language "Out of Bounds."

■

Some of these guys spend so much time in the woods, they have to carry 13 clubs and a jar of Calamine lotion.

■

This one guy is an avid golfer. He wants to bring his golf clubs to heaven with him. He's tried lessons; what he needs now are miracles.

He wants to be buried with his golf clubs and a brand new ball . . . and, of course, an old ball for going over water.

You've got to admire a man who wants to take his golf clubs with him to the grave. He refuses to believe it's an unplayable lie.

It takes a lot of courage to want to be buried with your golf clubs. Imagine carrying a bag of golf clubs and trying to convince St. Peter that you never told a lie.

■

Anybody who's been playing golf as long as this guy has has got to go to Heaven. He's already been through Hell.

Of course, all golfers want their clubs with them when they're buried. No golfer likes to see a hole that big and not have a putter in his hands.

■

There is golf in heaven you know. Anyplace that has "weeping and gnashing of teeth" has got to have golf.

Of course, golf is a lot different in Heaven. Everybody tells the truth on their scorecard.

I'm not sure golf and Heaven go together, though . . . not with my handicap

■

DANGEROUS GOLFERS:

I played today with a dangerous golfer. On the first hole he hit two Mulligans . . . Mr. and Mrs. Mulligan from Dubuque.

I played in his fivesome–four golfers and a nurse.

This guy can do more damage on a golf course than lightning.
. . . and he hits with about the same consistency.

His game is very exciting. It's a cross between karate and auto racing.

There's a poem written about his golf game.

"I hit a golf ball into the air
It fell to earth I know not where."

I always bring a special caddy when I play with this guy. He's the same blood type I am just in case.

I always play lousy when I'm in his foursome. I find it hard to take my natural swing when I'm wearing a flak jacket.

He played well today. He hit two birdies, an eagle, a Moose, an Elk, and a Mason.

You know what they call people who have played in his foursome? Survivors.

I always play it safe when he swings. I hide behind his last divot.

When he tees off, I hide behind a tree. I just ask his caddy to make room for me.

There are about 26 different golf courses in this area and this guy never knows which one he's going to play until his second shot.

He complained to me because I was talking during his back swing. I can't help it, when he starts his swing, I just have to recite the Lord's Prayer.

The nice thing about playing golf with him is that you don't have to keep score. You just look back along the fairway and count the wounded.

He drives the only golf cart in the world with a stretcher attached.

He's easy to spot on the golf course. His golf bag is white with a red cross on it.

In his golf bag he carries 13 clubs and a paramedic.

He averaged a 9 on each hole: 6 strokes and 3 letters of apology.

I was ready to play with him, though. I brought along a golf bag that converts to a fall out shelter.

When he yells "Fore" you never know whether he's telling you to get out of the way, or predicting how many people he's going to hit.

Some golfers run out of golf balls. He runs out of first aid supplies.

He's so dangerous to play with, before his first shot, he kisses his partner on both cheeks.

Of course, he's never hit me. I think that's because I'm the one he's aiming at.

His second shot is the nicest one to watch. It means you survived his first shot.

■

He was in the water so much today, by the time he finished the fourth hole, his ball had fins.

His caddy was Jacques Cousteau.

■

He hits a golf ball like Wade Boggs hits a baseball–take two swings and then pulls it right.

He's the only guy I know who can play 18 holes of golf and redesign the golf course at the same time.

When he plays golf he always carries his passport and his visa. He sometimes needs them to look for his ball.

He did something today, though, that should improve his game. He threw his bag of clubs in the lake.

He likes to play golf in the rain. That's because his swing can't get any rustier.

He's very serious about his golf, but the way he plays, he's the only one who knows it.

He gave up trying to shoot his age. Now he's trying to shoot his budget.

OUT OF SHAPE GOLFERS:

I played with a golfer today who's a little large. When he tees off on the front nine, he casts a shadow on the back nine.

He's built perfectly for golf. He's one man who always has his own foursome.

He's built like the front nine.

When I play in his foursome, I drive the golf cart. He rides in the U-Haul in the back.

I enjoy playing with a golfer his size. If just for the shade.

I'd rather play in the foursome behind him, though. After he walks a golf course, all the fairways seem wider.

He can walk into the woods to find his ball and create a new fairway.

When he gets into a sand trap, all the sand has to get out.

His biggest handicap in golf is trying to find a golfcart that comes in his size.
. . . extra whale.

I've heard of guys losing golf balls, but this guy can lose a golf cart.
. . . just by sitting in it.

The toughest part of his game is getting in and out of the golf cart.

He carries 13 clubs and a shoehorn. That's to get him back into the golf cart after each shot.

He was starting to hit the ball pretty good, too. A few times today he almost outdrove his beltsize.

He never goes into the woods, though. He doesn't fit.

GOLFERS WHO ARE OVER THE HILL:

I played with a guy today who's getting a little too old to play golf. He had to have two boy scouts help him across each water hazard.

He can only play on courses where the ball washers are filled with Geritol.

He drives a golf cart with a rocking chair in it.

He's so old he has trouble getting out of sand traps. Oh, he can hit the ball out; he can't get out of them.

He gave up trying to shoot his age. He's now trying to shoot his blood pressure.

HERE ARE SOME FOR A BALD GOLFER:

This guy helped us out today. We painted his head white and used him as one of the tee markers.

He has trouble on the golf course. With his hair-do, people keep mistaking him for a ball washer.
 . . . it's tough to concentrate when people keep sticking a golf ball in your ear.

GOOD GOLFERS:

I'm what they call a legendary golfer. "Legendary" means mythical or fictitious, and that's how I keep score.

■

I played today against a ringer. He gave me several strokes, then made them all back with his first tee shot.

He has a real smooth swing. He doesn't even have to sit down and rest between shots.

We played a friendly little game, and it's amazing how far he can hit that ball when he's got one hand in my wallet.

And I'm not a good loser. I get mad when I lose the dime I use for a ball marker.

He played well and he was always in the fairway. Sure, anybody can score well in golf when you've always got grass under the ball.

Today, this guy made some impossible shots. For me, that's what all shots in golf are.

He was 250 yards off the green today and used a 3-wood. When I'm that far away I use a cab.

Against him I even hit from the ladies' tees, but it was legal. It was always my second shot.

■

One guy was boasting to his playing mates about this great new ball he had. "If you hit it in the woods, it starts beeping, you know. You just keep listening for the sound, you go right to your ball. If you hit it in the water,

no problem. When it gets wet, it glows real bright, so you can see it under the water. You just reach in and get it. If it gets buried in the sand, that's no problem either. It has this little antenna that pops up and sticks out of the sand. You find it in a minute."
The other guys said, "That's great. Where'd you get it?"
The guy said, "I found it."

•

Another guy was complaining about this new golf ball he bought. It was cut proof, so it would never get worn out. It floated, so you couldn't lose it in the water. It beeped, so you'd never lose it anywhere on the course. The third time he hit it it caught fire.

HERE'S WHAT WILL ROGERS HAD TO SAY ABOUT THE SPORT:

"Golf is a wonderful exercise. You stand on your feet for hours, watching somebody else putt. It's just the old-fashioned pool hall moved outdoors, but with no chairs around the walls."

•

"I guess there's nothing that will get your mind off everything like golf will. I have never been depressed enough to take up the game, but they say you can get so sore at yourself that you forget to hate your enemies."

•

Two businessmen were on the first tee preparing to make their wagers for the day's round.
The first asked, "What do you shoot?"
The other answered, "I play in the high 70's."
The first said, "Honestly?"
The other said, "What's that got to do with it?"

SOME FAMOUS GOLFERS:

A friend once tried to convince Ulysses S. Grant to take up golf. He took him out to the club to show him what a fine game it was. They watched a hacker swing and miss at the ball a few times, chewing up a little bit of grass in the process. Grant said, "That does look like very good exercise, but what's the little white ball for?"

•

Justice John Marshall Harlan used to play golf at the Chevy Chase Country Club outside of Washington DC. A frequent playing partner was his friend, the Episcopal Bishop of Washington.

One time the good Bishop whiffed several times. Then he just glared at the defiant little white sphere.

Harlan said, "Bishop, that was the most profane silence I ever witnessed."

■

Bob Hope tells about playing golf with one of his good friends and fellow golfing enthusiast, President Dwight D. Eisenhower. Hope noticed that as they played Eisenhower kept glancing at his wrist. Hope said, "Mr. President, why do you keep looking at your watch." The President replied, "This isn't a watch. It's a compass."

■

After Eisenhower left office, someone asked him if leaving the White House affected his golf game. The former President replied, "Yes, a lot more people beat me now."

THERE CAN'T BE TOO MANY GOLF STORIES WITHOUT A PRIEST OR MINISTER:

As someone said: "Sunday is a day when we all bow our heads. Some of us are praying; some of us are putting."

■

A minister was scheduled to play in a golf tournament and his partner was a TV weatherman. After just a few holes, a thunderstorm broke and the rain came pouring down so hard that they had to retreat to the clubhouse.

They sat and waited for hours. Finally the minister said to the weatherman, "You'd think between the two of us, we could do something."

OFFICE ROMANCE

Sometimes office love affairs are hard to resist. They're tempting, they're enticing, and they're on company time.

■

I know a man who was very proud that he was faithful to his wife . . . and several of his office companions.

■

It's hard to avoid romance in some offices. The Muzak is almost irresistible.

■

They first met by the office Xerox machine. Since then they've had an urge to reproduce.

Their first children were triplets and they were born collated.

■

I wouldn't marry anyone I fell in love with at our office. You know the quality control in our company.

■

Many love affairs begin in the workplace. That's where I first fell in love with money.

■

Office romance is fun. It's something to do while you're making a living.

■

Office romance is killing two birds with one stone. Since you have to dress up anyway, you might as well be impressing someone.

■

Management hates to see people holding hands in the office. They're paying for four hands and getting the work of two.

■

Upper management doesn't really frown on legitimate office romances. In today's business world, they endorse anything that isn't a hostile takeover.

■

We have a very torrid love affair going on in our office at the moment. In fact, if it gets any hotter, they may have to get a secretarial chair that folds out into a bed.

These two are very much in love. Every day he has one dozen pink paper clips delivered to her desk.

They start each workday off with a kiss. Which is understandable if you've ever tasted the coffee in our office.

They kiss all the way home from work. That's difficult since he drives a Buick Regal and she drives a Mustang.

■

There's also the office Romeo. He told one fellow worker he was God's gift to women. She said, "I don't think so. God would have picked better wrapping."

This office Don Juan has two goals in life: to make a pass at every woman in the office, and to find a cure for staple-gun wounds.

This guy is single and deservedly so.

He's not really good looking, either. In fact, he looks surprisingly like the drawings of him on the ladies' restroom walls.

■

It's nice to see a little romance in the office. Maybe Labor and Management will learn from it.

■

Office romances happen between the unlikeliest candidates. In our office the fax machine ran away one night with our electric stapler.

■

A delivery boy once had to deliver a package to a Mr. Sexhauer in the accounting department of a large corporation.

When he came into the reception area, an attractive woman behind the desk said, "May I help you?"

The boy asked, "Do you have a Sexhauer here."

She said, "Pal, we don't even get a coffee break."

■

The boss came into work early one morning and found his bookkeeper in a passionate embrace with his secretary.

The boss said, "Is this what I pay you for?"

The bookkeeper said, "No, sir. This is totally free of charge."

■

When journalist, John Gunther, interviewed Fiorella LaGuardia, the Mayor of New York, he asked him about the inordinately large number of files in his office complex.

LaGuardia said, "I'll tell you a little story. Files are the curse of modern civilization. I had a young secretary once—just out of school. I told her, 'If you can keep these files straight, I'll marry you.' She did, and so I married her."

■

The CEO of a medium-sized manufacturing firm was a young, dynamic, executive. To stay in shape, he kept a bicycle in the parking lot and would ride that around the complex.

One day he discovered his bicycle was stolen.

It infuriated him so much that he organized an assembly of all the plant workers. He told an associate that he was going to give a scathing speech on ethics and morality. He was going to go back to basics. He planned to go through each of the ten commandments one by one with brief comments on each.

When he got to the 8th commandment, though—"Thou shalt not steal"—he would deliver an eloquent, impassioned lecture. He felt this would so move the listeners that whoever stole the bike would surely return it.

A few days later, the executive was riding around the plant grounds on his bicycle. The associate saw him and said, "I see your lecture worked. The 8th commandment got to them, huh?"

The CEO said, "Not really. I got up to the 6th commandment— 'Thou shalt not commit adultery'—and I remembered where I left my bicycle."

SEX IN THE OFFICE

Management frowns on sex in the office. If you've got that kind of time, it means they're not setting your quota high enough.

■

That's the one nice thing about computers in the office. It keeps everyone's hands up where we can see them.

■

You should make that a rule of thumb–never bring home from the office more hickeys than you left the house with.

■

Passionate romance in the executive office is dangerous. Sex was not designed for swivel chairs.

■

If you can successfully enjoy sex in the office, you must be getting a longer coffee break than you deserve.

■

There's no place for sex in the office—unless you've had one of your file cabinets converted to a rumpus room.

■

Sex in the office can be dangerous. It's difficult to explain paper cuts in hard to reach places.

■

Sex should be avoided in the office. Sex should be avoided in any place that has a paper shredder.

■

Illicit sex especially should be avoided in the office. It's hard enough to explain lipstick on your collar, but paper clips in your underwear?

One boss used to warn all his employees against inter-office affairs by saying, "Never dip you pen in company ink."

■

Management says that sex should be kept out of the office. They don't hold committee meetings in your bedroom, do they?

■

I knew one boss and his secretary who had a torrid inter-office affair. They claimed it was just their way of making up after typing errors.

■

Many executives religiously refrain from sex while on the job. They prefer to be incompetent at one thing at a time.

And some don't. They have desk chairs that convert to a water bed.

■

Some workplaces have effectively eliminated sex in the office. They have the thermostats in the office sprinkler system set very low.

■

One young lady effectively blackmailed her boss. She threatened to distribute Xerox copies of their affair.

■

Leave reproduction in the office to the copying machines.

■

I knew one executive who began each staff meeting with a prayer. While everyone had their eyes closed for a minute, he fooled around with the Public Relations Supervisor.

■

I knew one executive who was a real office Don Juan. It seemed like every three days or so he had to change his desk blotter.

■

One behind the times company finally promoted a woman to top management, and some of the members of that formerly all male establishment resented it.

One member was particularly discourteous to his new colleague. She confronted him.

He said, "I may be old fashioned, but I'm offended by your presence here. I'm embarrassed by it. I feel the same way I would if you intruded on me while I was naked in my own bedroom and had nothing to defend myself with."

She said, "Relax. You're not good looking enough to have those kind of worries."

Sir Thomas Beecham was a renowned conductor and founder of the London Philharmonic Orchestra. However, he was also like some of today's managers.

Someone asked once if it was true that he preferred *not* to have women in his orchestra.

He said, "The trouble is, you see, if they're attractive it will upset my players. If they're not it upsets me."

■

The boss called his secretary into the office and said, "We have to stop our affair. If I spend any more money on you, my wife might find out."

The secretary said, "If you don't spend more money on me, I *know* she will."

■

One worker was having a flagrant affair with one of the young women who worked in his office. The boss called him in.

The boss said, "You're a married man, right?"

The man said, "Yes."

The boss said, "You have children at home, right?"

The man said he did.

The boss said, "But you're having an affair with one of the young ladies in this office."

The man said he was, but he didn't think that was any of this man's business.

The boss said, "How would you feel if you found out your daughter was having an affair? Would you be shocked?"

The man said he would.

The boss said, "Would you be angry."

The man said he would.

The boss said, "What else would you feel?"

The man said, "I'd feel like somebody was lying because my daughter's only three years old."

■

An office romeo finally settled down and got married. It surprised most of his fellow workers. In fact, at the bachelor party they threw for him, some of his friends asked if he really thought the marriage would last.

The guy said, "Yes, I think it will."

They said, "But what if she finds out about all your other affairs. I think you've romanced every girl that works in our building."

The guy said, "It's no problem. My future wife knows all about my bachelor days. I've told her about every affair I've ever had."

One man said, "Wow, what courage."

Another said, "What honesty."

Another said, "What a memory."

The boss called one of his attractive workers into his office for a job review. He complimented her-he thought. He said, "I think you have the best mind of any woman who works in this department."

The woman was offended. She said, "Sir, the mind knows no sex."

The boss said, "You're wrong. I've seen the guys in the office look at you. Their minds know nothing else."

■

There's a story told that Noah Webster, who compiled Webster's American Dictionary of the English Language in 1828, was caught in mid-embrace with his secretary when his wife unexpectedly walked into his study.

The wife said, "Why, Noah, I'm surprised."

Webster said, "No, my dear, I'm surprised; you're merely astonished."

■

One gentleman was so henpecked at home that he used that as his excuse to have an affair with one of the women who worked in his office.

Then his wife came in unexpectedly one day and found them in a passionate embrace. She immediately ordered her husband into a closet. She slammed the door and the poor man had to sit there while the wife and the mistress had a fierce argument that lasted two hours.

Finally, the mistress stormed out and the woman said, "You can come out of the closet now."

The man shouted back, "I will not come out. I'll show you who's the boss in this family."

THE OFFICE TRAMP:

Most offices have one of these—the girl with the reputation. Rumors—true or false—circulate and titillate. You know the stereotype. This lady wears dresses that are so tight that if she gets a wart in the wrong place, she has to have all her skirts let out.

■

She wears mini-skirts that are so short the only thing they don't show is her nationality.

■

This girl's first words as a baby were "no-no," but she hasn't said them since.

■

Office gossip has it that her favorite hobbies are crawling into bed with a good book or a friend who has just read one.

And they say it's *every* night. Office tattletales say that she writes her diary with a rubber stamp.

They say of her that if her lover gets up in the middle of the night to go to the bathroom he has to leave a "reserved" card on the pillow.

■

I knew one girl like this. When she worked at a bank, they called her the "automatic teller."

■

She was a big football fan. She enjoyed anything that came in groups of eleven men.

■

I can't tell you how many lovers she had, but if they formed a volunteer army, we could all sleep safe at nights.

■

She's the kind of a vamp who can get any man she wants. She writes her diary two weeks ahead of time.

■

She never married. Her motto was, "Always a honeymooner; never a bride."

■

She's not the kind of girl who can't say "no"; she just prefers saying "next."

■

They say she only drinks in motel bars. She doesn't believe in commuting.

■

She's been on so many beds her nickname is "Chenille."

■

She keeps a list of all her lovers in a book. At the end of the year the phone company rents it just to see if they missed anybody.

■

She loves anything that wears pants . . . to start with.

■

They say that when she learned to drive, she spent the first two weeks learning how to sit up in the front.

You know the kind of girl. She was 24 years old before she found out that Drive-Ins showed movies.

■

She's a real office temptress. She has a walk that seems to say, "To whom it may concern."

■

She has a seductive walk. She's one of those girls who can wink at you while walking away from you.

■

She wears skirts that are actually tighter than skin. A person can sit down in their skin.

■

Around the office she's voted as the girl most likely to concede.

■

She dresses like a true exhibitionist, and the corridor gossip has it that she encourages peeping toms. They say the bedroom of her apartment has coin operated venetian blinds.

■

She wears so much make-up, she has to get two friends to help her smile.
In her purse she carries a compact and a putty knife.

THE OFFICE DON JUAN:

There's usually one guy in every office who thinks he's God's gift to women. And the women think: if he is, then God's one lousy shopper.

They think, "If this guy is God's gift to women, I sure hope God kept all the receipts."

■

This guy keeps saying to the female employees, "Wouldn't you like to get me in bed?" And they say, "Yes, if only to smother you with a pillow."

■

This guy has a one track mind, and it's a dirt track.

■

If it weren't for impure thoughts, this guy would have none at all.

■

This guy goes after anything in a skirt. He's been banned for life from the Scottish Bagpipe Festival.

He offers his body to everyone and so far the only ones who have accepted are the people at the organ bank.

■

This gentleman usually lives in a rich fantasy land. From an attractive woman, he considers "Good morning" a proposition.

■

He thinks every woman in the world is in love with him. He doesn't realize that even his own mother has to work at it.

■

This guy has been turned down more times than Joan Collins' bed.

■

This guy thinks about nothing but sex. He has a zipper that operates from a garage door opener.

■

This guy tries to hit on every woman he meets, figuring, "If I fail, I can always go home to the wife."

■

He's one step lower than "Wham-Bam-Thank you, ma'm." He's "Wham-Bam-Do you have any girlfriends you can introduce me to?"

■

The way he dresses reflects his attitude. He gets his suits from Hart, Schaffner & Sleaze.

■

Usually, this kind of guy is a bad grammarian. He ends almost every sentence with a proposition.

■

He's not romantic at all. He occasionally sends a woman a dozen roses, but he sends them in the form of a chain letter.

■

If he sends a box of candy, he doesn't consider it a gift; he considers it a contract.

■

Women generally don't like this guy. In an unofficial office poll, he finished lower than cracker crumbs as things they would least likely like to wind up in bed with.

PART FIVE

EXECUTIVE PERKS AND PEEVES

Each position has its good and bad features. The good you keep; the bad you delegate.

Happiness is the key to the executive washroom ...
whether you have to go or not.

LONG LUNCHES

Ideal working hours used to be considered from 12 to 1 with an hour for lunch. Today's executives don't agree. They need more time for lunch.

■

Some people take so long for lunch they could lose their seniority.

■

Here's a good rule of thumb for executives: Your lunches should never be so long that by the time you come back you need a new photo taken for the organizational chart.

■

Many executives thrive on long lunches. That's why someone had to invent the calendar watch.

■

Some executives treat lunch as a pleasant little break that separates the first hour of the workday from the last hour of the workday.

■

Some executives enjoy the "blue plate special" for lunch. They sit there until their plate turns blue.

Some executives correctly treat the lunch break as a form of R & R—rest and relaxation. Others make it last so long it becomes a form of R & NR—rest and near retirement.

■

Not too many executives conduct business during lunch. You know that, and I know that. Thank God the IRS doesn't yet.

■

Some executives stay away from their offices so long at lunch time that the first thing they do on their return is take a management refresher course.

■

My boss called me on it once. He said, "Have you heard of the book, *The One-Minute Manager*?" I said, "Sure." He said, "I read it 180 times while you were at lunch."

■

Some of us come back from lunch and say to our secretary, "Were there any calls?" Some of us come back from long lunches and have to say to our secretary, "You may not remember me, but . . ."

■

One boss told me to remember that I was eating on company time. That's as it should be. I worked up an appetite on company time.

Of course, in all fairness, there have been times when I've lost my appetite on company time, too.

■

One executive always stopped at his tailor's on the way back from lunch. His lunch breaks lasted so long his suits went out of style.

Also, he ate so much he had to have the seams let out on his desk chair.

■

I had one smart aleck secretary. I used to say, "I'm going to lunch," and she'd say, "Have a nice weekend."

■

Extra long lunches cannot only make the workday seem shorter, but many times your career, too.

■

One executive went to his boss and demanded longer lunch breaks. His boss gave him the rest of his life for lunch, and two weeks severance pay to leave as a tip.

Always bring your business cards to lunch. Sometimes you stay so long you may forget where you work.

■

One worker came back from an extra long lunch one day.
His boss said, "Where were you?"
The guy said, "I got my hair cut."
The boss said, "Do you mean to tell me you had your hair cut on my time?"
The guy said, "Why not? It grew on your time."

THE TWO-MARTINI LUNCH

The typical businessman's lunch is a three-course meal—two martinis and a check.

■

Overheard one executive saying to another: "I can't decide what kind of food to have for lunch today. I've got it narrowed down to either the olive or the twist."

■

Executive to his waiter: "I'll have the businessman's lunch. Hold the food."

■

Even if it's not a tax write off, most executives would still have the two-martini lunch. It'll just be a little harder to swallow.

■

The two-martini lunch is good for business . . . if you're a swizzle stick salesman.

■

Some executives who have their luncheon martinis straight up, wish they could walk out of the restaurant that way.

■

The two-martini lunch is as American as baseball or Mom's apple brandy.

■

There are many luncheon places that don't serve alcohol; they also don't serve many executives.

■

They say that many business deals are closed over the two-martini lunch. The reason they say that is because after two martinis, it's hard to say "consummated."

They call it the two-martini lunch, because after two you start to call them "martoonies."

■

I knew one executive who had so many two-martini lunches when he retired his favorite bar and grill lit an eternal flame in his honor. They set fire to his breath.

■

He and his pals would stop so often on the way home from work, his car had only 10,000 miles on it and already he'd gone through three sets of door handles.

■

We had one guy at work—nobody knew he drank until one day he came to work sober.

■

He cut himself shaving one day and bled so badly his eyes cleared up.

■

He came to work one day and I commented on his new beard. It wasn't a beard at all; it was his breath running down his chin.

■

He'd forget everything when he drank. Everyday when he returned from lunch he'd fill out another job application.

■

This guy used to go to lunch wearing very large cuff-links. I found out later they were actually curb feelers.

■

He passed out at a meeting once and they brought him to. Then they brought him two more and he was fine.

■

He got the recipe for his favorite meal at his favorite cafe. It began: "Take the juice from one bottle of gin."

■

The company got a great deal when this guy retired. They only had to pay pension for the years he remembered.

■

I once kidded a guy at his retirement party who like to brag about his drinking prowess. He didn't drink much, but even when he drank a little he took his glasses off.

"Bob and his wife have been married for 38 years. I said to her before the banquet, 'I guess you can always tell when Bob's been drinking anytime he comes home without his glasses on.' She said, 'What glasses?'"

■

Bob Hope kids Dean Martin about his drinking: "I like playing golf with Dean Martin. If he wins, we tell him."

■

Someone said that when they've had a little too much to drink, a Frenchman wants to make love, a German wants to sing, a Spaniard wants to gamble, an Englishman wants to eat, an Italian wants to boast, an Irishman wants to fight, a Russian wants to be friendly, and an American business person wants to make a speech.

■

A couple of guys had been invited out to lunch with their boss. It was a chance for them to make an impression on the boss, but it was also a chance for him to get to know a little more about them.

To try to find out a bit about their literary tastes, the boss asked one of them, "Do you care for Omar Khayam?"

The worker said, "Pretty much, you know, but with pasta, I much prefer Chianti."

Not too much more was said on the subject until the workers got back to the privacy of their office. Now the one chastised the other. He said, "You dumb klutz. Why don't you just say you don't know something when you don't know something?

The other guy said, "What did I say?"

The other worker said, "Omar Khayam isn't a wine, you nitwit. It's an imported Vodka."

■

The restaurant owner told his waitresses right before the lunch rush, "Girls, I want you all to look extra special today. Spend a little extra time on your make-up and be sure your hair is just the way you want it to look. Also, I want you to smile at everyone and be extra-special charming."

The girls said, "What's the occasion? Is this a special day or something?"

The owner said, "No. It's just that the government is cracking down on the two-martini lunch, and people may start realizing how lousy the food is."

■

Some day we'd like to see a waiter with enough of whatever it takes to lay the check face-up on the table.

■

A policeman noticed three well-dressed men sitting on a park bench in the early afternoon. Two of them were acting rather strange. One gentleman on the one end of the bench looked like he was casting for fish, but he had no rod or reel in his hand. The man at the other end of the bench looked like he was putting worms on the hook. The gentleman in the middle looked quite normal and unconcerned.

The policeman came over and asked the man in the middle what was going on.

The gentleman said, "Oh, I'm sorry, Officer. I know it must look strange, but everything is perfectly alright."

The cop said, "What's this guy doing?"

The man explained, "These gentleman had a very tough morning at work. They had a very disappointing business setback and they kind of drank too much during lunch–to forget, you know. They got to talking about how they'd like to retire and just fish for the rest of their lives. This guy thinks he's fishing for trout."

The cop said, "And this guy's baiting the hook for him."

The guy said, "Yes, but I'm here to take care of them."

The cop said, "Well, I understand, but it looks kind of strange. I think you'd better get both of them home."

The gentleman said, "Surely, officer." Then he rolled up his sleeves and started to row toward shore.

■

One poor gentleman got so upset at work and so relaxed after his more-than-two-martini lunch, that he got in his car, picked up his car phone and called the company he worked for. He was determined to tell them off.

He asked for the head man, and when he got him he told him off with all kinds of name-calling and obscenities. He told him the management stunk and that he was sorry he worked there.

The executive was stunned and angered. He said, "Do you know who you're talking to? I'm the President of the company."

The worker said, "Do you know who you're talking to?"

The president said, "No, I don't."

The worker said, "Good," and hung up.

■

One worker got so upset and angered at the way things were going at work that he indulged himself at lunch. He had too much to drink, went to his car phone, called the President of the company, and told him off.

He said, "I've been working for your company for 9 years now. It's the worst managed company I've ever seen and you're the worst chief executive officer I ever heard of. You've screwed up my career and my life, and I'm going to do something about it. I don't know what I'm going to do exactly, because I'm too drunk now to think of anything."

The CEO said, "I demand to know just who this is."

The guy said, "Forget it, Bozo. I'm not *that* drunk." And hung up.

PARKING

The bigger you are in the company, the closer your parking space is to your office. The nice thing about my parking space is that I build up frequent flyer bonus points.

■

I grew up on the wrong side of the tracks, now that's where my parking space is.

■

I can get from my parking space to my office in a matter of minutes—if the shuttle bus is on time.

■

I have such a remote parking space that when I park my car and walk to the office, I pass my house on the way.

■

I'm so low in the company hierarchy that I had to join a car pool to take me from my parking space to the office.

■

My assigned parking space is so far from the office that if they were arranged in alphabetical order, I'd be in Mr. Zygowitz's spot.

■

My Dad always used to tell me how he had it tough because he had to walk four miles everyday to get to school. I have to get three more promotions before I get a parking space that close to the office.

■

I asked for a parking space closer to my office, so they moved my desk down to the garage.
. . . I think my swivel chair is now dripping oil.

■

My last assigned parking space was so bad that when the company fired me, they let me keep the parking spot.

■

It used to be a status car was a symbol of success; now a place to park it is.

■

That's why a lot of executives aren't afraid of dying. At least then they're assured of a parking spot.

One sure way to get a great parking space right in front of your office building is to have your name legally changed to "Passenger Unloading."

■

The next best thing to having an assigned parking space near the building is to have a devoted secretary who's willing to run outside every two hours and erase the chalk marks from your tires.

■

The best jobs in the world are those that give you a reserved parking space close to the office with your name written on the slot–and also pay enough for you to afford a car.

■

QUESTION: What's worse than finding an unauthorized car parked in the parking space with your name on it?
ANSWER: Finding a maintenance truck parked there with the janitor removing your name.

■

In New York, parking spaces now cost what the car used to sell for.

■

In some cities the only way to be assured of a parking space is to leave your car in it and take a bus back and forth to work.

■

There's no such things as Sunday Drivers anymore. They're all Friday Drivers still looking for a parking place.

■

Every family has two cars. One for driving and one to hold the parking spot.

■

That's one nice thing about working late—you get to keep the parking space longer.

PEEVES FROM THE WORKERS

To paraphrase Mom—"Just wait. Someday you'll have employees of your own."

ABSENTEEISM

I like people who show up for work. They care enough to send the very best.

■

Those who believe that absence makes the heart grow fonder are forgetting that most people in management don't have hearts.

■

Chronic absenteeism makes you so mad you could scream. Unfortunately, the people you want to scream at are home.

■

Chronic absenteeism is as popular as a flat tire with a missing spare.

■

Being at work every day that one can be there is a duty, an obligation, and the best way there is to make sure that you hear the gossip first.

■

My mother always taught me that absenteeism was like stealing, except instead of wearing a mask, you wear a note from your doctor.

When I was a kid my mother thoroughly confused me about absenteeism. I was misbehaving on an outing and my mother said, "The next time I take you out with me, I'm leaving you home."

■

Some workers seem to worship absenteeism. To them, Jimmy Hoffa is a role model.

■

I had one worker who was absent so much the only time his chair was warm was when the air-conditioning broke.

I'll give you an idea how much he's absent. He's been working for me for six years and he's still on his first box of paper clips.

I'd turn in a missing person report on him but I haven't seen him enough to give a decent description.

He's absent so much he showed up for work one day and I asked if he was sick.

. . . it turned out he was ill. He said he wasn't feeling well enough to stay home and waste a perfectly good sick day.

■

Bad backs cut down on absenteeism. When they start feeling bad about it, they come back to work.

■

Some workers show up at the office religiously—once a week.

■

I have one guy who's been absent so much that I won't let him back into the office unless he brings a note from his pall-bearers.

■

He's been absent so much that I'd rather he didn't come to work. I don't have time to retrain him.

■

Some workers are like a blind date. You hope they show up, but after they do, you're not so sure you're glad they did.

■

One gentleman who worked for me had a valid medical excuse for missing work during the World Series. He got hit by a foul ball.

Management might fight absenteeism by inventing a paycheck that also calls in sick.

■

When Georges Clemenceau was appointed France's Home Secretary, one of his first projects was to tour his department. He arrived unannounced with an aide to inspect the offices and the staff.

As they walked around the offices, they found the place practically deserted. No one was in the office; no one was at work.

Finally, they opened one door and did find a worker. He was sound asleep with his head comfortably on the desk.

The aide rushed over, but Clemenceau stopped him. He said, "No, don't wake him. He might leave."

■

Studio boss, Samuel Goldwyn, hired a ghostwriter to write some articles under his name. Part way through the project the writer had to leave, and another writer was named to replace him.

When the new writer's work was presented to Goldwyn, he read it over and tossed it aside, saying, "It's not up to my usual standards."

■

Goldwyn also used to pass by two of his writers each day on the studio grounds. He never bothered to learn their names, but greeted them each day with "Hi, boys."

One day, one of the writers was absent. When Goldwyn passed the single writer on the lot, he simply ad-libbed, "Hi, boy."

■

One poor gentlemen was plagued with a terrible absentee record that bothered his employer. He called in sick so often that the boss reached the point where he refused to believe any of his complaints.

Nevertheless, the absences became more frequent and for longer durations. Each time the man's wife would have to call she'd get the same response.

She'd say, "My husband can't come in today. He's not feeling well."

The boss would say, "Your husband is not sick, M'am. He just thinks he's sick."

She'd call in again and the boss would say, "M'am, your husband's problem is all in his head. He's just convinced himself that he's sick."

The next time she'd call, she'd get the same response, "Your husband just thinks he's sick."

Finally, the boss fired the man.

A few months later he ran into this man's wife and politely inquired about the man's health. He said, "How's your husband doing?"

The wife said, "Oh, he thinks he's dead."

Many people who suffer from chronic absenteeism are accused of being hypo-chondriacal. None of them, though, will ever equal the master of that art, the late Oscar Levant.

Levant depended on medication, pain killers, and drugs of all types. He said of himself once that the time he hugged Judy Garland was probably the single greatest moment in pharmaceutical history.

Here are a few of his other self-effacing one-liners:

"I don't drink. I don't like it; it makes me feel good."

"I was voted 'pill of the year' by the American Pharmaceutical Society."

"I'm a study of a man in chaos in search of a frenzy."

"I'm a self-made man. Who else would help?"

"There is a thin line between genius and insanity. I have erased that line."

"I was once thrown out of a mental institution for depressing the other patients."

"Instant unconsciousness has been my greatest passion for ten years."

"Underneath this flabby exterior is an enormous lack of character."

"For exercise, I just stumble around the house and fall into comas."

■

Here's a classic tale of absenteeism:
George Bernard Shaw once invited Winston Churchill to an opening night performance of his play with this note:

"Dear Mr. Churchill,
Enclosed are two tickets to my new play which opens Thursday night. Please come and bring a friend, if you have one."

Churchill answered with the following note:

"Dear Mr. Shaw,
I am sorry, I have a previous engagement and cannot attend your opening. However, I will come to the second performance, if there is one."

SICK DAYS

A sick day is just a paid vacation that the company doesn't know they gave to you.

Because if they know they gave it to you, they wouldn't give it to you.

■

Sunday used to be the "day of rest;" now the fake sick day is.

■

Don't you love the men who put their foot down and boldly say, "I'm just not going to the office today and that's all there is to it." Then they have their wives call in sick for them.

■

Baseball lowers a person's resistance. Research shows that more workers get sick on opening day of the season and during the World Series than at any other time.

■

I had one worker call in sick with a fever. It must have been one helluva fever; it left him with a suntan.

■

You can't question every absentee, but when a worker calls in sick about all you can be sure of is that his phone's working and he's not.

■

Let's not say it's easy to lie on the phone, but it's one reason why the IRS won't permit you to call in your tax returns.

■

It's a good practice to remind those who call in sick that their absence means everyone else in the office will have to work that much harder. If the person is really sick, this news helps cheer them up.

■

This may be the boldest sick day lie ever: "Boss, I'm not feeling well and may not be in for a day or two, and if the folks in the office want to send a gift, I could use a dozen golf balls."

■

I've called in sick a few times when all I wanted was a relaxing day on the links. It's fitting that a day devoted to golf should begin with a lie.

■

My boss always sends me get well wishes when I call in sick. The only problem is he calls them in to the pro at my Country Club.

■

I once called in sick and the boss demanded that I bring a note from my doctor. It was easy to get; he was playing in my foursome.

The most common reasons given for legitimate stay at home days are the common cold, sore throat, upset stomach, and "It's the last time I ever behave like that at a party."

■

Hangovers are a common reason why people stay home from work. No one wants to be around a whole office full of people whose faces are all fuzzy.

■

One hangover sufferer called in complaining of a terrible headache. His head swelled up before he got a chance to take the lampshade off.

■

There is no cure for the common cold because it's such a convenient reason for taking a day off work.

■

There are some workers who will take advantage of sick days. When they sneeze, you don't say "Gesundheit"; you say "See you the day after tomorrow."

■

Most employees work when they have minor illnesses. They don't want to squander a perfectly good sick day on an illness.

■

The ultimate was the convention lecturer who was scheduled to speak on "Fitness and Health." He cancelled the talk because he was under the weather.

■

"In half of all cases, when an employee calls in sick, he's actually sick."—*Walter Pitkin, Literary Agent*

LATENESS

One worker blamed his chronic lateness on his back. He had trouble getting it out of bed each morning.

■

One worker was late for everything. He retired at age 66.

He was on time for his own funeral, but it took six people carrying him in to accomplish that.

One worker told the boss he liked to be late because by being a little bit late he missed all the traffic. The boss said, "That's because they're all sitting at their desks working."

■

This guy just couldn't be on time. He used to show up for work with a 5:06 o'clock shadow.

■

Anybody who got to work after this guy had already missed their coffee break.

■

If he was the Easter Bunny, you'd be getting your jelly beans around September.

■

One time our boss stood at the time clock and said to one of our late arrivals, "How come you were the last one to work this morning, but the first one to leave at night?"
The man said, "You want me to be on time tomorrow, don't you?"
The boss said, "Yes."
The man said, "Well, I'm getting a head start."

■

Our boss asked one employee at the end of the day, "How come you were the last one to work in the morning, but the first one to leave at night?"
The worker said, "I hate to make the same mistake twice in one day."

■

The boss tried to chastise one person who was chronically tardy. He said, "Do you know what time we start work around here in the morning?"
The worker said, "No, I don't. I'm never here for that."

■

The boss berated one late employee. He said, "Fifty people work in this office. Forty-nine of them can be at work on time, why can't you?"
The worker replied, "I'm the last to use the bathroom."

■

One chronic late arriver showed up on time one day through no fault of his own. He wanted to be paid time and a half for the first ten minutes.

■

One employee explained repeated lateness with: "I'm late every day because I have to look for a parking space."

The boss said, "From now on you can leave the car home, and stay with it to keep it company."

■

There is no valid excuse for lateness, but if you're the boss, you're going to have to listen to one anyway.

In fact, one guy said that's why he was ten minutes late each day. He could have been on time, but it took at least ten minutes to think up a good excuse for being late.

■

If you took all of the people who were late to work in the morning and laid them end to end, half of them wouldn't get there on time.

■

This guy was late so often that at his 25 year party, he only had 18 actual years experience with the company.

■

One worker had a chronic lateness problem throughout his entire life. He got through 8 years of elementary school, 4 years of high school, and 4 years of college, without once reciting the Pledge of Allegiance.

■

One employee was late for work every day of his life, but the company got even with him. They held his going away party two years after he retired.

He didn't even show up for it. He overslept.

■

An executive went into a barber shop for his usual.

The barber threw the cloth around his neck and as he was fastening it, the man said, "Can you get me done in about ten minutes? I have a meeting at 9 o'clock."

The barber took the cloth off and said, "The next time you want me to get you finished in ten minutes come twenty minutes earlier."

■

Sooner or later you hear every excuse for being late.

An employee showed up late and the supervisor questioned him.

The guy said, "It's the damn alarm o'clock."

The supervisor said, "The alarm clock, huh?"

The employee said, "Yeah. It didn't wake me up this morning."

The supervisor had heard it all before. He said, "And why was that?"

The guy said, "Well, it was set for seven, but there's eight in my family."

One innovative company began a policy of locking their doors at 8 AM. Anyone arriving after that had to identify themselves by name to gain access.

Each of the late employees was then sent a "Nastygram" during the day.

■

One supervisor get fed up with an employee who was late every single morning. He called him on it one day.

He said, "You're twenty minutes late for work this morning. You were about a half-hour late yesterday, and probably about fifteen minutes late the day before that. You're never on time for work. Do you have any idea of what time we start work in this office?"

The man said, "No, how could I. Everybody's always at it by the time I get here."

■

One employee had a great solution when his boss reprimanded him for lateness. The boss simply said, "You're late for work."

The man said, "That's all right. I'll make up for it tonight by leaving early."

■

A gentleman was pulled over by a cop for going a little too fast on the highway. The cop said, "Going to a fire?"

The driver said, "No. I'm trying to prevent one."

The cops said, "Oh really? How do you intend to do that?"

The guy said, "Well, that's what my boss said he would do to me if I was late for work again, so I was driving fast trying to get to the office in time."

■

One guy was driving as fast as he could to get to work on time. His boss wasn't going to like it if he was late again. A cop pulled him over.

The cop said sarcastically, "You know there are some pretty reckless drivers on these highways."

The man said, "I know there are, Sir. That's why I was driving so fast. I want to get safely to my office before all the accidents happen."

■

The punctual person always loses . . . about a half-hour waiting for the other person to show up.

OFFICE INEFFICIENCY

Too many employees think work is a place and not an action.

Too many employees think work is a noun and not a verb.

■

Efficiency is how much you get done over a certain period of time. It takes our office a certain period of time to get damn near anything done.

■

If two men can dig a ditch in 8 hours, and two other men can dig a ditch in 3 hours, why do the first two men give up ditch digging and come to work in our office?

■

Ask some workers to pick up productivity and they'll tell you they're not allowed to lift anything heavy.

■

The workers in our office are so inefficient, they give them three weeks for a two week vacation.
. . . it's the only way they can get it all in.

■

Our office is so inefficient if any worker puts in an honest day's work, we have to pay him time and a half for it.

■

One person came into our office just 15 minutes before quitting time. The boss said, "What can you do in 15 minutes?" The worker said, "Cook a 3-minute egg."

■

Our workers are so inefficient it takes them a week to get over the 24-hour virus.

■

If our office had fought the 100 Years War, they'd still be reporting casualties.

■

We asked the boss what our output was for last week. He said, "We don't know. It probably won't be done until later this week."

■

Our workers are slow at everything. We didn't have an office shower yet for one of our workers who is expecting a baby. Of course, we still have time. She's only 13 months pregnant.

■

Our office is so inefficient, it took us three months to discover that someone had stolen our office "out" basket.

You begin to suspect our group isn't on the ball when our office Christmas party is held in March.

■

Our office never had a Christmas party. Instead we held an office New Year's Eve party. We were so thrilled to get the year finished on time.

■

Our office efficiency record was so bad that the only reason the company kept us was to discourage hostile takeovers.

■

Our workers had such poor performance that if we asked for a raise, competitive companies offered to pay it.

■

Our boss's favorite expression was, "Up Your Output."

■

I yield to no one in my admiration for the office as a social centre, but it's no place actually to get any work done. —*Katharine Whitehorn, Sunday Best*

■

They talk about American efficiency, yet the secretary always answers the phone, and most of the time it's for her boss.

■

Henry Ford was an executive who couldn't tolerate inefficiency. Even though he was the boss, whenever he scheduled meetings with his executives, he visited their offices rather than have them come to his. He said, "I go to them to save time. I've found that I can leave the other fellow's office a lot quicker than I can get him to leave mine."

■

Abraham Lincoln was impatient with inefficiency. Toward the end of 1862, the President became more and more angered by General McClellan's inaction against the Confederate forces even though his army outnumbered them considerably. Finally, he wrote McClellan a brief letter that said: "If you don't want to use the army, I should like to borrow it for a while. Yours respectfully, A. Lincoln."

■

Early in his acting career, Leslie Howard worked for a small repertory company that did a variety of plays. Often they would do a different show each night, and sometimes two different shows in a day. It was invaluable training but not real conducive to remembering lines.

One afternoon, Howard "went up." That's show business slang for forgetting the lines. He began to panic onstage. He was obviously in trouble but no help came from the script prompter in the wings.

In desperation, Howard worked his way toward the wings and whispered, "What's my line?" The off-stage prompter whispered back just as desperately, "What's the play?"

■

Addison Mizner was an architect who made a lot of money and gained a lot of fame during Florida's great property boom. He was neither formally trained nor highly qualified, yet the rich and famous waited in line and paid handsomely to own a Mizner designed home–even though they often had glaring flaws.

In his obsession with unique design, Mizner sometimes ignored structural necessities. One two story structure he designed had no stairway leading from the first to the second floor.

One client, William Gray Warden, asked Mizner for a copy of the plans to his Palm Beach house. He wanted to show them to friends and boast a little. Mizner said, "The house isn't built yet. Construction first; blueprints afterward."

■

A publisher was arguing with one of his production people about the cost per page of a book that was on their schedule.

The worker said that the lowest bid they received was $1.00 per page. The publisher argued that the bid was too expensive. The worker defended the pricing. He said, "I've shopped around and this is the lowest offer I can get."

The publisher said that this particular vendor had done work for them before at lower prices.

The production worker finally said, "Boss, I have the proposal right here. It says '25 cents per page for design, and 65 cents per page for typesetting. Total cost is $1.00 per page.' "

The boss immediately said, "65 and 25 is 90 cents, not a dollar."

The worker said, "Oh yeah. Boy, the guy who drew up this proposal must really be an idiot, huh?"

■

An unfortunate construction worker was doing his job on a high rise building when a beam slipped, whizzed right by his head, and slammed to the floor. The man thought he escaped injury until he felt the side of his face and his ear was missing.

He rushed as quick as he could down to the bottom floor. The workers there asked what happened. He said, "I lost my ear."

They all began looking for it. Finally, one worker yelled, "There it is. It's on the ground over there."

The wounded laborer rushed over, looked at it, and said, "No, that's not mine. Mine had a pencil behind it."

•

I wondered about the competence of my boss once after a party we all attended. The boss was on vacation, but he came back into town just to attend this going away shindig for one of the workers. That was nice.

But after the party, the boss couldn't describe his car to the parking lot attendant. That wasn't the dumb part because the boss explained he had been on a camping trip, his car was hooked to the family trailer, and rather than disconnect it, he just borrowed his brother-in-law's car to come to the party. But he couldn't remember what kind of car it was, or even what color it was. The parking attendant was helpless.

The only solution was to wait until practically everybody left the party. That would narrow down the number of cars in the lot, and his would be easier to find.

I stayed with the boss, just in case he couldn't find it even then, and he needed transportation.

Eventually, the party thinned out and the boss did find the vehicle. As he drove by and waved a thank you to me I wanted to chase after and strangle him. The car had a canoe tied on top.

•

An owner was having trouble getting a decent amount of work out of a field labor crew, so he appointed one of the men as "Field Supervisor."

The man gladly accepted the position because it came with a small increase in salary. But then after about a week, he went to the boss and demanded that he be given a shovel.

The boss said, "You don't need a shovel now. You don't have to do any of the digging."

"But I want a shovel."

The boss said, "The other men have to do the digging. You don't, you see."

The man said, "But I want a shovel."

The boss said, "But you're making more money than they are. Not having a shovel sets you apart. They know you're the boss."

The man said, "I want a shovel."

The boss said, "Why do you want a shovel?"

The man said, "Everybody has something to lean on but me."

•

One manager perfectly described an arrogant but inefficient worker:

"If you could buy him for what he's worth and sell him for what he thinks he's worth, you could make a fortune."

An executive was called for jury duty and it looked like he might be called for an important case—one that might possibly drag on for some time. He didn't want to serve, so he asked the judge to excuse him.

He said, "Your honor, I would like to be excused from serving on this jury."

The judge asked the reason.

The executive said, "We're very busy at the office at this time of year. I'm not sure that I can afford to stay away for an extended period of time."

The judge said, "I see. You're one of those businessmen who have an exaggerated opinion of yourself. You've convinced yourself that your office, your business, your entire company just can't get along without your expertise. Is that right?"

The man said, "No, it isn't your honor. I know they can get along without me very well. I just don't want them to find out."

OFFICE MORALE

A happy office is one where both upper management and intermediate management both recognize and support worker enthusiasm and contributions. It's one where interoffice camaraderie is encouraged. It's one where workers support one another both in and out of the workplace. Either that or it's one where somebody is slipping something into the water cooler.

■

Morale is overrated. The happiest workers in the world were the seven dwarfs and they never made it to the Fortune 500.

■

Maintaining good morale is the art of keeping all the workers happy whether they like it or not.

■

One supervisor pleaded for happiness in his office, and one worker replied, "I'll be satisfied. That's 'happiness' after taxes."

■

Muzak was introduced to offices years ago to make the workers happier. Today removing it accomplishes the same thing.

■

Some say the happier you make the workers, the more productive your workers will be, which is hard to believe because I'm the happiest on my days off.

One supervisor had a no-nonsense approach to morale. He said, "Everybody in this office will either be happy or be fired."

■

A good manager promotes morale in the office. He should encourage his workers to do everything they can to keep him happy.

■

You show me a happy office and I'll show you one that doesn't know what the hell is going on.

■

Good morale produces good results. If everyone in the office smiles constantly, it can drive the supervisor bonkers within 6 working days.

■

Good morale is commendable, but it's a little extreme to have everyone singing "Hi-ho Hi-ho, It's Off to Work We Go" throughout the workday.

■

Your people should be contented. Why should Borden's cows be better off than your workers?

. . . except for those Borden's cows who do more than your workers.

■

Good morale is keeping everyone in the workplace happy with the possible exception of the shop stewards.

■

A good boss gets the workers all pulling together for a common cause. Although, come to think of it, that also describes a mutiny.

■

Our boss wrote a memo that said from now on he wanted to be greeted by smiling faces every morning. It wasn't for morale. It was to stop us from mooning him when he came to work.

■

A proprietor had ten men working in his factory who were not the most energetic of men. He felt he had to appoint a foreman to make sure that the other nine would give him an honest day's work.

Of course, the problem was that he had to select the most enterprising of the ten. How?

Finally, he came up with a device that he thought might work. He called a meeting of the workers and said, "Men, I have a project for one of you. It's kind of a nice easy position. It doesn't involve too much work, so I want to find a nice lazy kind of guy with an easy-going laid-back attitude to handle it. Do I have any volunteers for a nice relaxing job like that?"

∎

Nine of the men stepped forward. The proprietor immediately selected the tenth man.

He said, "I picked you because you weren't like the others. I want you to oversee the other workers. Make sure they work a full day, and work hard for that full day. There's extra money in it for you, and I'm giving you this job because you were the one man who didn't step forward. That showed drive, energy, ambition."

The worker said, "Well, thank you, sir. But I just figured that stepping forward was just too damned much trouble."

∎

The President of a small company had a number of signs prepared to be hung in strategic places around the workplace. They read, "Do It Now."

He tried to get a refund when he brought the signs back. The sign painter said, "Didn't they work?"

The boss said, "They worked too well. After the first week, my accountant skipped the country with $60,000, my sales manager eloped with my private secretary, three clerks came in and demanded a raise, and every night after work, I found the tires on my car were flat."

∎

The late Bear Bryant, Alabama football coach, once held a team meeting. He told his players want kind of conduct he expected from them on and off the field.

He said, "We're a class outfit here at Alabama and I want my players to respect that. I want your shoes shined. I want you wearing a tie. I want a crease in your pants and a decent haircut at all times. I also want you to go to class. I don't want any dummies on this team. If there's anybody in this room who is determined to be a dummie, I want him to stand up immediately."

Alabama's All-American quarterback, Joe Namath stood up.

Coach Bryant said, "Joe, how come you're standing up. You're not dumb."

Namath said, "I know that, Coach, but I just hate like hell to see you standing up here all alone."

∎

In 1862 Abraham Lincoln called together many of his closest advisers. Lincoln was reading as each of them arrived, and he paid little attention to them. When all were settled, the President began reading from the book by Artemeus Ward. It was a collection of humorous pieces called "A High-Handed Outrage at Utica."

It was a particular favorite of Lincoln's and he laughed heartily when he finished reading. No one else joined in. The cabinet members were not pleased with the President's frivolity at such a serious time.

The president reprimanded them. "Why don't you laugh? With the fearful strain that is upon me night and day, if I did not laugh I should die, and you need this medicine as much as I do."

Then Lincoln asked for their comments on a privately prepared "little paper of much significance." It was a draft of the Emancipation Proclamation.

■

Morale is important in the business place. Any dissension can cause problems with output and production. And sometimes the deterioration of office morale can be subtle.

There was a monastery somewhere in Europe in which the monks kept strict rules of silence. On just one Sunday each year, one monk was allowed to stand up at dinner and speak just one sentence.

One year the selected monk stood and said, "The mashed potatoes here are lousy." Then he sat down.

The following year, another monk stood and said, "The mashed potatoes here are delicious." Then he sat down.

The following year the chosen monk stood up and announced, "I'm leaving the monastic life because I can't stand this constant bickering."

THE MAIL ROOM

The mail room is the heart of any organization. It's the pumping station. It's the point at which all communication—incoming and outgoing—gets lost.

■

Some packages are lost in that mail room so long that they're delivered with moss on their northernmost side.

■

Our mail room is like mandatory retirement for packages.

■

I sent a package through our mail room and no one ever saw it again except as a picture on a milk carton.

■

I have a serious philosophical difference with the mail room. I believe in collecting stamps, too . . . but not until after the package is delivered.

I won't say our mail room is slow, but if you send away for some Burpee seeds, be prepared to receive a bouquet of flowers.

■

Our mail room is a fun place to work because every time they find a package, they throw a party.

■

If you ever want to hide out from the law, just put a couple of stamps on your cheek, write "rush" on your forehead, and throw yourself into one of our mail bins.

■

The mail room always has been and always will be there. It's just amazing that in today's world, we're not forced to call it the "person room."

■

Our mail room is so far behind the times, it's one of the few places in the world where you can still buy a penny postcard.

■

Our mail room is fairly efficient except for one flaw. They think the terms "rush" and "do not deliver until December 25th" are interchangeable.

■

To give you an idea how slow our mail room is, I just received a letter telling me I might have a chance to win one million dollars, and the envelope had a picture on it of Ed McMahon when he was a boy.

■

Our mail room has a one-day delivery department. They just don't tell you which day that's going to be.

■

When you send anything marked "rush" from our mail room, it just means they try to lose it sooner.

■

Our mail room reminds me very much of Thom McAn's shoe stores. They're both well stocked with loafers.

■

To them, "Fragile" is a Latin word meaning, "How far can you toss it?"

■

The word "Fragile" stamped on packages is supposed to be a caution, a warning. Our mail room considers it a challenge.

I went down to pick up a package in our mail room and the clerk kept shaking it. He said, "We always shake them. We can tell from the rattle what's in it."

I said, "But this package doesn't rattle."

He said, "It will. We've only had it a week."

∎

Many of today's giants of the business world graduated from the mail room. Which proves that things can come out of the mail room provided they don't have an address on them.

∎

The mail room is an excellent starting point in business . . . for everything but mail.

∎

The boss was not pleased with the way things were progressing in the mail room. Work there was slow and it was not dependable. It was the bottleneck of the entire company and the boss felt it was because the youngsters who worked there were lazy and unmotivated.

He took a group of his associates on an unexpected tour of the mailroom. Sure enough he pointed out countless examples of sloth and carelessness.

Then the group came upon one animated, happy, energetic worker. This guy was zipping through the mail. The letters would fly through his hands and into the various slots for distribution throughout the building. He looked like a magician doing card tricks.

And through it all he was smiling, singing, and whistling. He was a shining example of an ambitious, contented, efficient workman.

The boss went to him and said, "Excuse me, son."

The youngster kept working, "Yes sir, can I help you?"

The boss said, "You're already helping me. I'm the President of this company and I want to applaud you on your work."

The lad said, "Thank you, sir, but this isn't work; it's fun."

The boss said, "That's the attitude we need in this department. And because you enjoy your work, you're good at it."

The kid said, "Thank you, sir."

And letters kept flying past the boss's head.

The boss said, "I've never seen anyone sort mail as quickly as you do."

The kid said, "This is nothing, Sir. Wait'll you see how fast I go once I learn how to read."

THE SUGGESTION BOX

The suggestion box is still a good idea. Anything the employees have to say should be kept under lock and key.

■

The old fashioned suggestion box was small, empty, and had a hole in the top. It reminded a lot of people of the boss.

■

You know what executives get who put up suggestion boxes? Exactly what they deserve.

■

You should summarily dismiss any suggestions that are crude, lewd, or anatomically impossible. However, there may some worth to the other 2 percent.

■

Suggestion boxes still exist in many companies because the executives feel the employees are entitled to their own stupid opinions.

■

Never open a suggestion that is smoking, ticking, or rattling.

Never open a suggestion that has breathing holes cut in the lid.

■

A suggestion box is a place where employees can say about you sober what they say about you when they're drinking.

■

You can compose a standard form letter that will respond to most suggestions you receive. It reads: "Dear Employee, the same to you."

■

You'll find that most suggestions you receive from employees are the same as you receive from passing motorists on the freeways.

■

When opened, most suggestion boxes yield one or two sensible suggestions, 3 or 4 impractical suggestions, 30 or 40 immoral suggestions, and 600 or 700 candy wrappers.

Employees treat the suggestion box as a halfway house between trash receptacles.

Workers need a place to voice their suggestions. Especially when space starts getting limited on bathroom walls.

■

Study all suggestions at your leisure and in privacy. It removes the burden of having to read them with a straight face.

■

The suggestion box is a perfect forum for those employees who are either too shy to speak up or who don't use that type of language in public.

■

Workers should be encouraged to voice their opinions. Why should management be the only ones who come out looking like fools?

Maybe 1 in 100 suggestions will be practical. That's no big deal. It's about the same record as management.

■

Some companies have suggestion boxes, but rarely open them. I saw one suggestion written on yellowed paper that had an idea to relieve the parking problems outside the plant–add more hitching posts.

■

All suggestions should be hand-written. If the suggestion is bizarre enough, it helps the FBI track down the author.

■

A suggestion box serves a purpose. If nothing else it helps keep the damned shop steward out of your office.

PEEVES FROM THE HIGHER-UPS

Most people in business feel that the word "superior" is an honorary title.

PERSONNEL

"Personnel" is now "Human Resources." It's the only department in all of industry that operates under an alias.

·

Personnel has a tough job. They deal with people—the only item in the business world that hasn't been improved over the past 200 years.

·

It's not easy dealing with people, but someone has to hire the employees to sit in front of the computers.

·

Personnel workers are to be applauded. They are the people movers of industry. And you know how hard it is to get some of the people who work for you to move.

·

Personnel hires people and send them to other departments. It's kind of like selecting someone else's spouse, isn't it?

They hire a person and then put him to work in another department. That's kind of like voting a town dry and then moving.

■

People who work in personnel find it hard to make new friends. Every time they meet someone new, they ask him to fill out 6 or 7 forms.

■

You have to fill out a half a dozen forms even if you go to the personnel department just to get change for the coffee machine.

■

Personnel–that's where all blank forms go to be filled out.

■

Personnel has solved the age old problem–you can't get a job without experience and you can't get experience without a job. By the time you get done filling out all of their forms, you've got experience.

■

Personnel is a trusting department. They administer lie detector tests and chain all the pens in their waiting room.
... do they know something we don't?

■

Personnel is a risk free department. No matter who or what they hire, they send them to work in some other department.

■

Once you hire people today, they're hired. Personnel should try to learn never to make the same mistake once.

■

Personnel hires the people for other departments. It's kind of like letting someone else pack your parachute.

■

Personnel is where all the new employees go through when they enter the company. It's like the Ellis Island of the business world.

■

Personnel is where they keep all the records of the employees. They know more about you than Santa Claus's helpers.

■

At the last judgment, God will arrive on a fluffy white cloud, and seated next to Him will be the Personnel Manager with your folder in his hand.

Personnel knows more about you than you know about yourself. That's logical, though. You would give yourself a promotion.

... they know better.

■

One speaker addressing a convention of personnel workers said: "What a great audience this is. 350 people here and not a shop steward in sight."

■

There was a respected Personnel Manager who always had a habit of opening his desk drawer and glancing in at something before signing his name and official title to anything important.

Years later, when he retired, curious employees opened the desk to see what mysterious words of wisdom were written there. It was a small piece of paper that said, "2 N's—1 L."

■

Part of being a good personnel manager is knowing your people and their potential.

President Lyndon Johnson once invited Jack Benny to perform at the White House. Naturally, Benny brought his violin with him.

However, the White House guard stopped him at the gate and asked, "What do you have in that case, Mr. Benny?"

Jack said, "A machine gun."

The guard said, "Then you may enter. I was afraid for a minute you had your violin."

■

Will Rogers once said, "We have eleven million unemployed, counting the four million that do nothing but keep statistics on things that we would be better off not knowing."

THE COMPANY LINE

The official company line is the logic you use when employees question company practices. Mothers have used it successfully for centuries. Theirs goes: "Because I said so, that's why."

■

The official company line is so hokey if you used its equivalent to try to pick up girls, you'd still be a virgin.

Any employee who believes the official company line should not have been hired in the first place.

■

An executive must learn the official company line, practice reciting the official company line, then practice reciting the official company line with a straight face.

■

Sometimes you have to present the company line even when you don't believe in it. It's a lot like telling your children the evils of sex.

■

No one really believes you when you recite the official company line. It's kind of like a politician reciting the Oath of Office.

■

Sometimes there's only one good reason for supporting company policy. Because they're the one who signs your paycheck.

■

It can seem at times that the company position is both feet planted firmly on the ground with the head buried securely in the sand.

In that position, they do make an inviting target, don't they?

■

It's kind of tough advocating a position you don't believe in. You feel like an atheist praying to have an audience with the Pope.

■

Most companies are not democratic. They don't believe that everyone is entitled to their own stupid opinion.

No, they insist that the only stupid opinion be theirs.

■

You are supposed to obey all company directives blindly, which is fitting. Many of them look like that's how they were drawn up.

■

You know, when the blind are leading the blind, anyone who can see is considered insubordinate.

■

Sign seen in an office: "I've made up my mind. Don't confuse me with facts."

Remember no one ever went wrong blindly believing the official company line
. . . except maybe customers.

■

It's ironic how there's always enough blame to be spread around, but rarely
enough credit.

■

I like the musician who had a colorful way of describing official company policy.
He asked his bandleader if he knew the difference between a bull and a band. The
bandleader, of course, said he didn't. The guy said, "With a bull, the horns are in
front and the big ass is in back."

■

Of course, we all have to be able to sell something we don't believe in. Otherwise
we'd never be able to get through a job interview.

■

Remember, companies don't pay you to think. They hire computers to do that.

■

Here's a guy who thought the employee should think on his own.

A man was riding in a cab in New York, and it stopped for a red light. While it
was stopped, a blind man with a seeing eye dog started to cross the street. They got
right in front of the cab, when the light changed to green.

The cabbie started hitting the horn and yelling obscenities out the open window.

The passenger was a little embarrassed and told the driver to take it easy. He said,
"After all, the poor man is blind."

The cabbie said, "Yeah, but the dog should know better."

■

TRUMAN'S LAW: If you can't convince them, confuse them.—*Harry S. Truman*

■

Somebody said, "Liberty don't work as well in practice as it does in speeches."

■

Sometimes it's not what you say but how you say it.

Thoreau wrote a book called *A Week on the Concord and Merrimack Rivers* that
didn't sell well. The publisher printed 1000 copies, but couldn't unload them, and
needed the shelf space for newer books they were publishing. Thoreau bought the
unsold copies–706 of them.

However, he recorded the transaction in his personal journal as follows: "I now
have a library of nearly nine hundred volumes, over seven hundred of which I wrote
myself."

Sometimes company spokesmen are as one-sided as the Southern matriarch who spoke to her grandchildren, grand nephews and nieces at a family gathering. She wanted to instill in them the love of the South that was so much a part of her family upbringing.

She said, "Children, the South is gracious and gentile. All things that are good and virtuous originate in the South."

One child asked, "Grandmom, was Jesus a Southerner?"

She answered as honestly as she could, "He was good enough to be a Southerner."

■

One biased alumnus was praising his beloved Harvard, when a heckler said, "You know something? I started out going to Harvard, but I switched to Yale."

The speaker quickly added, "And raised the Academic standard of both institutions in the process."

■

Here's a gentleman who explained the "company" line forthrightly. A friend from 'up north' who had just graduated law school wrote to him and asked what the prospects were for a legal practice in Alabama.

The gentleman wrote back saying, "If you are an honest and competent lawyer with good qualifications, willing to work hard and withstand decent competition, you'll find the business community will support you and afford you every opportunity for success in the fine state of Alabama. And on the other hand, if you are a Republican the game laws will protect you."

■

Bob Hope used a version of the "company line" in one of his telecasts back in the days when the United States was struggling to mount a viable space program.

Several of our test launches had failed. In fact, one comedian noted that we should change the names of our missiles. We were putting too much pressure on our program with impressive names. The headlines would read: "Thor missile fails in test launch." This comic said, "Name them Irving or Eugene, or something. Then it's not so depressing to read: 'Irving Fails.'"

In any case morale was low because the Russians had already launched Sputnik and we still hadn't gotten anything off the ground. Another comedian said that we should let the Russians steal our space secrets. That way, they'd be two years behind us.

That was the background when another of our launches from Florida was aborted into the ocean and Bob Hope went on the air. He began with:

"Well, I guess you heard the good news from Cape Canaveral? The United States just launched another submarine."

REPORT WRITING

Report writing is the art of saying nothing and putting it in a binder.

■

Remember the essays you used to write in school on "How I Spent My Summer Vacation?" Business reports are the same type of writing except titled "How I Earned My Summer Vacation."

■

A well written business report doesn't allow facts to get in the way of progress.

■

Most reports have three facets: what you know, what you think you know, and what you think the boss wants to hear.

■

Every argument has two sides and a well written report should contain enough facts to support both of them.

■

Your report should contain your conclusions. Conclusions are what you arrive at after you've stopped thinking.

■

Reports are a collection of fiction supported by facts.

■

Reports are said to be like bikinis. What they reveal is interesting, but what they conceal is vital.

■

Statistics can be made to resemble anything. They are adult Tinker-Toys.

■

Remember that any bottle that's half full, is also half empty. So are most reports.

■

Numbers may not lie, but they sure wink a lot as they're telling the truth.

■

In any good business report, two and two should add up to four–if it's expedient.

Two numbers can only add up to one sum; but pages full of numbers can add up to damn near anything.

■

Remember, whole numbers can add up to half-truths.

■

When you read that "9 out of 10 dentists recommend . . . " it could be that the 10th one is the only one who still has his teeth.

■

Most reports have to be rewritten. The boss generally asks the authors to go back and attempt a non-fiction version.

■

Some reports are held together with paper clips; some reports are held together with staples; some reports are held together with binding. All reports are held together with wishful thinking.

■

A good executive can read a report, separate fact from fiction, and utilize either one.

■

Report writers should remember that there are two types of facts–those that support the writer's premise, and inconclusive.

■

George Burns at the age of 93 summed up reports. He said, "I've read a report that said cigar smoking, drinking, and carousing with younger women were bad for one's health; so I'm going to do something about it. I'm going to give up reading."

■

Dynamics Corporation of America plagiarized Charles Dickens in writing their 1975 annual report. They weren't worried about a suit by the author because they were already in Chapter Eleven. Their report began:

"It was the best of times, it was the worst of times, it was the age of wisdom, it was the age of foolishness, it was the epoch of belief, it was the epoch of incredulity, it was the season of Light, it was the season of Darkness, it was the spring of hope, it was the winter of despair, we had everything before us, we had nothing before us, we were all going direct to Heaven, we were all going direct the other way—in short, the period was so like the year 1974 for Dynamic Corporation of America that one might suspect that Mr. Dickens had premonitions of DCA's travail in mind as he started *A Tale of Two Cities*."

Will Rogers said: "We are always reading statistics and figures. Half of America do nothing but prepare statistics for the other half to read."

■

Some of the best have employed creative fiction writing in reports.

Winston Churchill was once asked by a member of the Labor opposition for some statistics about his government programs that could be potentially embarrassing.

Churchill said, "I'll have an answer for you tomorrow."

Sure enough, he did rattle off statistics for the better part of an hour.

An associate later said to Churchill, "How could you gather so many statistics in so short a time? It would have taken me and my staff six months to gather that much information."

Churchill agreed and said, "And it will take them six months to figure out that they're all false."

■

Doublespeak works nicely in reports.

One girl told her friend, "I'm terribly worried. I wrote Jack in my last letter to forget that I had told him I didn't mean to reconsider my decision not to change my mind, and he seems to have misunderstood me."

SCHEDULING

No business schedule has ever been adhered to. God created the world in six days. He promised it in four.

In fact, no schedule has ever been adhered to. Even twenty-four hour viruses often stay twenty or thirty minutes past their check-out time.

■

The difference between "date of completion" and "scheduled date of completion" is the difference between "chicken" and "chicken pox."

■

Scheduling is the easiest duty that a manager has. It consists of taking an assignment and writing after it a day, a month, and a year. Naturally, though, that's not all there is to it. Whoever gave you the assignment will not be satisfied with the date you promise. So you haggle and you negotiate and then you write down another day, month, and year. *That's* all there is to it.

"Estimated date of completion" for any business project is that day that other people can legitimately start asking why it's not done.

■

Santa Claus is the idol of every business person who has to make a schedule. Santa has to cover the entire world once a year, yet he always puts it off until Christmas Eve.

■

You don't have to adhere to any scheduled date. You pick out any day of the year and look at it on the calendar. You'll find it always has another day following it.

■

The most realistic scheduler in the world is the guy who had a signmaker paint him a placard that said "The World Will End Tomorrow" and wanted to pay for it on the installment plan.

■

No one will respect the first business person who meets a promised schedule. It will throw everybody else's schedule off.

■

Schedules are contradictory. I've had people come to repossess furniture that hadn't been delivered yet.

■

There is no task so complex, no assignment so confusing, and no job so difficult that some executive can't put a completion date after it.

■

When an executive says, "You'll get this when hell freezes over," he really means two days after hell freezes over.

■

I like the guy who had an answer for his boss's impossible schedule. The boss said, "You have three days to finish this project." The guy said, "Okay. I'll take Halloween, Thanksgiving, and Christmas."

■

Meeting a promised date is like walking on water. Even if you could do it, nobody would believe you anyway.

■

Some business people are so bad at scheduling it takes them an hour and a half to watch "60 Minutes."

There is one schedule that's strictly kept. It still takes business men and women 9 months to have a baby. But that's because embryos never go on strike.

■

I like the boss who understood scheduling. When he gave an employee an assignment, he said, "I need this tomorrow, but since you're always a day late, pretend I gave it to you yesterday."

. . . The employee said, "I'll have it done for you next Monday. That'll give you the whole weekend to pretend it's tomorrow."

. . . they were both happy to get it out of the way by the following Thursday.

■

I saw this sign over the supervisor's desk in an office I visited:
"If I wanted it tomorrow, I would have given it to you tomorrow."

■

This story defines scheduling:
A woman was helping her parents clean out their garage. She came across an old shoe repair ticket of her father's, dated 1942. The little shoe repair shop was still in business so she thought she'd take the ticket there just to see what would happen.

She presented the ticket and asked the clerk if he had the shoes. He went into the back of the shop, came out after a minute or so and said, "Yeah, we have the shoes. They'll be ready next Tuesday."

■

Here's a story of some creative scheduling:
A young bull and an old bull were on a hill overlooking an entire herd of cows. The youngster got a little excited with so much bovine pulchritude on display and said, "Hey, Oldtimer, what say we run down there and service a few of those beauties?"

The old bull said, "No, why don't we just walk down and service them all?"

■

Here's some real advance scheduling:
An old couple—they were in their 80's—appeared before a divorce judge. They'd been married over 50 years and the judge was upset that they wanted to dissolve such a long marriage, and he told them that. He said, "Why do you want to get a divorce now?"

The woman said, "Your honor, we've been unhappy with each other for almost 50 years."

The man said, "That's right, Judge. This ain't a spur of the moment thing."

The Judge said, "Well, in that case, why did you wait so long?"

The woman said, "We wanted to wait until the children died."

President Lyndon Johnson had a colorful expression to explain a scheduling dilemma he had. He said: "Handling this situation is like being a bitch in heat. If you stand still, you get screwed; if you move, they bite you in the ass."

■

Here's a good example of reversed scheduling used as an attack device:

A gentleman came home from work and found the house a mess. Nothing was cleaned, junk was scattered all over the floors, and his wife was sitting on the living room sofa with a pile of dirty laundry heaped on the coffee table in front of her.

The man said, "What happened?"

His wife said, "You know how you always wonder what I do all day? Well, here it is. I didn't do it."

■

An American manufacturer was entertaining a prospective client from the Soviet Union. As they were touring the factory, the noon whistle blew and most of the workers abandoned their work stations to go to lunch. The Russian visitor was worried and said, "Your workers! They're all escaping."

The host said, "Don't worry. We have ways of getting them back."

They continued their tour and their meeting, then the whistle blew again. All the workers returned to their stations.

Now the manufacturer wanted to get back to business. He said, "About those machines you were interested in buying. . . "

The visitor said, "Forget the machines. How much do you want for that whistle?"

■

When Thomas Edison opened his first plant, he noticed that most of the employees spent a lot of their time–his valuable time, actually–watching the one clock in the factory.

Edison was a tireless worker, and clock-watching both baffled and annoyed him.

However, rather than express his displeasure to the workers, he simply had more clocks installed, all with different times.

From then on clock-watching became so confusing that no one bothered to do it.

RESPONSIBILITY

How come top executives delegate most of the authority, but keep all of the salary?

■

Have you ever noticed? Responsibility is delegated; perks are kept.

When the boss says, "I'm making you totally responsible for this?" what's *he* responsible for?

■

Responsibility is a commodity that easily sours. When it does, it turns to blame.

■

All executives crave responsibility; none of them wants any blame.

■

Delegating responsibility is a euphemism for turning over something you don't know how to do to someone who does know how to do it without letting anyone know you don't know how to do it.

■

Don't let responsibility swell your head. It just makes it roll further if the project fails.

■

Authority is different from responsibility. The person with responsibility is the one the person with authority blames when the project fails.

■

A boss who gives responsibility without authority is saying, "I hope you do a good job because I'm really sticking your neck out for you on this one."

■

Responsibility without authority is like being sent into a cage full of lions without a whip, a chair, or a prayer.
. . . It's worse if the lions are unionized.

■

Responsibility without authority is like trying to rob a bank with a fake gun. It only works until people start to catch on.

■

Being given responsibility without authority is like being challenged to a duel where there's only one pistol.
. . . and it's being used.
. . . by the other guy.

■

It's like the Captain of a sinking ship saying, "I have the authority to get in the life boat. I'm giving you the responsibility of getting the ship safely to shore."

It's like the boss saying to you, "Get up there and walk that high wire. If you need a net, it'll be in my office."

■

A boss who gives responsibility without authority is saying, "Let's divide this one equally. You take the kicks in the ass; I'll take the pats on the back."

■

If you want a person to do a job, give him authority and responsibility. If you want to do a job on a person, just give him the responsibility.

■

Authority means you can say "yes" or "no." Responsibility usually means you can just say "good-bye."

■

Sometimes authority doesn't work. In California, the pedestrian is authorized to cross the street in a marked crosswalk even if traffic is coming. The pedestrian should still be responsible and look both ways. Have you ever seen a white line stop a truck?

■

Sometimes, neither works. Custer had authority and responsibility. The Apaches apparently remained unimpressed.

■

"Whenever a man's failure can be traced to management's mistakes, he has to be kept on the payroll."—*Peter Drucker*

■

A General was once testing a new flying boat. He took it up for a short spin, did a few maneuvers, and then began to land it at the airport.

The Colonel who was accompanied him, screamed, "General, this is a sea plane . . . land on the water! Land on the water!."

The General immediately pulled up circled around and set the plane down on the water's surface. Then he glared at the Colonel and said, "Don't you ever yell at a superior officer like that again. I'm an experienced flyer and I would have discovered my error without your help, and certainly without your panic and insubordination."

With that said, he opened the door, and stepped out of the plane and into the water.

■

There's a story told about Abraham Lincoln when he was a military Captain during the Black Hawk war. He was not much of a military tactician, but he was a leader even then.

Once he was marching his men in platoon formation. They came upon a locked fence and Lincoln had no idea what the proper military protocol was.

Nevertheless, he gave this order: "Company dismissed for two minutes. At the end of that time, fall in on the other side of this fence."

PEEVES FROM EACH OTHER

It can be depressing to glance around at our co-workers and realize that technically they're considered our equals.

ANNOYING COLLEAGUES

FINGER DRUMMERS:

People who drum their fingers on the desk at meetings are annoying. You keep hoping a stick-man comes in just so everybody will have to put their hands in the air.

■

I hate to chair meetings that include a finger drummer. It's too tempting to sit there with a gavel in my hands.

■

Everybody hates it. You sit there and want to give the guy a free manicure with "Krazy Glue."

■

The steady rhythm gets to everyone. All the reports are read like a Run D-M-C recording.

■

If I get a guy like that on any of my staffs or committees, I immediately change the dress code–to shirt, tie, and straight jacket.

Either that or I conduct all meetings as a seance. Having everybody join hands helps keep him quiet.

LOUD VOICES:

I worked with a guy who was so loud he cost the company a lot of money in overtime. When he was speaking nobody could hear the quitting bell.

■

Everything he did was loud. When he sneezed the bomb squad arrived.

■

His telephone voice was so loud he could override a busy signal.

■

His voice was so loud he could dominate any meeting–even those he wasn't attending.

■

This guy was annoying no matter where we put his office. His voice could have been heard over World War II.

■

His voice was so booming it could shatter a glass, an ear drum, and a friendship.

■

He was great to have along on a business trip, though, because when he hailed a cab, the taxi not only stopped, but all its doors popped open.

■

He could get a bartender's attention and a drink in front of him in no time at all–whether the establishment was open or not.

■

This guy was so loud we all figured it was because of his heritage. His mother was Irish and his father was bull horn.

■

He was a nice guy, though. After he greeted you with a hearty, loud hello, he'd help you look for your glasses.

UNWANTED VISITORS:

Some office colleagues insist on visiting when you're busy. Like bills, they generally arrive when you can't handle them.

■

Sometimes you can get rid of these people by dropping subtle hints–like calling "Security."

Nothing deters them. They consider a closed and locked door with an armed secretary nearby an invitation to come in for a friendly chat.

■

When you say, "I'm too busy to talk now," they say, "That's all right. You just listen."

■

I finally put a sign on my door that said, "This is a business office, not the 'Phil Donahue Show.' "

One guy thought that was so clever that he insisted on coming in and talking about it.

BORROWERS:

There's always the borrower. He borrows books, staples, pens. The only thing this man brings to work with him that is his is skin.

■

There's usually one in every office. He's known as the "Corporate Kleptomaniac."

■

The picture on his desk is not even of *his* wife and kids.

■

I tried to nail down everything in my office just to protect against this guy, but I couldn't. He had borrowed my nails.

■

The last time he was fired they gave him one hour to gather up his belongings. He had 58 minutes to kill.

■

Things just disappear when they get to his office. His desk must be made from driftwood that floated in from the Bermuda Triangle.

THE OFFICE SLOB:

Then there's the office slob. He's the opposite of Johnny Appleseed. He wanders from office to office sprinkling coffee stains to the wind.

■

He has more rings around his office than a Zsa Zsa Gabor garage sale.

■

When this guy visits your office he always leaves coffee stains–even when he's not carrying coffee.

When this guy washes his hands he leaves a coffee ring around the soap.

■

He's trying to improve, though. The coffee rings he leaves on my desk are getting closer to the coaster I give him.

■

He drops cigarette ashes on the floor and says, "They're supposed to be good for the carpeting." I say, "Well, I guess we'll know once we put this fire out."

■

He can just look at a document on your desk and it will get a stain of some kind on it. He's a "smudge-voyant."

JUST PLAIN OBNOXIOUS:

Then there are some office neighbors who are just obnoxious. The kind of person you'd be embarrassed to introduce to your parole officer.

■

You'd rather have a termination notice come into your office than these people.

■

They're just unlikable people. The kind of a person Mother Theresa would punch in the mouth.

■

You know the kind of people. When they go to the beach, the tide goes out and doesn't come in again till they leave.

■

They're loud, they're rude, they're obnoxious, they're ignorant. You know they're just bucking for a promotion.

■

They should be eliminated. Every office building should have a resident exorcist.

COMMITTEES

You can tell this is a management meeting. I stopped a fellow in the corridor and asked him how to get to this room. He immediately appointed a committee to get back to me in three months with an answer.

■

My Dad always had two safe answers. At work he would say, "We'll have a committee study it," and at home he'd say, "Go ask your Mother."

Forming a committee to attack a problem is exactly like forming a posse to catch an outlaw . . . except the posse uses *complete* horses.

■

Somebody once said a camel was a horse that was built by a committee. I doubt that. The camel is finished.

■

A committee is a group of people who meet in the same room at the same time to do the same thing differently.

■

Usually a committee is a group of people separated by a common goal.

■

An executive forms a committee so that he'll get either a solution to his problem or someone to blame.

■

If at first you don't succeed, appoint a committee and let them worry about it.

■

"We've appointed a committee to look into the matter" is the same as saying, "Next."

■

Committees are confusion with a gavel.

■

Committees get rid of annoyances for awhile. It's like sending your business problems to summer camp.

■

The idea behind a committee is that a small group of highly trained and dedicated people, if they band together, can conquer any problems no matter how numerous, ferocious, or troublesome they may be. Custer and his men are good examples.

■

I wouldn't use committees too often. You notice every time a bunch of baseball players gather on the mound, the pitcher's usually in trouble.

■

There is only one "best solution" for a problem and every committee member has it.

Two heads *are* better than one. It's the other ten or twelve heads on the committee that slow things down.

■

Committees don't usually solve problems. They let them die of old age.

■

No great decisions have ever come out of a committee except where to adjourn for lunch.

■

If committees were really effective, cars would be built with a steering wheel in front of each seat.

■

Committee reports don't usually solve anything. They just take already existing problems and put them in book form.

■

Committee reports take a long time to write. It's not easy to say "We don't know" in 85 pages or more.

■

The boss was reading an exhaustive report handed in by one of his committees.

He said, "I see a name on this committee that I've never heard of before."

The committee chairman replied, "Oh, that's probably just the guy who actually does the work."

■

"I see a committee that was investigating the high cost of living, turned in their report: 'We find the cost of living very high and we recommend more funds to carry on the investigation.' "—*Will Rogers*

■

"There is quite an argument in Rome over the exact spot of Caesar's death. Some say that Caesar was not slain in the Senate; they seem to think that he had gone over to a senatorial investigation meeting at some committee room, and that is where Brutus gigged him. The moral of the whole thing seems to be to stay away from investigations."—*Will Rogers*

■

"At the Pan-American Conference they have done nothing but form committees, and then those committees would form advisory committees, and the subcommittees would form advisory committees, and they have just committed their self to death.

"In years to come, the question will be asked by some fond child of its father, who was a delegate to this conference: "What did you do, father, at the big conference?"

" 'Why, I was the fellow who thought of all the different names for all the different committees. If it hadent been for me, they wouldent have known what to call their committees, and if they hadent had names for the committees, the conference would have been a failure–for forming committees was the sole accomplishment of the conference.' "—*Will Rogers*

■

A businessman was travelling by train and got stuck in a bar car with a group of Chamber of Commerce Boosters from Phoenix, Arizona. They weren't at all shy about promoting their fine city.

They told him, "We're the committee that's been appointed to travel around the country, gather information, and come up with a plan to beautify our fair city."

The businessman said, "That's nice."

Another one boasted, "Yes sir, we've been travelling, and meeting, and conferring, and making plans, and boy, do we have a doozy of a program to beautify the great city of Phoenix."

The businessman said, "That's nice."

Another one said, "We have plans to redesign our roads and relandscape them." Another one said, "We have plans that will have major corporations flocking to Phoenix."

Another one said, "We have plans for the airport that will make Phoenix one of the major transportation hubs of the world...the world, I say."

The businessman said, "Why don't you turn Phoenix into a thriving seaport?"

They all stopped. They didn't know whether to laugh or call for medical help. Finally one commmittee member said, "How could we turn Phoenix into a seaport?"

The businessman said, "Lay some two-inch pipe from your city, through California, out to the Pacific Ocean. Then if all you fellas can suck as hard as you can blow, you'll have yourselves a seaport before nightfall."

■

Here's the kind of gentleman who should be handling committee meetings:

He was travelling on a coast-to-coast non-stop flight that was being terrorized by a five-year-old youngster. The boy ran up and down the aisles disrupting business people who were doing paper work, waking those who were sleeping, tearing headsets off of people who were trying to listen to music.

The passengers complained to the flight attendant who insisted that the child be controlled, but when the boy was belted into his seat, his screams were more disconcerting than his antics.

The passengers were desperate. They suggested that he be locked up somewhere, that he be bound and gagged, that the parents be arrested–anything to make their trip more pleasant.

Finally, this one gentleman spoke to the flight attendant who spoke to the flight crew. They made room for the boy in the first seat on the plane, and with some creativity, fashioned a steering wheel from a plate, a rudder from some sort of stick, and several other flying instruments from different odds and ends.

Then the pilot came back and asked the lad if he would help him fly the plane. The kid was delighted. He sat up front with the pilot next to him and was "taught" how to fly.

The pilot excused himself and left the boy in charge of "flying" the plane the rest of the way. The boy enthusiastically and reasonably quietly piloted the plane into a safe landing at San Francisco.

Many of the passengers thanked the gentleman for his ingenuity. One asked how he ever thought of it. The man said, "You were all trying to solve your problem. I tried to solve the boy's."

MEETINGS

An executive without a business meeting to go to is like a fish in a jelly jar while his tank is being cleaned.

■

All executives should have important meetings to go to. A briefcase is a terrible thing to waste.

■

If you put a bunch of rats in a maze, they'd immediately begin looking for the cheese. If you put a bunch of executives in a maze, they'd immediately call a meeting to find out where the cheese is.

■

Executives have discovered that deciding what work to do is more fun than working.

■

I know one executive who attended so many meetings, he got tennis elbow just from raising his hand and saying, "Present."

■

An executive meeting is nothing more than a bull session with an agenda.

A meeting is when executives are behind closed doors keeping minutes while the employees are outside wasting hours.

■

Some executives spend three days a week at meetings trying to figure out why their employees are only doing two days worth of work.

■

If all the people who attended meetings were laid end to end, they'd get about as much done.

... but it would make taking notes more fun.

■

A business meeting is just like the old-time general store except with a big table where the cracker barrel used to be.

■

Most meetings begin with a note pad before each seat–blank. Could that be symbolic?

■

The best way to solve a big business problem is to call a meeting to discuss it. Soon the meetings become such a big pain in the ass that the original problem starts looking smaller.

■

Having a meeting to increase productivity is like pulling your car over to the side of the road to find out why you're not going faster.

■

If business meetings are supposed to be productive, why do the executives always come out and give the work to someone else to do?

■

White collar crime is an executive, who has spent all week attending meetings, picking up his paycheck.

■

Good ideas will come out of good meetings early. So will good executives.

■

Never speak at a meeting unless you have to. A good rule to remember is that it's better to remain silent and be thought a fool than to speak and remove all doubt.

■

A good rule of thumb at most meetings is to keep your briefcase and your mouth shut.

To appear intelligent at meetings, suck on something, such as the end of a pencil, the earpiece of your eyeglasses, or almost anything that isn't attached to your or anyone else's body.

... with the possible exception of doorknobs.

■

Seating at a business meeting is important. If you can't hear what the chairperson is saying, don't bring it up. You're not important enough to know what's going on anyway.

■

Behind the closed doors of the executive meeting, the manager is impervious to the attacks of his natural predator, the people under him. Surely you, at some time, have tried to see a superior, only to be told by his secretary that "Mr. So-and-so is in a meeting." Translated into the vernacular, this means that Mr. So-and-so is in his fortress. It cannot be penetrated by arrow, brick, burning oil, mortar fire, rocket, laser beam, or shop steward. He cannot be reached by phone, messenger, telegram, smoke signal, mental telepathy, or sky writer. He cannot be called from the meeting for any reason short of a death in the family, and even then only if it is his own.

■

Someone once said, "The only difference between most business meetings and a funeral is you know when you're at a funeral."

■

COMING UP WITH IDEAS: New idea meetings need five people, and preferably twelve. Mix ages and backgrounds. When the group runs dry, restate the problem. At the end, go back to the wildest two ideas and see what innovations they inspire.—*J. Geoffrey Rawlinsons, Creative Thinking and Brainstorming*

■

Will Rogers summed it up well, as usual: "Congress ought to pass a law to prohibit us conferring with anybody on anything–till we learn how."

■

When Calvin Coolidge became Vice-President of the United States, Channing H. Cox succeeded him as Governor of Massachusetts. In that position, Cox met with many people and worked long hours to get his official duties done.

He visited his predecessor in Washington once and was surprised to see that Coolidge saw many visitors each day, yet finished his work at a normal hour. Cox asked, "How can you see so many people and finish so early, when I have to stay until at least nine o'clock each night?"

Coolidge said, "You talk back."

Jean Giraudoux was France's Minister of Information shortly before World War I. In that capacity he attended a meeting to discuss the troublesome problem of national unemployment.

The speakers debated the problems for a long time. Then one said, "If things continue this badly for another year, we'll all be on the streets begging."

Giraudoux said, "From whom?"

■

A very successful businessman, who was nearing retirement age, gave a glorious wedding reception for his only daughter. He allowed time for a sort of business meeting with his new son-in-law, though.

The two met in a private room and the man said, "I love my daughter, and now I welcome you into the family. To show you how much we care for you, I'm going to make you a 50-50 partner in my business. You are now half owner of a very successful business."

The man continued, "All you have to do is go to the factory and learn the operation . . . "

The son-in-law interrupted him. He said, "I hate factories. I can't stand the noise, the confusion."

The father-in-law said, "I see. Well, then you'll work at the office. You'll be in charge of some of the operations . . . "

The kid interrupted again. He said, "I hate office work. I can't stand being stuck behind a desk."

The father-in-law said, "Wait a minute. I just made you half-owner of a money making organization. You can't stand factories; you can't stand offices; you hate desks. What am I going to do with you?"

The youngster said, "Buy me out."

■

Someone said it. "Meetings are like Panda matings. The expectations are always high, but the results are usually disappointing.

MEMO WRITING

If you don't have anything to say, don't say anything–write it in a memo.

■

Memos are the backyard gossip of the business world . . . minus the substance.

■

If an executive has nothing to say but attaches a mailing list to it, it becomes a memo.

The memo is a form of communication in business just as jungle drums are in the wild, except that jungle drums don't run up your xeroxing bill.

... Besides you can't do erotic dancing to memos.

■

In diplomacy it's a communique; in the military it's a dispatch; in business it's a memo. Everywhere else, they just call it bulls___.

■

In business, the memo is a way of transmitting information from those who have none to those who don't want any.

■

A memo lies somewhere between an official document and a perfectly good blank sheet of paper.

■

The business world feels that paper is cheap and it becomes even cheaper after you write a memo on it.

■

Save your memos. They make excellent scratch paper ... on both sides.

■

In the business world, memos are a form of communication, although you wouldn't know it to read some of them.

■

Memos should be short, sweet, and to the point, if any.

■

The best way to write memos is to put in them only what is absolutely necessary. It's also the best way to eliminate most of them.

■

Some executives write lots of memos because they say it promotes communication and all communication in business is good. Does the Tower of Babel ring a bell?

■

A memo is the official written version of "something better left unsaid."

■

You all know what a memo is ... that's inter-office junk mail.

■

You can make paper airplanes out of memos, but usually, like the information on them, they don't fly.

Memos are a record of communication. So if another executives claims he never received your memo, you have a written record of what he never read.

■

When another executive asks for one, what he's really saying is: "I don't have time to deal with that issue now. Send me a memo and I'll ignore it later."

■

The only things that should begin with "From" and "To" are gift cards and prison sentences.

■

Here's a memo that's short and to the point. It was written by Cornelius Vanderbilt to some businessmen who had tried to pull a fast one.

"Gentlemen: You have undertaken to cheat me. I will not sue you, for law takes too long. I will ruin you. Sincerely Yours, Cornelius Vanderbilt."

QUALITY CONTROL

Quality control is a business euphemism for "Hey, we're trying, OK?"

■

Quality control doesn't eliminate errors; it just gives you a department to blame them on.

■

Quality control is sort of an oxymoron. Shouldn't quality be uncontrolled?

■

Quality control is a strange thing. I bought a shirt with a slip of paper in it that said "This item was inspected by No. 6." The word "inspected" was misspelled.

... besides, if someone is good at inspecting, shouldn't they give their name, not their number.

I don't believe those things anyway. I've never seen anything that wasn't inspected by No. 6.

... Have No. 1, 2, 3, 4, and 5 retired?

■

Quality control is doing their job if the item they're making lasts one day longer than the warranty.

■

Quality control is less important now than it was years ago. Thanks to modern technology, we can now blame everything on the computer.

To err is human. To err a thousand times an hour is technology.

■

Quality control has determined that most errors are not serious, unless you happen to be the one who bought that product.

■

It's important to remember that quality control is not a service to the customer; it's self-defense against your competitors.

... errors would be perfectly acceptable if we'd all agree to make them.

■

Perfect quality control is attainable. Have you noticed whenever you get a defective product, the billing is always correct?

■

I once bought a pen that came with a lifetime guarantee and it broke. I was afraid I was going to die that night.

... or the pen company would have me eliminated.

■

Lifetime guarantees do make sense. If the thing breaks the day after you die, who's going to bring it in for repairs?

■

The quality control department doesn't really want to eliminate all errors. If they did, who'd need them?

■

I don't trust companies that handle customer complaints with alacrity and precision. I'd much rather deal with a company that's genuinely surprised to get one.

■

There's no such thing as absolute quality control. Even in nature, some snakes are born with two heads. The big difference is, they get the two heads at birth; not the day after the warranty expires.

■

Companies are very strict about quality control. One man was fired for cheating in quality control. It happened to be with his manager's wife.

■

A farmer gave one of his hands a jug of hard cider as a Christmas gift. After he had drunk it all down, the farmer asked him what he thought of it.

He said it was just right.

The farmer said, "What exactly do you mean by 'just right?' "

The hired hand said, "Well, if it was any better you wouldn't have given it to me, and if it was any worse I couldn't have drunk it."

■

A construction supervisor had hired a local laborer to dig a long ditch to lay some pipe work in. They agreed on a price and the supervisor began to walk away.

The laborer said, "Wait a minute. How deep do you want this ditch?"

The supervisor said, "Just about four feet."

The laborer said, "How wide?"

The supervisor said, "Oh about two feet wide."

The laborer said, "Where should I put the dirt?"

The supervisor said, "Just lay it alongside the ditch."

The laborer said, "But now do you want the sides to be nice and smooth, or what?"

The supervisor said, "Can't you just dig a hole?"

The laborer said, "No sir, I take pride in my work and I want to do the job right. If I'm going to dig a ditch proper-like, I have to know what that ditch is going to be used for."

The supervisor said, "Look, we just want a hole dug so that we can take all the nitwits who are working on this project and bury them in it. Now just dig, will you."

The laborer said, "Well, then, I want an extra day's pay."

The supervisor said, "What for?"

The laborer said, "Because from what I can see, I'm gonna be the only one left around here to fill this ditch in again."

We may be hard on ourselves, but we'll never be our own worst enemies as long as there are other people working in the company.

DECISION MAKING

A decisive business executive is one who can make a logical choice after outlining a specific problem, gathering and sorting relevant information, and analyzing all possible and feasible options . . . I think.

■

Making a decision is like going to the dentist–once it's over, you're surprised at how painless it really was, and most executives only do it twice a year.

■

Experts claim that there are three elements that go into making a decision: defining the problem, gathering relevant information, and logically analyzing that data. But the experts can't decide which is most important.

■

You can make a good decision that no one else agrees with. If you don't believe that just listen to the way most people talk about the groom at a wedding.

■

You know what happens to people who can't decide to make a decision quickly enough? They become best men and bridesmaids.

Executive is constant decision making. What to do, how to do it, when to do it, and who to blame when it doesn't work.

■

There is no one correct solution to any problem. Or if there is, I haven't found it yet.

■

A good manager knows that there is more than one way to skin a cat. A *great* manager can convince the cat that it's necessary.

■

Don't be afraid to make a decision. Bosses realize that people make bad decisions. Hell, you may be one of theirs.

■

Top management does nothing but make decisions all day long. They decide who they're going to appoint to make their decisions for them.

■

Appointing a committee is to decision making what sticking a pin in the back of the head is to a laboratory frog–totally paralyzing.

■

If you want to see decision making at its murkiest, watch four executives try to decide where to meet for lunch on a day when all of their secretaries are home sick.

■

I had one boss who loved decision making. He'd make several decisions on the same problem 5, 6, 7 times a day.

This executive was so indecisive, his memos used to read: "To all of the staff . . . to most of the . . . to some of the . . . Dear John."

This guy could jump out of a plane and not know whether to go up or down.

For years we thought he came to work in slacks and a sports jacket, but he didn't. He just couldn't decide which suit to wear.

Of course, he always stood by his decisions. That's because he could never decide whether to change his mind or not.

■

My superior once accused me of being indecisive and lackadaisical. I said, "I'm not so sure about that, and furthermore, I don't care."

I was so angry at that indecisive crack that I quit on the spot. I gave him 48 weeks notice.

. . . with options.

I couldn't decide whether to burn my bridges or not, so I just heated them up a bit.

■

Some decisions are tougher than others. One executive got two ties for Christmas from his Mother.

She said, "When you come over for Christmas dinner, will you wear one of them?"

He agreed. When he showed up at the house, his mother said, "What's the matter? You didn't like the other one?"

■

"If all economists were laid end to end, they would not reach a conclusion."
—*George Bernard Shaw (attrib.)*

■

TRUMAN'S LAW: If you can't convince them, confuse them. —*Harry S Truman*

Richard M. Nixon, as quoted in *Time* Magazine–"I make it an absolute rule not to make decisions that somebody else can make. The first rule of leadership is to save yourself for the big decisions."

■

There are three valid answers to a yes or no question: yes, no, and no decision right now. Eighty percent of all bad decisions are snap decisions. Good managers make the best decisions after "sleeping on it." —*Joseph Stein, business consultant*

■

Someone once asked John Foster Dulles if he had ever been wrong. He thought for a while and said, "Yes, once–many, many years ago. I thought I had made a wrong decision. Of course, it turned out that I had been right all along, but I was wrong to have thought I was wrong."

■

The most dangerous people in the world are those who are often wrong, but never in doubt.

■

"Many executives are convinced that Business Administration is not really a science, but more of an accident."—*Frank Hughes*

■

A student once asked Richard Fuller, noted architect and engineer, if he considered aesthetic values when making a technical decision. Fuller answered, "No. When I'm working on a problem, I never think about beauty. I think only of how to solve the problem. But when I have finished, if the solution is not beautiful, I know it's wrong."

■

Not all of the decisions we make are of the business variety. One of the most basic and important decisions is which religion we will subscribe to.

Once Al Smith, Jimmy Walker, Herbert Lehman, and several other politicians attended a convention. They spent the night partying and drinking.

However, the next day was a Catholic Holy Day, and the politicians even then were mindful of their image. Al Smith, Jimmy Walker, and a few of the other Catholics, decided that they should appear at Mass. They rose early, dressed for Church, and tiptoed through the living room of the suite. They didn't want to wake Lehman and the other Jewish politicians who were "sleeping it off."

Looking at them sleeping peacefully, Al Smith turned to Jimmy Walker and said, "I sure hope we're right."

■

With regards to religion, sometimes no decision is the best decision. Bob Hope says he does benefits for all religious faiths. He says, "I'd hate to be sent to hell on a technicality."

■

Sometimes we shouldn't question the decisions of our superiors. It just might be possible that they know more about what they're doing than we think they do. An umpire in the minor leagues once illustrated that graphically.

He had called a batter out on strikes and the batter disagreed–fiercely. He yelled and gestured and kicked dirt on the umpire. Finally, the umpire had had enough. He grabbed the youngster and said, "Calm down, Boy. Let me show you something."

He took a deck of cards out of his pocket, fanned them, and told the kid to pick a card–any card. The kid was confused, but intrigued. He picked a card. It was the king of spades.

The umpire said, "Put it back in the deck." The ball player did.

The umpire said, "Your card was the king of spades." The kid had forgotten all about the called third strike by now. He was astounded.

He said, "That's great. How did you figure that out?"

The umpire said, "The same way I figured out that last pitch was a strike. Now go sit in the dugout and leave smart matters to smarter people."

■

"A conclusion is a place where you got tired of thinking."—*Fischer's Law*

One small businessman had a problem that needed some creative decision making. He was sandwiched between two tough competitors.

His tiny store was between one establishment that just put up a large sign that read: "Going out of business. Prices reduced 60 percent," and another store that put up a huge banner that read: "Year-End Clearance. Unbeatable Prices."

He attacked the problem creatively and since he was located right between the two he simply put up a banner that read: "Main Entrance."

■

Here's a good example of creative problem solving.

In the War of 1812, the British defeated an American Army that outnumbered them badly and they captured and imprisoned the American General who led those troops.

Then they realized that any General who was that incompetent was more valuable to them as an opponent than as a prisoner.

They released him and later attacked and burned to the ground the American Capitol. It was being defended by the same General.

■

Sometimes it's just as important to know when not to do something as when to do it.

There's a story, probably apocryphal, told about President Lincoln. He was going into the field to inspect the troops. They presented him with a spirited stallion.

However, when he mounted the horse, it showed no respect for his office. It began bucking, and jumping and kicking, and the President had all he could do just to hang on for his own protection.

Finally, the horse reared up so violently that he got his own hind leg caught in the stirrup. That stopped his bucking.

Lincoln looked down, saw the horse's leg caught in the stirrup, and said, "Well, that settles it. If you're getting on, I'm getting off."

SPEAKING

I don't do a lot of speaking, and I think after this talk you'll know why.

■

Most experts advise that a speaker should open with a joke. Those experts have never heard me tell a joke.

My Dad used to say, whenever he had to punish me, "This is going to hurt me more than it's going to hurt you." I wish I could say the same thing about my speeches.

... Unfortunately for you, I can't.

■

People ask me, "Where do you get the jokes you use in your speeches?" Well, at most conventions I attend, people like you tell me a few. I take them back to my office, clean them up ...

■

I always like to open with a little joke. That way, when people start laughing at me in the middle of my speech, I assume they're still laughing at the opening joke.

■

I don't speak in public very often. It's the public's choice.

■

Thank you very much. I always thank my public for that opening round of applause. I may not get the chance again.

■

Probably not too many of you out there have heard me speak before. I get very few people in my audience who have heard me before.

I asked one gentleman why that was. He said simply, "Life is too short."

■

Years ago a western town had a public hanging scheduled and it turned out to be fortunate for a travelling politician who was campaigning for re-election. Because of the public hanging everybody would be assembled in the public square. He could reach all of the voters at once.

So he asked the mayor permission to address the crowd. The mayor said it was all right with him, but he felt morally obliged to ask the condemned man's permission, too.

He said, "Is it all right if the Senator here borrows your audience for a little while. He'd like to give a little talk to the crowd."

The prisoner said, "It's okay with me if he talks, but could you do me a favor? Hang me first; I've already heard him talk."

■

I'm going to try to keep today's talk very simple. I always try to match my speech to the audience."

Thank you very much. I'm happy to be here today. I hope as the talk progresses that you are too.

■

As an experienced speaker, I can usually judge how my speech is going over by the audience's body language. I know if your arms are folded that you're not accepting my message. If you're leaning forward in your seats, then you are accepting my speech. If a few of you are walking towards the door, we all know what that means.

. . . It means that the speaker who preceded me was so bad that people are still walking out on him in the middle of my speech.

■

I want to thank you for a very nice introduction. I wish my parents could have been in the audience to hear it. My Dad would have been so proud of those words, and my Mother, God bless her, would have believed them.

■

There's probably no skill more important in business than the ability to communicate. As one executive used to say, "I don't care if you agree with me or not, so long as you understand what the hell I'm talking about."

■

There was one business executive who used to open his talks by saying "Eighty-five percent of what I'm about to say will be brilliant; fifteen percent will be baloney. The problem is I never know which is which.

". . . I'm hoping that you will."

■

Robert Frost said: "Education is the ability to listen to almost anything without losing your temper or your self-control."

■

Someone said: "Good listeners are not only popular everywhere but after awhile, they know something."

■

One manager used to advise his employees: "If you have something to say in business, stand up and say it calmly, confidently, and articulately. If you don't have anything to say, shout."

■

William Evarts, a 19th century Secretary of State, once opened an after dinner speech with, "You have been giving your attention so far this evening to a turkey stuffed with sage. Now you're being asked to direct your attention to a sage stuffed with turkey."

■

There was a brilliant scientist who delivered many discourses on his subject. On one tour he had a driver who was outspoken.

The driver said, "You know, you got life pretty easy. You travel around to these places, you give a talk for a half an hour or an hour, you answer a few dumb questions, and you make a fortune. Meanwhile, I gotta bust my buns working 8, maybe 10, hours a day, and I don't get half the bread you do."

The scientist said, "Well, you've heard my speech many times, haven't you."

The driver said, "Yeah."

The scientist said, "Do you think you could deliver it?"

The driver said, "Sure, I could. What's so hard about that?"

The scientist said, "Then at the next stop, you'll give the speech, and I'll sit in the back. Then you'll see how easy life on the lecture circuit is."

So they pulled a switch. The driver got up and delivered the speech word for word. The scientist sat in the back of the hall.

Everything went well, until the question and answer period. The first question was on an extremely complicated scientific procedure that was surrounded by much controversy. It was a difficult question for even an expert scientist, let alone this untrained driver.

The real scientist sat in the back and chuckled. He said to himself, "OK, wise guy, let's see you get out of this one."

The driver, at the microphone, chuckled, too. Then he said, "Sir, that question is so simple that I would guess that even my chauffeur could answer it. Sir, would you please come up to the microphone and respond to that?"

■

There are some hazards that people who speak a lot have nightmares about.

A professional speaker appeared at the lecture hall, went inside, and was stunned to see that there was only one person in the audience. However, he followed the old show business adage, "The show must go on," and the speaker's precept, "You deliver your all, whether there's one or a hundred out there." He went to the microphone and worked as hard as he could.

He finished his prepared speech, accepted the modest applause from the one listener, and said, "Thank you. I'm sure there are no questions." There was a question.

He answered it. There was another question.

This went on for some time, and finally the speaker couldn't take the frustration any longer.

He said, "Why are you doing this to me? I delivered the best speech I could, but it's very difficult for me to stand up here before only one person. Now you keep me up here by asking question after question. I have a question for you: Why?"

The person in the audience said, "Because I'm scheduled to be the next speaker."

■

A good business speaker makes sure that what he's saying is what he wants to say.

A political candidate once spoke to a group of voters. He told about his early life, his past accomplishments, his hopes and dreams, and what he would accomplish if elected to this office he sought.

After the speech he asked, "Are there any questions?"

Someone yelled, "Who else is running?"

STRESS

Authorities say people and circumstances don't cause stress; our reaction does. Those authorities have never met my boss.

■

I hate my boss. When he walks by, even my feet make a fist.

■

One man summed it up. He said, "almost every day at work something happens that makes me disgruntled. Just one day I'd like to spend a full eight hours at work gruntled."

■

Stress is when you get a queasy feeling in your stomach the whole time you're at your workplace. It's called "churn and earn."

■

Stress is a double-edged sword in business. Some workers can't get rid of it and some managers can't induce it.

■

People who feel music helps relieve stress have never worked in an office with a guy who hums all day.

■

Stress is when you have soup every day because a one-hour lunch break doesn't allow you enough time to get your teeth unclenched.

Stress is something gnawing at you from within while your boss is gnawing at you from without.

■

Job related stress is a nervous breakdown that can't get a day off from work.

■

Stress is nature's way of reminding you that Maalox comes in pleasant tasting flavors, too.

■

Stress becomes troublesome when rather than asking your boss for a transfer, you ask your druggist what's good for an upset stomach.

■

Stress is when you have to get home from work and have two martinis before your hair begins to unwind.

■

You know stress is affecting your life when the wife and kids meet you at the end of the workday waving a white flag of truce.

■

One executive knew stress was getting to him when he got home from work one day and found his wife had left him a tape recorded message: "Hi Honey, the kids and I went out for a little while. How was your day at the office? We'll be home when you've finished answering that question."

■

Even the family dog notices when you bring stress home with you. He used to greet you each night with your pipe, newspaper, and slippers. Now he greets you with a packed overnight bag and two airline tickets to Monterey.

■

It's unfair to take your stress related frustrations home with you, so shout them out the window at the guy driving next to you on the freeway.
. . . like everybody else does.

■

A sense of humor can help alleviate stress. Laugh at your problems while you're still rational enough to know what you're laughing at.

■

If you have a superior who rules with an iron fist, don't let him upset you. Just relax and pray that some day he gets jock itch.

Stress is more commonplace now than it was years ago when people worked harder. All that leisure time must be making us nervous.

■

Are you stressed out? Think about it. When *was* the last time you blinked?

■

An executive went to a psychiatrist and complained: "I have so much pressure and stress put on me at work, I can't take it anymore. I'm beginning to get grouchy and irrational. I always feel uptight and I'm even beginning to forget things—names of friends, my children, my own wife."

The doctor said, "How long have you had this problem."

The man said, "What problem?"

■

An executive got so upset about work that he finally visited a shrink. On his first visit he said: "My work is driving me crazy. My boss is a tyrant, he's incompetent, and he doesn't understand me. None of my fellow workers are any comfort because they're more incompetent than the boss. They not only don't help the problem; they add to it. They annoy me almost as much as management does. My family, the wife and kids, are completely insensitive. They expect things from me that I can't deliver. They don't understand the pressures that exist at work. Nobody likes me. And I get no fair pay. Why I can hardly afford to pay for this visit."

The doctor said, "Don't worry about that. This visit is free of charge."

The man said, "But why?"

The doctor said, "Because it's your last visit. You see, I don't like you, either."

■

One executive was telling a few of his co-workers how wonderful his psychoanalysis was going. He recommended that they all begin it. A fellow worker said, "Has it relieved all of your job related stress?"

The executive said, "No, but now I know why I have it."

■

One executive was assigned such demanding quotas and unreasonable deadlines that it began to tell on him. He was stressing out and the company feared a breakdown. They sent him to the company psychiatrist.

The doctor said, "You don't have enough faith in yourself. You're afraid that you can't meet the demands the company has set on you."

The man said, "Right."

The doctor said, "Wrong. You can accomplish what they ask. You simply have to know what you want and then believe that you can do anything you want to do."

The man said, "I can't do it."

The doctor said, "You can."

At each visit the doctor would drum into the executive that he had to know what he wanted and believe he could do what he wanted. This was repeated time and time again.

Finally, the executive shouted, "Yes! I know what I want to do and I'm going to do it."

The doctor cheered him on. He said, "That's it. You've got it. Now what is it you want to do?"

The executive said, "I want to do 40 percent less work each week."

PART SIX

BUSINESS PROTOCOL

Just remember there are business ethics just as surely as there are rules in professional wrestling.

ETHICS

Ethics: that's morality divided by profit.

■

Every profession has ethical standards. They have to. How else would we know what to violate?

■

Even old-time gunfighters never shot each other in the back. And they weren't even patrolled by OSHA.

■

Executives shouldn't feel a need to lie or cheat on the job. They should get all of that out of their system at their weekly golf game.

■

Business people should be ethical, but they don't have to pray all the time. Although that would be nice. It keeps their hands up where we can see them.

■

Ethics should be a part of your business life. The Golden Rule applies from 9 to 5, too.

■

You should live your business life as if the company accountant were addicted to Sodium Pentothal.

■

It's best to be squeaky clean because you never know when someone might decide to squeal.

■

There are dishonest executives. They'll do something for a profit whether it's right or wrong. Then there are stupid executives. They'll do what's wrong whether it shows a profit or not.

■

I knew one proprietor who boasted he was so above board that he would gladly throw open either set of books.

■

There is such a thing as white-collar crime. That's where you steal armed with only a staple gun.

There are some ethics offenders in the business world— a few black sheep in white collar jobs.

■

One rotten apple can spoil the barrel. What really gets your goat is when they're so rotten they own the barrel.

■

Upper management often wants their executives to live like saints, but show profits like sinners.

■

Ethics is an individual thing. It's one of the few things you can do as an executive without a committee.

■

Bob Hope had a good definition of ethics. He said, "Ronald Reagan is one politician who doesn't have to lie, cheat, or steal. He's always had an agent to do that for him."

■

Will Rogers had a pretty good definition, too. "Live your life so you can will your parrot to the town gossip."

■

One businessman was so unethical if they ever made a coin in his honor it would have a face on both sides.

■

One gentleman defined an ethical dilemma to me. He told me he had performed a service that earned him a commission of $100,000. By an oversight he was paid twice...once by the client and once by the customer. The ethical dilemma that he was faced with was: "Should I tell my partner?"

■

One youngster learned a valuable lesson in ethical behavior after he and some friends played a prank. They went through the neighborhood turning over out-houses.

When his father confronted him, the boy remembered the lesson of George Washington and the cherry tree. He said, "Father, I cannot tell a lie. I did turn over the outhouse behind our house."

His father pulled down the boy's trousers and gave him a memorable spanking.

The youngster asked, "But Dad, when George Washington told his father the truth, he didn't get punished."

The father said, "George's father wasn't sitting in the cherry tree at the time."

Once there was a judge with a questionable reputation. He was trying a particular case and the lawyer for the defendant, thinking the judge could be bought, sent an envelope to his chambers containing $1000.

The plaintiff's lawyer also figured the judge could be bribed so he sent an envelope with $1500 in it.

But the judge proved to be a man of principle. He returned $500 to the plaintiff's attorney and then tried the case purely on it's merits.

■

Sometimes honesty pays.

Frederick the Great once toured a prison in Berlin. As he walked along, the prisoners fell on their knees beseeching him to free them. They all protested their innocence, except for one man. He remained silent.

Frederick had the quiet man brought to him.

He asked, "Why are you here?"

The man said, "For robbery."

Frederick said, "Are you guilty?"

The man said, "Yes sir. I am guilty and I deserve the punishment I'm receiving."

Frederick ordered that the man be set free immediately with a full pardon.

The man thanked him, but asked why.

Frederick said, "You are a guilty man. I will not have you in this prison corrupting the fine, innocent people who occupy it."

■

Jesse James and his henchmen were riding hard to escape a posse after a bank robbery. They stopped at a farmhouse for some rest and refreshment.

The woman there offered them what little food she had and apologized that she couldn't be more hospitable. She was a widow who had fallen on hard times, and was even now awaiting the representative from the mortgage company. She couldn't raise $1400 to pay off her debt and was about to lose her farm.

Jesse James gave her the money, part of the booty from the bank robbery they were escaping from. He told her this was money she was to use to pay off her mortgage and for nothing else. He also reminded her to obtain a receipt for the payment.

The woman paid off her debt. Jesse James and his men met the banker as he rode from the house, robbed back their money, and continued their escape.

■

One merchant had ten pair of slacks that he couldn't sell at the end of the season. They only cost $10 per pair, and he would have gladly accepted $5 a pair if he could just unload them, but he couldn't. So he did an unethical thing. He packed them up and sent them to an unethical buyer. He told him he was enclosing *nine* pair of slacks *for $10 a pair. He felt sure that the dishonest buyer wouldn't be able to resist the "free" pair of slacks.*

Instead he got a package with a letter enclosed. The buyer said, "I received your shipment and found them perfectly suitable as far as quality and price. However, I feel they are not right for me at this time of the season, so I'm returning the shipment in full."

There were only nine pairs of slacks returned.

■

A businessman returned from a trip abroad. While he was there he purchased a few yards of material at a good price. When he returned, he wanted to have a suit made.

He went to one tailor and asked if there was enough material there for a business suit. The tailor inspected the material, measured it, measured the man quickly and said, "Nope. Not enough."

The man went to another tailor on the same block just to get a second opinion. This tailor measured the material and measured the man and said, "Yep. I can make you a nice suit with that.

When the gentleman went to pick up the merchandise he noticed the tailor's young son running around with a pair of trousers made out of this cloth.

He asked the tailor, "How come you can make a suit with this material and have enough left over for a pair of trousers for your son, and the gentleman across the street says there's not enough material?"

The tailor says, "For him, there wasn't enough. He has two boys."

Every business has some practices that are borderline, too.

There was an antique dealer who was shopping around several rural junk shops when he spotted a cat sipping milk out of a very valuable bowl.

He wanted to buy that bowl, but he didn't want the junk shop owner to know just how valuable it was, so he decided to trick him into selling the bowl.

He said to the owner, "That's a very cute little cat you've got there."

The owner just said, "Yep."

The dealer said, "My granddaughter used to own a cat that looked just like that but it ran away."

The owner just nodded.

The dealer said, "I'd give anything to surprise her by bringing a cat like that home. Would you consider selling that cat?"

The owner said, "Might."

The dealer said, "I'll give you fifty bucks cash."

The owner said, "Sold."

They exchanged the money and the antique dealer said, "You know the cat seems pretty attached to that bowl. You don't mind if I take that along, too, do you?"

The owner said, "Oh, I couldn't let you have that. That's my lucky bowl. You wouldn't believe it, but since I've been putting the milk in that bowl, I've sold 15 of them fifty-dollar cats."

TELEPHONE ETIQUETTE

Telephone etiquette died with chivalry. Some people answer the phone as if they have a black belt in conversation.

■

Some switchboard operators are blessed with the ability to say "Amalgamated Manufacturing Incorporated," and have it sound like, "What the hell do you want?"

■

Too many people who answer business phones think that "What?" is a contraction of "Good morning, may I help you?"

■

Most people answer the phone like they've just had their request for a raise turned down.

■

The way some people answer the phone, if I call from a pay phone, I just ask for my money back.

■

If my wife answered my call the way some businesses do, I would immediately know that I left the milk out that morning.

■

Some people answer phones with security in mind. The way they bark their greeting would scare away terrorists.

■

I've been in shouting matches on the Freeways where angry motorists have spoken nicer to me than some people who answer business phones.

■

Either a lot of business people need more phone training or courtesy just can't be transmitted over telephone wires.

■

Be courteous in answering the phone. Remember that the person calling in is probably no happier with her job than you are with your's.

Phone courtesy pays. One telephone operator asked me so nicely to please deposit another 75 cents that I did it even though I wasn't using a pay phone.

■

We had one worker who was so loud on the phone, you could hang up on him without losing volume.

■

Many times you have to speak to five, six, seven, or eight people before you finally get the person you want. Some companies have their phone systems designed by the same person who plans Elizabeth Taylor's weddings.

■

You know your phone system needs work when people say, "I'll take a day off from work and call you sometime."

■

You should at least wait until you pick up the phone before you start speaking. The accepted phone salutation used to be "hello"; in business today it's "—old please, click."

■

If Alexander Graham Bell could have foreseen the hold button, he would have strangled his invention at birth.

■

The telephone is a great invention, but I'd rather have invented the anti-hold button.

■

Some executives have more people on hold than they have under contract.

■

The phone is the umbilical cord that connects your company to the outside world. Can you imagine the trouble the world would be having today if umbilical cords came with hold buttons?

■

I especially hate hold buttons that play music. It's disconcerting to call the Vice-President of International Sales and Marketing and get Guy Lombardo.

If I wanted to hear boring music, I wouldn't call; I'd take an elevator.

■

After your third day on hold, you can safely assume the person doesn't want to talk to you.

I learned in Catechism Class that Purgatory is really Heaven with a hold button.

∎

A gentleman by the name of Burnham Kelly said, "You can be fairly sure you are dealing with a bureaucrat if he or she has to dial 9 to get an outside line."

∎

Rockefeller once made a collect call from a pay phone, but the phone failed to refund his coin when the call was completed.

He called and told the operator what happened. Naturally, she asked for his name and address so that she could mail the money.

He said, "My name is John D. Rock . . . oh, forget it. You wouldn't believe me anyway."

∎

A telephone operator at a national charitable organization answered one call very pleasantly. She identified the organization and then said, "May I help you?"

The caller said, "Yeah, I'd like to talk to the dumb bastard who runs this organization."

The operator said, "Sir, I'm sorry, but I can't put you through to anyone with that attitude. We are a non-profit organization, but if you wish to speak to any executives here, you'll have to ask for them by their proper titles and with respect. Now to whom do you wish to speak?"

The caller said, "I told you. The dumb bastard who's in charge."

The operator said, "Sir, I've already told you that you'll have to refer to any official here with proper respect. I won't put you through unless you do. Now who would you like?"

He said, "The dumb bastard who runs things."

She said, "Sir, I told you once; I told you twice. I will only tell you one more time. You must refer to our officials by their proper titles. Now to whom do you wish to speak."

He said, "Look, I respect the work you do. I'm a wealthy man and I want to donate one million dollars to your cause, but I'll only do it if I can speak with the dumb bastard who's in charge of things."

The operator said, "Here comes that stupid son-of-a-bitch now."

∎

When Alexander Graham Bell first invented the telephone in 1876, financiers weren't eager to invest in it. His company, Bell Telephone, was so desperate for cash that they were willing to sell all the patents to Western Union for $100,000.

However, Western Union considered it an "electrical toy" and refused.

Later, though, Western Union reconsidered and bought a similar patent from another inventor. Bell Telephone sued for patent infringement and won. The settlement froze Western Union out of the telephone business.

PETTY THEFT IN THE OFFICE

The room where the stationery is kept in the office is called the "supply cabinet," not the "sample case."

■

Petty office theft is one crime that does go unpunished–except for paper cuts.

■

Office theft is when you take something home that isn't yours. Withholding tax is when you don't take something home that is yours.

■

Office theft is getting so bad, the government may add a line to the tax form: "income from paper clips."

■

One office held an essay contest offering prizes. The topic was "Why Office Theft is Wrong." All the entries were written on company stationery.

■

Petty office theft is too costly to patrol. Probably the only solution is to make paper clips and staples that are too large to fit into a briefcase.

A briefcase is sometimes called a valise. It can also sometimes be called an accomplice.

■

The problem is petty office theft is rarely considered a crime. It's considered a fringe benefit.

■

No company condones petty office theft . . . except, perhaps, a paper clip manufacturing company.

■

Almost everyone "steals" incidentals. That's why there are no stores in the shopping malls called "Paper Clips-R-Us."

That's today's philosophy: If it ain't tied down, take it. If it is tied down, take the rope, too.

■

I know some people who were tempted to take an early retirement, but they couldn't. They needed the rubber bands.

■

Petty theft is so rampant some employees should leave the office wearing a ski mask.

■

There's so much petty office theft going on that some company parking lots have special spaces marked "getaway cars only."

■

Some employees plan to take so much each week that they consider their salary only a down payment.

■

Some executives feel petty office theft is an organized thing. They call it "The Great Paper Clip and Paper Caper."

■

Office theft may be considered a petty thing, but I have a friend who owns a home built entirely out of paper clips.

In his fireplace, he burns nothing but No. 2 pencils.

■

The government wrote a startling report on petty office theft, then found out they had no loose leaf binders left to put it in.

■

One thing puzzles me: Do people who work for a burglar alarm manufacturing plant have the courage to steal things?

■

Appealing to the workers sense of decency doesn't work. If it did, Moses would have come down from the mountain carrying the Ten Suggestions.

■

Groucho Marx said, "There's only one way to find out if a man is honest–ask him. If he says 'Yes,' you know he's a crook."

Once there was an office worker who would leave work each day pushing a wheelbarrow full of sand. The guard at the gate knew that he was stealing something, so he'd go through that sand thoroughly. He found nothing, so he had to let the guy pass.

Then the guard got a rake and raked through the wheelbarrow of sand. Still he found nothing.

He got a sieve. He sifted through the sand—nothing.

Finally, when the guard was retiring, he spoke to this guy. He said, "Look, I know you've been stealing from the company, but I can't find anything in that sand. Do me one favor before I retire and tell me what you've been sneaking past me."

The guy said, "Sure. I'm stealing wheelbarrows."

∎

One guy retired from his job and gave this speech at his going away party: "Everything I have today I owe to this company. And someday if my conscience bothers me, I may send some of it back."

∎

One company was having so much trouble with office thievery that they hired an actor to play the part of Diogenes. You remember him—he was the Greek philosopher who carried a lamp around the world searching for ten honest men. They thought this would dramatize to the workers the seriousness of the situation.

They had this guy roam around the offices. He went into the accounting department and the manager said, "Diogenes, what are you doing here?" He would answer, "I'm searching for honest men."

The next day he went to the marketing department and the manager said, "Diogenes, what are you doing here?" He said, "I'm searching for honest men."

The next day he went to the shipping department. The manager said, "Diogenes, what are you doing here?" He said, "I'm searching for my lamp."

∎

A burglar was caught red-handed by the police. He was leaving a house with a satchel full of stolen loot.

When he was brought into court the judge asked if he had an accomplice.

The crook asked, "What's an accomplice?"

The judge said, "a helper, an assistant, a partner. Did you have a helper with you or did you commit this crime alone?"

The thief said, "I did it alone, Your Honor. It's hard to get help you can trust nowadays."

∎

During his days as a rancher, Teddy Roosevelt and one of his cowhands were roaming the range looking for strays. They lassoed one two-year-old steer that had never been branded.

They found the maverick on land that belonged to Roosevelt's neighbor, so according to the rule among cattlemen, the animal belonged to the neighbor.

When they began the branding process, though, the cowhand was going to brand the steer as one of Roosevelt's.

Roosevelt said, "Wait a minute. You're branding that steer as one of mine."

The cowhand said, "That's right, Boss. I always put my boss's brand on 'em."

Roosevelt said, "Drop the branding iron, get back to the ranch, get your belongings and get out. I don't need your services anymore."

The cowboy protested, but Roosevelt insisted.

He explained later, "Any man who will steal for me will steal from me."

BUSINESS DRESS FOR SUCCESS (MEN)

Always dress for the office as if you're going to get that big promotion today. And then hope that you don't wear out too many outfits before you turn out to be right.

■

Neat dressing is important for the executive. It gives the appearance that the business world is civilized.

■

My boss read a book that said, "If you're going to be a leader, dress like a leader." Next day he came to work in a drum major's costume.

. . . He was fired two months later, but boy could he twirl a baton.

■

"Dress for success" is the battle cry of the 80's. How many of you really expected to get there naked?

■

Remember the good old days when a briefcase was something used to carry your papers in, and not a fashion accessory?

■

Some people feel they can put on a dark suit, white shirt, and red tie, and they're ready for a promotion. Put these same people in satin shorts and a pair of boxing gloves, and see if they're ready to fight Mike Tyson.

Just because you dress the part doesn't mean you have the ability. Some people can glue feathers all over their body and walk with a waddle, but they're never going to lay an egg.

■

Dressing in a dark suit, white shirt, and red tie doesn't make you a better executive. Remember, everybody who lost a war wore uniforms, too.

■

Clothes don't necessarily make the man. When I put on a $150 tennis outfit, I still have a lousy backhand.

■

When I was a kid a power suit was blue leotards with a red "S" on the chest.

■

I know one executive who took the power suit concept to extremes. He had pinstripes and a red tie tattooed on his body.

■

Your dark suit, white shirt, and red tie might be useless if you run across a cantankerous customer who's color blind.

■

The trouble with a power suit, white shirt, and red tie
Is that it does no good
When I remember
Underneath is just I.

■

Not everybody follows the "dress for success" principles. I know one high ranking executive who has never let success go to his wardrobe.

■

Some executives dress poorly. I worked for one gentleman who would give you the shirt off his back . . . out of spite.

■

One point of fashion controversy is: should you have your initials on your custom-made shirts? Who else's?

■

One expert made the statement that the two things that all men look good in are tuxedoes and military uniforms. So if you really want to look your best, enlist in a formal war.

Wouldn't it be nice if clothes did make the man? An expensive tie could replace years of character building.

■

George Gobel had a fantastic line about dressing and life. He said, "Did you ever have the feeling that life is a tuxedo and you're a pair of brown shoes?"

■

Here's an old-fashion put down that works:
Feel the material on a friends clothing and say, "That's a nice suit. I hear they're coming back in style."
It is old, though.
I said it to a friend once and he replied, "So's that joke."

■

A young lady once asked Bob Hope, "What are you wearing that smells so nice?"
Hope answered, "Clean socks."

■

Bing Crosby once showed up on the set of a Road picture wearing a gaudy, multi-colored sports jacket. When he saw it, Bob Hope commented, "Nice jacket. It's the first time the rainbow ever covered up the pot."

■

I showed up at work one day with a pair of funky shoes. I thought they were funky; everyone else just thought they were funny. I took a merciless ribbing. Finally, in an effort to stop the extemporaneous roast, I tried a joke of my own. I said, "You guys can kid about my shoes if you want, but my father gave these to me on his death bed."
They stopped for a moment, then one of them asked, "What did he die of? Embarrassment?"

■

Dress codes serve a purpose. Bob Uecker told a story about his first major league start. As his team was about to leave the locker room, the manager asked Uecker if he was feeling alright.
"I feel fine," Uecker said.
"You're not nervous?"
"No, I'm raring to go."
The manager asked again. "Are you sure you're not nervous?"
"I feel great."
"Well, this is your first major league start. I just wanted to make sure you were alright."
Uecker said, "I feel fine. Let's go."

The manager said, "Well, alright then, but I just wanted you to know that the rest of the team took a vote and we all decided we'd wear our jockstraps *inside* our trousers."

.

Some men carry this successful appearance to extremes. One executive not only had his clothes custom tailored, but he also had his teeth recapped so they'd be straighter and brighter, he bought an expensive new toupee to cover his bald spot, he had his nose surgically altered to look more authoritarian.

He was driving to work one day, failed to see the red light, and crashed in an intersection. He went flying out of the car. The teeth went in one direction, the hair went in another, and the new nose scraped to a halt on the highway.

As the poor man lay on the road, he looked to heaven and said, "Lord, why did You let this happen to me."

A voice from the clouds came down and said, "To tell you the truth, Sam, I didn't recognize you."

.

The minister of a Baptist church labored long and hard to try to get one of his fold to come back to Church on Sunday. Finally the man admitted that he felt embarrassed. He had no decent clothes to wear and he didn't want to be seen each Sunday looking like a pauper.

The minister took some money from the Sunday offerings and gave it to this gentleman.

"Buy yourself a new outfit. Get a shirt, tie, suit, socks, shoes–the whole works– and sit right up front next Sunday."

The following Sunday, the man still didn't appear, so the minister went to visit him.

He said, "We gave you plenty of money to buy clothes. Why weren't you at the Baptist Church yesterday?"

The man said, "Well, Reverend, I looked so damned good in those clothes, I became a Presbyterian."

.

A guy is crawling in the desert, dying of thirst. First, he sees a man, and asks for water. "No," says the man. "I have no water, but I can give you a shirt."

The man refuses the shirt and keeps on crawling. Not soon after, he comes across another man. "I need water," he begs.

"I have no water," the man says, "but I have a necktie."

The guy refuses and keeps crawling. After several hours, he comes upon an oasis, but it is barred by a guard and a gate. "Let me in," he begs the guard.

The guard looks him over. "Sorry, sir, " he says. "Shirt and necktie are required."

Groucho Marx was entering an elegant Los Angeles restaurant when the Maitre'd stopped him.

"I'm sorry, Sir," he said, "But you have no necktie."

Groucho said, "Don't be sorry. I can remember when I had no pants."

■

Part of good grooming is a healthy, energetic appearance. Sir Alec Guinness appeared in a movie on television. The role he played called for him to look weary and haggard. His wife watched the show, then rushed upstairs to her husband who was dressing to go out. She said, "Are you all right?"

He said, "Of course I am. Why?"

She said, "You look terrible downstairs."

BUT YOU OUGHT TO SEE THOSE GOOD DRESSERS ON WEEKENDS . . .

Guys that look sharp in the office dress the grungiest on the weekends. Have you ever seen the Lone Ranger? Well, they look like the cloud of dust he rode off in.

■

You've heard of getting up on the wrong side of the bed? They look like they *are* the wrong side of the bed.

■

I visited one of those sharp dressers in my office early one Sunday morning. He came down the stairs looking like he'd been hit by a Kamikazi pilot.

■

Some of them look so bad they could have breakfast in bed every weekend. It would be served to them by the Red Cross.

■

They dress in such ragged clothes that it would take several hours of repair work just to make rags from them.

■

They even wear the rattiest underwear. It's Fruit of the Loom, but it's overripe.

■

One guy's wife complained about his weekend wardrobe. She said, "Those trousers are 20 years old. Why don't you throw them away." He said, "My skin's twice as old as that, and I'm still wearing it."

She said, "Yeah, but you don't put your skin through the wash and dry cycle every Tuesday."

The wives can't get rid of these weekend grungy clothes. One woman took her husband's favorite weekend knockabouts and threw them in the Good Will Bin at the supermarket. It threw them back out.

▪

One of these slick dressers never wears shoes on the weekend. Well he can't. What kind of footwear goes well with twenty-year-old trousers and a torn undershirt?

▪

Some guys wear weekend clothes that are so covered with grease, if you ring them out you could start a cartel.

▪

Some of them wear those suburban Bermuda shorts which is a mistake. They have legs that obviously never passed quality control.

▪

They never shave. All week long they deal with trouble; on the weekend they like to sit and scratch their stubble.

By dinner time on Saturday they begin to look like the Wolf-Man at half past a full moon.

▪

One gentleman's wife finally issued an ultimatum. She said, "On Sunday morning you have two choices: either shave or start a revolution."

▪

These guys work hard during the week, so on the weekend, many of them just sit around the house. One wife said, "I thought my husband would help with the housework on the weekends. Instead, he's just something else that has to be dusted."

▪

One wife said, "My husband goes from Mr. Fashion Plate to a total slob on the weekends. I never see his navel on weekends. It's always covered by a beer can."

When he gets ready for work on Monday morning, he has to shower and rub Lemon Pledge on his stomach . . . to get rid of all the beer can stains.

▪

One spouse said, "My husband just sits around the house in those ratty clothes on the weekend and I'm ashamed of him. If company comes, I paint a black line on top of his bald head and tell them he's a piggy bank."

"Or I just stick a piece of ivy in his beer can and tell them he's a planter."

BUSINESS DRESS FOR SUCCESS
(WOMEN)

Try to wear clothes that are so nice that men will feel compelled to fold them neatly when they undress you with their eyes.

If male executives think ties are a pain in the neck, you wonder what they'd think of panty hose?

Panty hose are different from ties. You don't tie a knot in panty hose; they just feel like someone did.

t ride up on yo't ride up on you every time you sit down.
And on warm days you can loosen a tie.

It's hard to describe panty hose to a male. Try to imagine a cross between Jockey shorts and a Venus Flytrap.

■

A power suit for women executives is one that makes you look tough enough to smile despite your panty hose.

■

Male executives are lucky. They can go all through their business careers without ever having to worry about what "sensible shoes" means.

■

Men get all the breaks. They can go through their entire business life looking perfectly acceptable in "flats."

■

Women in the office should appear attractive but not seductive. Unfortunately, they have to dress for success and self-defense at the same time.

■

Women should look attractive, but not seductive. Unfortunately, it's always men who decide which is which.

■

Sexy attire is not proper for the work place. Some women not only look like they were poured into their dresses, but forgot to say when.

■

Women shouldn't hide their figures, though. It's hard for some male executives to hide their figures; most of it hangs over their belt.

Women have to dress in that fine line between "attractive" and "seductive." Some male office workers find anything in skirts seductive–including a Scottish bagpipe band.

■

Women's business attire reveals more of their body than a man's. All you can see on a properly dressed male is the head and face–which is often too much.

■

Dressing for success is more difficult for women than it is for men. Men don't have to worry about what length trousers will be worn at next year.

■

Men's clothes stay in fashion. Women are lucky if their clothes stay stylish through the first three payments.

■

Men can always be in fashion-no matter what their legs look like.

■

If mini skirts return, some women executives will have to opt for early retirement.

■

Women's fashions are revised almost as often as the tax laws.

■

Women can add a flair to their dress with attractive accessories. The only flair a man can add is a boutonniere, a pocket scarf, or if you're big enough in the company, a beanie with a propeller on it.

■

The male chauvinist pig is still around, but humor won't let him be much more than a ham. As John Wayne used to say, "A woman's place is in the home and she ought to go there just as soon as she gets off work."

■

"I've determined it's not God's will for women to wear miniskirts. If it were His will, He would have created flesh-colored varicose veins."— *Erma Bombeck*

■

A meat packing firm demanded for health and safety reasons that the workers wear specific uniforms on the job. Many of the women objected because the proscribed dress was neither sexy nor flattering.

The company had to enforce the dress code strictly, but attempted to keep morale up by offering to buy a new dress for every female employee. They were told to pick out a dress and send the bill to the company.

They all did, but one employee got somewhat extravagant. She sent a bill to the company for $300. The bill was brought all the way to the company president. Although he agreed the employee was a little greedy, he ordered that the bill should be paid anyway. He said, "I've packed a great number of hogs in my day, but this is the first time I've ever dressed one."

■

One female employee was chastised for her flamboyant dress on the job.
"What's wrong with the way I dress?" she asked the boss.
He said, "It's a little too sexy."
She said, "I can't help it if I have an alluring figure."
He said, "Besides, you're too large a woman to wear sequined dresses."
She said, "What do you mean, too large?"
He said, "Well, the other day you bent over to pick something up, and several people mistook you for a Sparklett's truck."

■

One woman was asked to tone down her dress for the office. She asked why and the boss told her it was a little too sexy.
"That's not true," she said.
He said, "Then how come every time you file something in the bottom drawer, the smoke alarms go off?"

■

There was a sexy redhead who worked in our office who always wore provocative clothing. She was an attractive woman who wore her hair in bangs, but always wore form fitting clothing that somehow or another always revealed some part of her voluptuous anatomy.
However, her boss thought it was becoming too much of a distraction, and asked her to tone it down.
She asked, "What makes you think my outfits are too revealing for the office?"
Her boss said, "Because I've been keeping tabs on your costumes. In this past week, I've seen every part of your body except your forehead."

■

I once attended a meeting where a motivational speaker was trying to make a point with a mixed audience of insurance brokers. He was telling of his own success as a speaker. He told how it was difficult to get bookings at the beginning. He came close to abandoning his career many times because it didn't seem as if it would be fruitful.
"But," he went on, "I continued. I persevered. I worked harder, and today I'm working so often and am on my feet lecturing for so many hours that I have to wear panty hose to protect the veins in my legs."
He went on, "I'll tell you, it's not pleasant wearing them day in and day out."
A woman in the back of the hall shouted, "No kidding."

PART SEVEN

OFFICE SQUABBLES

Put two people in an office and you have a feud. Put three people in an office and you have a feud with a clique.

OFFICE FEUDS

Offices have feuds just like the Hatfields and the McCoys except they don't go on forever. They usually end when either Hatfield or McCoy is made manager.

■

Some inter-office feuds make labor versus management look like puppy love.

■

I've been in offices where so many people weren't talking to each other that they took up office collections by mail.

■

I knew one executive who wasn't talking to his secretary. He had to write out his dictation.

■

If you get along with your secretary, you can always slip a little something extra into her paycheck. If you're feuding with your secretary, she can always slip a little something extra into your coffee.

■

Offices are just like families. They have their petty squabbles–except your family can't fire you.
. . . on the other hand, in a family squabble, you can't hide behind the union, either.

■

Everyone in an office is disliked by someone. Whoever's disliked by everyone is generally put in charge.

■

I've seen offices where the feuds were so bad it took an inner office memo to get the sugar passed in the cafeteria.

■

It's silly to get frustrated, angry, and near violent in the office. Save that for the drive home.

■

Some offices are famous for internal strife. They have to hire a food taster for the company picnic.

■

I've had some employees feud so badly that I should have reported them to my superiors, but I wasn't talking to them at the time.

Managers get angry at office feuding. They'd like to send a few of their employees to bed without their paychecks.

■

Serious office feuds can hurt production. It's hard to hold a pencil when you're wearing boxing gloves.

■

Someone once said, "When two people always agree, one of them is unnecessary." I'm not sure his partner agreed with that statement.

■

I knew one veteran executive who'd been through so many office feuds he had his chest tattooed. It read, "Stab other side."

■

Keep an open mind in the office. Remember what some wise man once said, "Everyone is entitled to their own stupid opinion."

■

I used to tell my employees to find other ways to release their aggression and hostility, and they did. We had a tug-o-war at one company picnic that went all the way to Cleveland.

■

I used to force my employees to like me. It was part of their job descriptions. And they all did except one—the one I used to get to start my car for me.

■

There are two things I can't stand: office feuds and this one guy in the marketing department.

■

When Calvin Coolidge was Governor of Massachusetts, two senators were feuding. During a bitter argument one of the politicians told the other, publicly, that he should "go to hell."

The offended politician took the debate to the Governor. He said, "My colleague told me to 'go to hell' in an open forum. What should I do?"

Coolidge told the senator, "I've looked up the law on this, senator. You don't have to go."

■

One office worker visited a workmate in the hospital and decided to play a prank on him. He told his office mate that while he was recuperating a few of the people in the office had gone to the manager complaining about the small amount of work this guy was getting done and the many errors that he was responsible for.

The worker was furious. He demanded to know who was responsible. Of course, the prankster wouldn't name any of them.

The worker said, "It had to be Charlie. Charlie is that kind of lily-livered coward that would go behind my back and do something like that."

His friend said, "It wasn't Charlie."

The guy said, "Fred. Fred is a sneaky, back-biting kind of guy that is jealous of anybody who has more talent and drive than he has. Fred was one of them, wasn't he?"

His pal said, "Nope. Fred wasn't involved."

The guy said, "OK, then it had to be Ralph. Ralph is a lazy, good-for-nothing kind of worker who knows he'll never get ahead unless he bad mouths every other guy in the office. Ralph would definitely do something like that."

His friend said, "No."

The guy said, "Let's see then. It could be Gene; he's a sneak and a thief. Or it could be Don. Don's the kind of guy who would sell his mother to get ahead. Or maybe it was Frank. Frank's always been a disgrace to this office."

His friend said, "Look, this was a joke. I've been putting you on. Everybody in the office loves you and they would never say anything like that. "

Now the guy was angry. He said, "Damn. Now why did you go and make me say all those terrible things about the nicest bunch of guys a fella could ever want to work with?"

■

Two managers didn't like one another. They disrupted any meeting they attended with their personal finger-pointing and name calling. Any time a problem arose, they'd spend most of their time trying to fix the blame on the other's department rather than trying to solve the problem.

Finally the boss called them in for a meeting. They'd hardly taken a seat before the invectives started flying. The boss quickly and decisively put an end to it.

He said, "Let's get one thing straight here—I'm the one who's at fault. I hired both of you."

■

The manager called one of his supervisors into his office for a private discussion. Two of the supervisors had a personal feud going that was interfering with production. The boss spoke to each individual and warned that the vendetta had to stop or these men would be replaced.

The one supervisor agreed to the truce, but couldn't leave the office without adding, "I never liked this guy, and I always will."

■

Several workers were complaining about conditions during one of their coffee breaks. One of them finally spoke wisely about office morale:

He said, "Look, anytime you get a group of people working on the same project in the same office, you're going to have problems like this. It always happens. Except once. My work partner and I worked in the same office with 4 other people for 25 years. All of us worked on getting the payroll out and there was never a problem in that office. There was never an argument. We just did our job and enjoyed one another's company."

Everyone was duly chastised until this guy finally added, "Although my partner and I knew that we were doing most of the work."

■

Charles Steinmetz was an electrical genius who worked for the General Electric Company. His fellow office workers voted on a new rule and Steinmetz showed up for work one day to be greeted by a sign that said, "No Smoking."

Steinmetz left another sign that said, "No Smoking—No Steinmetz."

They repealed the rule.

OFFICE GOSSIP

Gossip is a good thing in an office. It cuts down on absenteeism.

■

Every office has gossip. If you never hear any, you're it.

■

If all you have to say is good about people, then what's the point of taking a coffee break at all?

■

The coffee break is the prime office gossip time. It's when the vending machine coffee is not the only thing that's overly acidic.

■

There's only one reason why people talk behind other people's backs—because they can say juicier things than when they're there.

■

If it weren't for gossip in an office, football pools would be the only form of recreation.

■

When gossip starts, "I hate to say this but . . . " it really means, "You're going to love hearing this . . . "

Real gossip is something you wouldn't believe for a minute, but it sure is fun hearing it.

■

We had so much gossip in one office I worked in that I had a tattoo on my chest that read, "Please bite other side."

■

You show me someone who has never said anything bad about another person and I'll show you Marcel Marceau.

■

Office gossips are dastardly people who go about the office spreading the truth behind our back.

■

You can usually spot the office gossip. That's the person who uses their medical insurance periodically to have their tongue retreaded.

■

The office gossip is a person whose conversation should be labeled with a skull and crossbones.

■

The office gossip is generally a person with few friends but unlimited listeners.

■

The office gossip was out sick last week so we all had to sit around and say nice things about one another.
. . . Rarely have we ever sent a Get Well card that was so sincere.

■

How can you tell when the office gossip is spreading scandal? Easy. His lips are moving.

■

The office gossip is kind of a local edition of the National Enquirer published verbally.

■

Columnist Earl Wilson summed up office gossip when he said: "Gossip is hearing something you like about someone you don't."

■

Company rumors are sort of like gossip, too, except that they usually come true.

Rumors have about as much to do with company policy as eggs have to do with chickens.

•

If it weren't for rumors, upper management would have no creativity at all.

•

A supervisor from another department called an old friend in for a chat. He said, "Do you know Harry Katt?"

The guy said, "Sure I know him."

The supervisor said, "What do you think of him?"

The guy said, "Harry's OK. He drinks a little too much, and he's got a furious temper."

The supervisor said, "What kind of a worker is he?"

The guy said, "Well, he's not the brightest man in the world and he's not the most industrious. If there's a way of getting out of work, Harry'll find it. If there isn't and he has to do the work, he'll do it wrong."

The supervisor said, "Can he be trusted?"

The guy said, "Not by me. I wouldn't trust him as far as I could throw you and the desk your sitting at."

The supervisor said, "How can you be sure all this is true?"

The guy said, "How can I be sure? Harry's my best friend."

OFFICE AIR CONDITIONING

There are three kinds of people who work in offices–those who want the air conditioner turned up, those who want the air condition turned down, and the boss who has to decide.

•

That's why it was easy for Solomon to be so wise. He lived before they started putting thermostats in offices.

•

The office where I worked was always either too hot or too cold. I finally complained to my manager and he had a perfectly logical explanation. He told me the building was having a change of life.

•

The Good Lord should have made office temperatures the same way He made socks-one setting suits all.

I've worked in some companies where I wish the stock would have gone as high as the thermostat setting.

■

In some offices, if you yell "Fire," people will rush to turn the thermostat setting down.

■

This sign I saw posted near an office thermostat made sense: "If you're not with me, you're against me."

■

One would think 72 degrees Fahrenheit would be the perfect office thermostat setting, but it pisses off those who prefer 71 or 73.

■

That should be one of the standard questions on all job applications: "What position are you applying for?" "What salary do you want?" and "What office temperature will you tolerate?"

■

Some employees expect to do a day's work and take a sauna all at the same time.
. . . Others aren't happy unless they can see their breath when they holler, "Turn the air conditioner up."

■

The "hotties" and the "coldies" of today's offices have replaced the "cattlemen" and the "sheepherders" of yesteryear.
. . . Come to think of it, barbed wire fences could be the answer in the workplace, too.

■

You show me an employee who is always comfortable and I'll trade you two secretaries who work under blankets and a shop steward in a down jacket for him.

■

Some workers like the office cold. They begin complaining as soon as the icicle on the tip of their nose melts.

■

Others like it hot. If you tell them to go to hell, they pack a sweater.

■

Blue is their favorite color . . . for lips.

■

Air conditioning is in the office what Mother-in-Law is at home.

Newton said, "Give me a fulcrum and a lever and I can move the world." I say, "Give me two people in an office and one thermostat and I can start World War III."

■

Some people were discussing the world's most ingenious invention. One person said it was the telephone. It allowed instant yet private conversations between people in different corners of the world. Another said it was the wheel, a simple device that was the foundation of all travel modes. A third said it was the thermos bottle. "If you put hot coffee in there," he said, "it keeps it hot. If you put a cold drink in there, it keeps it cold. What's amazing is---how does it know?"

OFFICE COLLECTIONS

They took up so many collections in the office where I worked that for the first three months I worked there, I genuflected.

■

The first day I went to work they took up a collection for a girl who was getting married; the second day for a guy who was retiring; the third day for a girl who was having a baby. I said to myself, "What more can they ask?" The next day the Red Cross Bloodmobile came.

■

That was the most money I ever put in a collection basket without at least getting to sing a hymn.

■

Some people are so good at taking up office collections that their right hand is shaped like a cigar box.

■

Some office workers love to take up collections. They come to work with a portable vacuum cleaner with an attachment for cleaning out pockets.

■

Some people can take up an office collection so smoothly your wallet hardly feels the incision.

■

We had a fellow faint in our office one day. We had a bouquet of flowers on his desk before he hit the ground.

. . . Of course, we were a little lucky that day. He happened to fall out a window.

Some office workers love giving gifts. They'll even take up a collection for a girl who *wants* to be pregnant.

■

We've given "going away" gifts to people who didn't even know they were going.

■

One office formed a "Sunshine Club." They'd collect a certain amount weekly and just hope that someone would get sick.

■

Some offices collect so often that employees hope for a semi-serious illness just to break even.

■

In some offices the employees work at only 80 percent of productivity because 20 percent of the time their hands are in their pockets.

■

You can get blood from a rock if you tell the rock it's to buy flowers for a sick friend.

■

I've given money I didn't have for an employee I didn't know to buy a gift I never saw.

■

You know they're taking up too many office collections when you wear out your pockets before you wear out the seat of your pants.

■

That's one reason why I never got promoted. Every time opportunity knocked, I couldn't open the door because I had my hands in my pockets.

■

I finally told them to just throw my paycheck into the cigar box and I'd take some money out any time I needed it.

■

The office collection ritual is the closest man has yet come to the bottomless piggy bank.

■

I've had some jobs where the office collection box made more money than I did. ... but it probably worked harder, too.

A charitable organization went to visit with a wealthy businessman. They explained the good they did in the community, but also how difficult it was to continue to do that good for the poor unless they had the support of those who were more fortunate, like this man.

He was pleasant and polite, but said, "I can't give even a penny for your organization. You see, I have a brother and sister who are destitute."

Later this man's brother and sister applied to the organization for financial aid. The administrators said, "Wait a minute. How can you need our help? Your rich brother takes care of you."

They said, "Yes, we have a rich brother, but he doesn't give us a nickel. We're broke, baby."

These fund-raisers were furious. They went back to see the businessman. They said, "How dare you tell us that you can't help us because you give to your brother and sister."

He said, "I never said that. I said I have a poor brother and sister. The point I was making is if I don't give them a dime, why would I give it to you?"

■

Some people are better at taking up collections than others. One office worker was taking up a collection for a fellow worker. He went to the top manager's office, but the manager knew he was coming. He told his secretary to find an excuse why he couldn't see the person.

The secretary said, "I'm sorry, but Mr. Wilson can't see you at this time. He has a sprained back."

The collector said, "Tell Mr. Wilson I don't want to wrestle with him; I just want to ask him for some money."

SMOKING AND NON-SMOKING

Smoking has become a problem in many work places. A little smoke can set off the smoke-alarms and half of the non-smokers in the office.

■

Remember the old days when "Do you mind if I smoke" was a rhetorical question and not a declaration of war?

■

I like the answer one person gave. Someone asked, "Do you mind if I smoke?" He said, "I don't mind if you burn."

In one office, non-smokers went around and put up signs that said, "Thank you for not smoking." The smokers went around and set fire to them.

■

Some people in the office are very militant about non-smoking. If they catch you smoking they throw the cigarette out the window...with you still attached to it.

■

Some people are very militant about smoking. If you have a cigarette in your hand, their stare is more of a carcinogen than the tobacco smoke.

■

Some anti-smokers are as militant as Smokey the Bear, and they use the same protocol. If they catch you smoking, they hit you in the face with a shovel.

■

It's easy to spot the militant non-smokers in a work place. They're the ones who swagger around with a fire extinguisher strapped to their belt.

■

Then there are the very tough militants. They have a fierce looking tattoo on the back of their hand that says, "Born to breathe."

■

You can tell the militants. They hate smoke in any form. They're the only group of people in the world who call Smokey the Bear by his real first name.

■

Many people want to treat smoking like a traffic violation. After three offenses they take away your lips.

■

Some people in an office if they catch you smoking will take the cigarette right out of your mouth. The *real* militants will push it in.

■

Some people are too fanatical about it. When they go into their own kitchen, they get mad at the pilot light.

■

Smoking does foul the air in the work place. One gentleman was absent. He called his boss and said he was taking a "health" day.

■

Smoking can foul the air in the work place. Some people long to get fired, just for a breath of fresh air.

Some offices have so much smoke in them they look like a national convention of Indian pen pals.

■

Some offices have separate smoking and non-smoking sections. All important meetings are held in the de-militarized zone.

■

Some offices do have separate smoking and non-smoking sections and the people in the non-smoking area always get to go home first. That's because the people in the smoking section are coughing so much they never hear the quitting bell.

■

Some offices seem to encourage non-smoking because that section is painted in bright, lively colors–red, blue, orange–while the smoking section is painted in various shades of nicotine.

■

Every office has a chain smoker. You know the type: He smokes so much when you put the lights out, his tongue glows.

■

The inside of his mouth is so hot, he can bite raw meat and cook it while he's chewing it.

■

People who have dated him say his goodnight kiss is like Mexican food.

■

He's the kind who goes to burning building and inhales.

■

He coughs so much he's got a bloodshot mouth.
He claims it began with his Army physical. The doctor told him to cough, but never told him to stop.

■

His fingers have so much nicotine on them, for him, nail-biting could be fatal.

■

I've tried to get him to give up cigarettes and smoke crayons. They're just as unhealthy, but the stains on his fingers would be prettier.

■

I had a manager once who liked to smoke. One of his greatest pleasures in life was lighting up a fresh, expensive cigar. It was also one of his rarest.

The cigars he used to smoke were so cheap and malodorous that three of the exhaust fans on his floor turned in grievances for upgradings.

■

His cigars smelled so bad that none of the workers would work evenings. They couldn't hold their breath that long.

■

This guy smoked cigars for years, but never inhaled. In fact, with the cigars he smoked, nobody inhaled.

■

But there is one good thing about having a boss who smokes cheap cigars–you always know when he's in the area.

PART EIGHT

BUSINESS ON THE MOVE

Whoever said, "Getting there is half the fun," has never had a connecting flight in Chicago.

COMMUTING TO WORK

It used to be the worst part of the day was the 8 hours spent in the office. Nowadays it's the four hours spent driving to and from work.

■

America now has a chicken in every pot, but so much traffic on the freeways that we can't get home to eat it.

■

The law says there should be five car lengths between you and the car in front of you. In order to get that, you have to talk four people into staying home.

■

Everybody is always on the freeways nowadays. It's getting so the off-ramps are only used for emergencies.

■

Congestion is getting so bad, you can now change a flat without losing your place in traffic.

■

All across the country rush hour traffic is bumper to bumper. The next thing they'll be selling is anti-perspirant to put under your car's fenders.

■

Some of the more heavily travelled roads are like the Army. Once you get one of them, you're there for a two-year hitch.

■

The brake used to be something you used to stop your car. Now it's something you take your foot off of when traffic lets up.

■

I remember how embarrassed people used to get when traffic stalled. Now it's no problem. You just blend in with normal traffic.

■

Traffic is always heavy in both directions. There are just as many people trying to get to whatever you're trying to get away from.

■

You have mixed feelings now when you see an opening in rush hour traffic. You're glad for the opening, but you wonder who died.

It's typical of America. All of the freeways are loaded with cars, and neither the cars nor the freeways are paid for yet.

■

It's useless to print roadmaps anymore. You just get on the highway and go wherever the other cars take you.

■

Traffic is really heavy. Remember those little dogs in the back seats that used to blink their eyes for turns? They now just foam at the mouth.

■

The only way to get home from work on time now is to take the day off.
. . . even then, you're cutting it close.

■

Traffic is so bad nowadays, a pedestrian is someone in a hurry.

■

Cars are jammed too close on the highways during rush hour. I pushed in my cigarette lighter the other day and the woman in the car in front of me slapped my face.

■

You don't even have to brush your teeth anymore. Just get in rush hour traffic, smile, and let someone else's windshield wipers do all the work.

■

You can sit on the highways forever nowadays. In fact, some places have little exit ramps where you can pull over and make another payment on your car.

■

Roads are getting packed. During rush hour the only way you can change lanes is to buy the car driving next to you.

■

Remember the good old days when traffic used to be bumper to bumper? Now it's windshield wiper to windshield wiper.

I watched a young couple in front of me necking all the way home on the freeway. They were in separate cars.

■

Our highways have become insane asylums with turn signals.

■

They shoot at each other in Los Angeles. They have places on the freeways where you can pull over to reload.

That's right. In Los Angeles people say, "I'm going to drive to work now; cover me."

■

In Los Angeles, when a guy puts his hand out the window, if it doesn't have a gun in it, it means he's going to turn left.

■

They say that 40% of the drivers in L.A. are on alcohol and 40% are on drugs; the other 20% are shooting at them.

■

They have two different gauges on the cars in L.A.–one to tell you when you're out of gas; the other to tell you when you're out of ammunition.

■

I've told my wife if I leave the office at 5 o'clock, the height of rush hour, it takes me about an hour and a half to get home; but if I go to the little bar across the street and sit there until about . . . say . . . 11, there's no traffic whatsoever.

■

Anybody who says "Getting there is half the fun" doesn't have to travel to and from work during rush hour.

■

Look it up. "Commuting" is 2 and 1/4 four-letter words.

■

"We had quite a panic here the other day in New York, in the subway. Several people were trampled on and crushed. The cause of the trouble was that someone hollered out: 'Here is a vacant seat!' "—*Will Rogers*

"Another way to solve the traffic problems of this country is to pass a law that only paid-for cars be allowed to use the highways. That would turn our boulevards into children's playgrounds overnight."—*Will Rogers*

■

A gentleman was so frustrated by the early morning commuting traffic to work that he desperately tried every sort of bypass and shortcut around the traffic that he could.

Eventually, he turned onto a strange onramp only to discover that it was really an offramp. He wound up on the freeway driving against oncoming traffic.

Fortunately, a police car pulled him safely off to the shoulder of the road, and directed traffic around him.

The cop went to the driver and said, "Where the hell are you going?"

The man said, "I don't know, but it must be over. Everyone else is coming back."

■

One employee moved far out into the suburbs. It was away from the city noise and confusion, but it was also far away from work. Another guy who worked in the office asked how he liked it.

The commuter said, "Well, it's nice, you know. I live out in the country. It's peaceful and quiet, but it also has some inconveniences."

His friend said, "What do you miss most?"

The guy said, "The last train home at night."

■

One businessman was very anxious about missing an important meeting. He jumped into a cab at the airport and screamed to the driver, "I want you to go top speed. I don't care how recklessly you drive. There's a $15 bonus in it for you if you get me there on time."

The driver stepped on the gas, and the cab screamed out of the airport. He drove like a madman through some pretty hectic traffic.

Then the guy in the back seat realized he never told the cab driver what his destination was. He said, "Hey, do you know where you're going?"

The cabbie said, "No, sir, but I'm driving as fast as I can."

■

Ferenc Molnar enjoyed sleeping in until the early afternoon. Rarely did he awake before 1 P.M. Once, though, he was subpoenaed as a witness in a lawsuit and he had to be in court by 9 A.M.

His servants awakened him, dressed him, and loaded him into a car for the drive to the court room before he even realized what was happening.

When he finally came to his senses, he looked out the window and saw that he was in the middle of the morning rush hour traffic. He said, "My God, are all these people witnesses in this stupid case?"

TRAVEL

I never realized how dumb my boss was until I travelled with him. After the flight attendant showed us how to operate the seat belts, he had questions.

. . . It'll take him two or three more flights to get the hang of the oxygen masks.

■

Modern air travel is nature's way of saying, "You didn't really have to get there on time anyway."

My mother always taught me that people who tell lies never amount to anything. But they do. They get jobs making out airline schedules.

■

The best way to assure that your flight will leave on time is to arrive two minutes late for it at the airport.

■

Airlines perform a great service for mankind. If it weren't for air travel, the world would now be knee deep in honey-roasted peanuts.

■

Modern travel is very convenient. The entire world is shrinking. I hope that explains why my trousers are a little snug.

■

They say that flying is the safest way to travel, but I've yet to see an insurance vending machine outside a bicycle shop.

■

I like what Bob Hope says about it: "Travel is very educational. I can now say Kaopectate in seven different languages."

■

In flight meals answer the age old question: "What do the airlines do with their old tires anyway?"

■

When you travel you learn that home is where your heart is. God only knows where the luggage is.

■

I travel extensively. I've been to almost half as many places as my luggage.

■

They say that getting there is half the fun. Now if they would just tell that to our luggage.

■

An inventor friend of mine tried to cross a suitcase with homing pigeons. Your luggage would find it's way home despite the airlines.

■

This story says a lot about today's air travel: A man scheduled to fly to Cincinnati checked three bags. He said to the clerk, "I want this one to go to Pittsburgh, that one to go to Miami, and I want you to send that other one to Honolulu." The clerk said, "We can't do that." The man said, "Why not? That's what you did with them last week when I flew to Phoenix."

■

Business people travel too much. That's why so many have back problems. Their spine keeps wanting to return to its full, upright, and locked position.

■

If the Good Lord meant for us to travel this much we would have been born with luggage tags instead of ears.

■

You know you're doing too much business travelling when you show up at home and the kids think you're there to read the meter.

. . . So does your wife, but she invites you into the bedroom anyway.

■

You know you're doing too much business travelling when you shout to your wife as you go out the door, "Good-bye, mother of four;" and she shouts back, "Good-bye, father of three."

■

You know you're doing too much flying when you go to an elegant restaurant and complain because your silverware didn't come wrapped in plastic.

■

You know you're flying too much when you promise to take your kids on a picnic and you begin boarding the family car by row numbers.

■

You know you're flying too much when you write your will and leave each of your heirs just enough to be comfortably stowed beneath the seat in front of them or in the overhead compartment.

■

I knew one businessman who was very apprehensive about flying in small aircraft, until one flight when the pilot explained to him that more accidents happen in the kitchen of the home than happen in the air. Now the guy's afraid to make a salad.

■

A sportswriter told the story about some trouble the Kansas City Chiefs had while flying to an away game. The plane had some trouble with its landing gear and the pilot announced that they should prepare for an emergency landing. "As a precaution," he explained, "the runway will be coated with foam."

That news upset Bobby Bell who was a Hall of Fame linebacker with the Chiefs. "Oh no," he shouted. "I'm allergic to foam."

There was a time when there was a rash of collisions and near misses between two airlines. I stood in line behind two businessmen at the counter of one of the beleaguered carriers. One man said, "I'll take two chances to Pittsburgh."

•

A friend of mine was offered a new job assignment with a hefty increase, but it meant travelling overseas. He was going to refuse the offer because he was afraid of air travel. I argued with him. I said, "You've got to get over this fear. You can't jeopardize your career just because of a silly phobia." He didn't want to listen.

Finally he got an idea and called an airline. He asked, "What are the chances of a bomb being on a plane with me." The young lady at the other end of the line chuckled and said, "Oh, I would guess about a million to one." My friend didn't like those odds. He still was going to turn down the offer.

I argued some more, then he got a bright idea. He called back, got the same girl, and asked, "What are the chances of two bombs being on the same plane with me?" Now the young lady laughed out loud. She said, "That would probably be about 200 million to one." Now those odds he liked.

Now he'll fly anywhere, but he always carries one bomb with him.

•

A businessman who was never too fond of flying was on a flight that was going through some very choppy air. He tightened his seat belt, but that didn't make him feel any safer. As the turbulence worsened, he began to pray out loud. He said, "Lord, I'm a rich man. Lord, if you'll just let this plane land safely, I'll give you half of everything I own."

The plane did land safely, and this gentleman was the first one off. As he hurried along the airport corridors, another gentleman came up behind him, tapped him on the shoulder, and said, "Excuse me, Sir, but I was on that plane with you. I heard you tell the Lord that if He let the plane land safely, you would give Him half of everything you own. Now I'm a man of the cloth, and I'm here to collect."

The businessman said, "No, I made the Lord a better offer. I told Him if He ever catches me on another plane again, He can have it all."

•

One diminutive businessman didn't enjoy flying. He was afraid of it and it made him sick. On one flight he was assigned the window seat, and the gentleman seated next to him was immense, built like a wrestler but dressed like a Dude. He wore an exquisitely tailored western suit, a big ten-gallon hat, and beautiful, expensive snakeskin cowboy boots.

The plane went through some moderate turbulence that bothered the tiny businessman, but didn't upset the western traveller at all. He just pushed his seat back and went to sleep.

The businessman got sicker and sicker, but he couldn't wake his seat mate. Finally, the poor man got so ill that he couldn't help himself. He lost his lunch all over the Texan's beautiful, costly snakeskin boots.

Now he had another worry besides the flight. What would this giant do when he woke?

The plane landed and taxied to a stop. The Texan woke up, and the businessman leaned over and said to him, "Feeling better?"

■

Author, Fran Leibowitz observes: "Twenty-four-hour room service generally refers to the length of time that it takes for the club sandwich to arrive. This is indeed disheartening, particularly when you've ordered scrambled eggs."

■

Sometimes the worst part of travel is the ride from the airport. I once had a guy pick me up, and the first red light he came to, he zoomed right on through without stopping or slowing down.

I said, "You just went through a red light."

He said, "Yeah, I always do. My brother taught me how to drive and he always does that."

Then we came to a stop sign and he zoomed right through that. I told him about it, and he said, "My brother taught me and he always does that."

He went through another red light and told me the same thing: "My brother always does that."

Finally, we came to a green light and he screeched to a halt.

I said, "Why did you stop for a green light?"

He said, "My brother might be coming."

■

Even dignitaries are not exempt from problems when they travel.

Once Prime Minister Lloyd George was travelling through Wales and had to make an unscheduled stop in a small town. He couldn't find a hotel in the village so he inquired at a large brick building. "Can you put me up for the night?" he asked.

"This is an insane asylum, sir," the man answered.

The Prime Minister wasn't put off. "I have to sleep somewhere for the night. Can't you accommodate me? I'm David Lloyd George."

The man answered, "Well, we have five Lloyd Georges here already. I suppose we can always make room for a sixth."

■

In his late eighties, Justice Oliver Wendell Holmes was relaxing during a train ride when the conductor asked for his ticket. Justice Holmes began searching in every pocket, but couldn't produce the ticket.

The conductor, recognizing him, said, "That's all right, Mr. Justice. When you find it, mail it to the company."

Still Holmes searched frantically for the ticket. The more he searched the more upset he became.

The conductor felt sorry for him. "It's all right, Mr. Justice," he assured him. "Don't worry about the ticket."

"I know I have that ticket and I have to find it," said Holmes. "I want to know where in the world I'm supposed to be going."

•

A man who worked on a farm all his life finally surrendered to the lure of industry. He took a corporate job and that meant travelling for the first time in his life.

On his first trip to the big city, he took his wife and his ten-year-old son. It was the first time any of them had ever been inside a hotel.

The father and son stood in the lobby and were fascinated by the panorama. The boy asked, "Daddy what are those doors that keep sliding open and closed?" The father said, "I don't honestly know, Son."

So they stood and watched as an elderly lady pushed the button, the doors open and she stepped into the device and the doors closed behind her.

They watched the dial above the door go up to 2-3-4, then come back down again, 3-2-1. The doors opened and a beautiful young lady stepped out.

The father said, "Go get your Ma, Son. I want to run her through this thing one time before we leave."

•

A young executive told his wife, "I have to go to New York on business, but I'll only be gone 5 or 6 days. I hope you won't miss me too much while I'm gone . . . "

She said, "I won't miss you at all. I'm going with you."

He said, "Well, now, I don't think you should. I'll be terribly busy and won't have much time for you."

She said, "That's all right. I'll be out shopping. I have a lot of things I have to buy."

He said, "But that's nonsense. You can buy all the clothes you want right here on Main Street."

She said, "Have a nice trip, Honey. That's all I wanted to hear."

TRAVEL-ON OLD AIRCRAFT:

Business travel is getting to be a little scary nowadays because the airlines are allowing their planes to get very old. I've heard of planes being de-iced before takeoff, but de-shingled?

Most business people don't like it. For some strange reason they're superstitious. They like the plane to land with the same number of wings that it took off with.

■

They don't like to take off in a sedan, and land in a convertible.

■

Planes are getting so old now they fly on a mixture of jet fuel and prune juice.

■

On one plane they opened the emergency door and instead of a rubber chute, a large truss inflated.

■

One plane was so old they had trouble lowering the landing gear. It kept getting tangled up in the plane's truss.

■

When frequent flyers get on a plane now they ask for a boarding pass and the plane's birth certificate.

■

Here's a good rule of thumb: Don't ever fly on any plane you've seen in a Grandma Moses painting.

■

The airlines try to keep the planes flying as long as possible. They just wash them down occasionally with soap and oil of olay.

■

You have reason to worry if you hear the pilot say to the flight attendant, "Bring me a cup of coffee and a quart of Geritol for the plane."

■

Many of the commercial planes are getting a little old and tired. They're beginning to match some of the flight attendants.

■

They do keep a lot of older planes in the air. I got on one the other day that had running boards.

■

Be wary of any aircraft where the safety instruction card is written in olde English.

■

It's getting pretty bad when one airline's advertising slogan is "Coming in on a wing and a prayer."

On flights years ago they used to hand out chewing gum so you could keep your ears from getting clogged. Now they hand out chewing gum so you can keep the wings on.

■

Planes are getting so old that frequent flyers shouldn't take any chances. Always carry a tube of Krazy Glue in your briefcase.

■

It was bad enough when the airlines used to lose luggage; now they lose landing gear.

■

The airlines are concerned about it. In addition to the lecture on safety procedures now, they also give you a lecture on airplane repair.

■

You know the maintenance is getting a little lax when you hear the flight attendant say: "Your seat cushion may also be used as a flotation device . . . I mean, those of you who have a seat cushion."

She went on to announce: "Please note that there are emergency exits either over the wing or where the wing used to be."

■

The pilots are aging, too. Many of them qualify for pre-boarding privileges.

■

Some travelling executives feel a little uncomfortable when they discover their flight crew will be a pilot, a co-pilot, a navigator, and a nurse.

■

They announced on one flight that no passengers would be permitted to operate any electronic equipment during the flight. It interfered with the pilot's hearing aid.

■

Some frequent flyers say they like to see a grey-haired pilot. It gives them a feeling of security and trust. Not me. My mother was grey-haired and she couldn't fly worth a damn.

■

Some travellers feel that grey hairs mean that a pilot is mature and has been flying safely for some time. Not necessarily. It could mean that he's a young man who's just had a lot of close calls.

On one recent flight I had a pilot who was not only older, but had been drinking. I could smell the prune juice on his breath.

TRAVEL—SUPER ECONOMY STYLE:

Some companies will do anything to save travel costs. There was one that flew several young employees to North Carolina for free. All they had to do was pass a physical and go through 6 weeks of basic training.

■

Those low cost trips are excruciating. Have you ever flown from Detroit to Los Angeles in a rumble seat?

■

One company booked passage on a flight that flew from Detroit to Washington in 7 hours and 14 minutes . . . at an altitude of 14 feet.

The captain explained, "If we go any higher, the sun melts the wax wings."

■

Some company travel departments find the strangest deals. One trip I heard of was very cheap. The only catch was you had to bring your own landing gear.

■

I've heard executives complain they were on trips that were so economical, instead of in-flight movies, the airline put on high school plays.

■

On one trip, the plane didn't even have a toilet on board. It was followed by a flying outhouse.

■

One company travel department worked with an airline that had three different types of planes: steel, wood, and stucco.

On this airline you could fly anywhere in the continental United States for $24.02. The 2 cents was for the deposit on the plane.

Some of the flights are exciting. You can even see the Mississippi River from the air . . . on a flight from Los Angeles to San Francisco.

■

Some companies will do anything to cut travel costs. They don't even use a plane. They just issue their executives an LSD pill with a rudder.

■

I flew on a company flight that was so cheap when they rolled the stairs away, the plane tipped over on its side.

I solved the problem for them. I said, "Why don't you take one of those two wings, and put it on the other side of the plane?"

•

A number of executives were on one of those super economy flights when they suddenly experienced quite a bit of turbulence.

Suddenly the pilot came running down the aisle wearing a parachute.

He said, "Don't be alarmed, but we're having a little trouble with the aircraft. I'm just gonna run on ahead and warn the people at the airport."

•

Of course, you can get some powerful drinks on those economy flights. They don't carry those little tiny bottles on board; they just tap into the plane's fuel supply.

RELOCATION

The business world today has adopted the Navy's old motto: "Join the exempt employees and see the world."

•

You can always spot the yuppie housing developments. They feature quaint, comfortable little homes completely surrounded by shade trees and "For Sale" signs.

•

One executive has been relocated so many times, the last four numbers of his zip code are question marks.

•

The last time this man relocated, his wife said to the moving van drivers, "Just unload three months worth, and keep the motor running."

•

They've lived in 12 houses in the past 10 years. This family goes to bed at night with directions to the bathroom under their pillows.

•

Like all of us, this executive has a favorite easy chair, but he spends more time waving goodbye to it than sitting in it.

•

He came home from the office one day and said to his wife, "I'd love a good home cooked meal." She said, "I'm not going to bother unpacking the cartons just for that."

He relocated so many times, the only time he could relax was when he went on a business trip and the company provided a round trip air ticket.

Even then, he kissed his wife goodbye and said, "If we're relocated before I get home, leave a forwarding address."

■

One kindly manager finally asked him, "Where's your favorite place to work?" He answered, "I don't know. I've never been in any one place long enough to form an opinion."

■

He would get changed so often, he'd come home from the office at night and say, "Hi Honey, I'm home . . . I think."

■

He moved so often that his closest friends over the years were real estate brokers.

■

He was raised in Idaho, but spent his entire adult life in escrow.

■

It made his weekends pleasant. He never stayed in any house long enough to have to mow the lawn.

■

He moved so often that his was the only phone listing in the telephone directory that was in pencil.

■

The kids kind of liked it. They could get in trouble at school and move before their punishment was assigned.

■

The kids had a perfect excuse for not handing in their homework assignments: "It blew off the moving truck."

It helped some of their grades. They not only studied geography; they lived it.

■

The kids had the ideal excuse for not getting good grades. They spent all their study time learning the new school yells.

■

They complained to their Dad that they never had time to make friends. He convinced them that was good management training.

EXPENSE ACCOUNTS

Studies show that "Mother" is the most revered word in the English Language. "Reimbursement" runs a close second.

■

A generous person is one who leaves a big tip even when the expenses aren't covered.

■

Being on an expense account is often the difference between leaving a fair tip and your usual one.

■

An expense account is the secure feeling that no matter where you travel in the world, you can still reach into the company's pocket.

■

Will Rogers said it about taxes, but it applies to expense accounts, too: Expense accounts have made liars out of more Americans than golf has.

■

Some executives think the expense account is the opposite of generosity–"Take till it hurts."

■

Many business people treat the travel expense account as a Bon Voyage gift.

■

Many executives treat the expense account as the company's way of saying, "Have a nice trip and buy yourself a little souvenir."

■

Some business travelers treat the company expense account exactly as it says in the Bible: "Cast your bread upon the waters and it will come back to you a hundredfold."

■

Some people cheat just a little bit on their expense accounts just like they do at golf. Like the guy who got a hole in one and wrote a zero on his scorecard.

■

Most expense accounts won't pay for anything that is illegal, immoral, or unethical–unless, of course, it's for the benefit of the business.

Companies want you to follow your conscience in submitting expenses for reimbursement. If the travelers had followed their consciences, the expenses wouldn't have been so high in the first place.

■

Companies don't really want to reimburse you for your expenses. You'll notice very few of them are called "I'll Get the Check, Inc."

■

Businesses want you to treat expense accounts like spies treated the cyanide capsule hidden under their false tooth—even though the company pays for it, you try not to use it.

■

The company wants the expense account to be like the fire extinguisher in the corridor. It's there for you, but they'd rather you didn't use it.

■

The company enjoys paying your expense account about as much as parents enjoy paying a teenage daughter's phone bill.

■

The company pays your expense account just like Santa Claus: You submit a list, they check it twice; they want to find out who's naughty and nice.

■

Always tell the truth on your expense account. The money you save could be your job.

■

Pad the expense account too much and it might turn into severance pay.

■

If you must pad your expense account, at least do it creatively. The accounting department can always use a good laugh.

■

A very successful entrepreneur used to meet with his financial advisor regularly. They'd have lunch at the Beverly Hills Hotel, and the businessman would always pick up the check.

The advisor chided him. He said, "You have to watch your generous spending habits. For instance, every time we meet, we come here to the Beverly Hills Hotel and you pay. That's an unnecessary expense."

The man thanked him for his counsel and promised to be more diligent.

The next time they met they went to a fast food chain. The entrepreneur gave the clerk behind the counter and said, "Give this man whatever he wants and keep the change."

Then he said to his advisor, "When you've had enough come over to the Beverly Hills Hotel, I'll still be finishing my lunch."

PART NINE

OCCUPATIONS WE ALL DEAL WITH

*We are all brothers under our skin, and that's where most
subcontractors usually get.*

ACCOUNTANTS

An accountant is a person who tells you exactly how much money you have and how much of it you owe to him.

■

Accounting is one of the few professions where you know how much your clients can afford to pay.

■

It's fun having lunch with your accountant. It's one of the few times when you know what to leave as a tip.

■

Accountants are kidded unmercifully about not having a sense of humor. Thank goodness they don't understand most of the jokes.

■

An accountant is someone who can take everything you own and put it in a form you don't understand.

■

Accountants are valuable. They take all of our dumb mistakes and put them in neat little columns.

■

Accountants take your finances and rearrange them slightly. They're plastic surgeons to your money.

■

Accountants always have a pencil in one hand and an adding machine in the other. When people are working with our money, it's comforting to be able to see both hands.

■

Some accountants charge 5% of your gross income. That's not bad. It's only 2.5% for each set of books.

■

I've been rich and I've been poor. And I've had accountants who could show me as either.

■

Accountants are rarely judgmental. Nothing is either right or wrong so long as you have a receipt for it.

Anyone who thinks accounting is boring has never had an IRS audit.

∎

Accountants work mostly with taxes. Their job is to keep *your* dollars from becoming *our* dollars.

∎

Accountants are to the IRS what goalies are to the opposing hockey team.

∎

Accountants know all the *legal* ways to avoid taxes, which for most citizens is a last resort.

∎

Accountants try to get a handle on your finances so the government can't find the handle on your finances.

∎

I once had an accountant who was so good with numbers he eventually got to wear one for ten to fifteen years.

∎

The best accountant I ever had was very hard to get an appointment with. His office hours were from 9 to 5 every visiting day.

∎

My accountant has a plaque on his desk that reads: "The buck stops here-at least long enough for me to figure out which column to put it into."

∎

One friend told another, "If you want to make a small fortune, look up my accountant."
The other guy said, "He's that good?"
The guy said, "No, but there's a cash reward for his arrest and conviction."

∎

My accountant called and quoted the bible to me. He said, "Have you ever heard the quote: 'What does profit a man if he gain the world and lose his soul?'"
I said, "Yes."
He said, "I got good news. You don't have to worry about your soul."

∎

Robert Frost had this to say about accounting:

Never ask of money spent
Where the spender thinks it went

Nobody was ever meant
To remember or invent
What he did with every cent.

■

Accountants, unfortunately, have the reputation of being the "squares" of the business world. Again, unfortunately, this story won't help to dispel that myth:

An executive was attending a convention and he struck up a conversation with a fellow attendee who happened to be an accountant.

The executive said, "Would you like to stop down to the bar? I'll buy you a drink."

The accountant said, "No thank you, I don't drink. I tried it once, but I didn't like it."

The executive said, "Well, then let's just sit here and talk. May I offer you a cigar?"

The accountant said, "I don't smoke. I tried tobacco once and didn't care for it."

The executive said, "Fine. Listen, tonight a few of us are going to play a little poker. How about sitting in?"

The accountant said, "I don't gamble. I tried it once and it didn't appeal to me. However, my son may be arriving later today. Maybe he'd like to join you."

The executive said, "It's your only son, I presume."

ADVERTISING

Advertising can sometimes be promoting the outstanding features of a product that doesn't have any.

■

Advertising is a con job with illustrations.

■

Advertising is the show & tell of the business world.

■

Lincoln said, "You can't fool all of the people all of the time," which is why he made it in politics and not advertising.

■

Advertising is half-truths . . . usually told by a celebrity spokesperson.

■

Advertising is the art of holding the box up so that it puts both its name and its best foot forward.

Advertising puts the name in big print and the warranty in small.

■

Everyone's in advertising. It's the basis of a successful courtship.

■

The greatest examples of advertising can be seen at any singles bar on a Friday night.
That's the original "point of purchase" campaign.

■

The purpose of advertising is to make every product look good. It's the plastic surgery of sales.

■

Good advertising is supposed to enhance any product. It's the padded bra of the marketing world.

■

All of advertising can be reduced to the maxim: "A fool and his money are soon parted."
. . . your ad should help in the parting.

■

It's a toss up which advertising generates more of–sales or ulcers.

■

Advertising is a pressure packed world. It's not for those whose stomachs are weaker than their products.

■

Anybody in advertising who doesn't bite his nails either has great will power or the General Motors account.

■

The only advertising job that's free from pressure is carrying a sandwich board advertising "Joe's Deli."
. . . and that's only free from pressure when Joe's out of town.

■

Advertising is for those who like the challenge and excitement of looking for new work.

■

Otto Kahn was incensed to see a sign in the window of a run-down store in a dilapidated neighborhood that read, "ABRAM CAHN—COUSIN OF OTTO H. KAHN."

Kahn immediately took legal action to have that sign removed.

Later Kahn drove by to see if the offending sign had been removed. A new sign was in its place. It read, "ABRAM CAHN—FORMERLY COUSIN OF OTTO H. KAHN."

■

It's a good thing that Lee Iacocca, who starred in his company's commercials, never saw this poem by an anonymous author.

When the client moans and sigh,
Make his logo twice the size.
If he still should prove refractory,
Show a picture of the factory.
Only in the gravest cases
Should you show the clients' faces.

■

"Doing business without advertising is like winking at a girl in the dark: You know what you're doing, but nobody else does."— *Edgar Watson Howe*

■

"Let advertisers spend the same amount of money improving their product that they do on advertising and they wouldn't have to advertise."—*Will Rogers*

■

Some advertising is purposely deceptive. Like the immigrant who opened a small tailor shop in his new neighborhood and had to attract new customers. He put a sign in the window that said,

My name is Fink
What do you think
I alter your clothes for nothing.

The primitive, hand-written advertising worked. Many customers came in with old clothes that needed a tuck here, something let out there.

Fink did all the work, but when the first customer came to pick up his clothing, Fink said, "That'll be $2.25."

The customer said, "What are you talking about. Your sign says that you alter clothes for nothing."

Fink said, "No. You're misreading the sign. It says, "My name is Fink. What do you think? I alter your clothes for nothing?"

■

Fred Allen said, "An advertising agency is 85 percent confusion, and 15 percent commission."

Pacific Air Lines, a west coast commuter airline, was looking for a fresh, inventive advertising campaign that would lift their profits. They called on Stan Freberg who had a string of wacky commercials that brought astonishing results.

Freberg liked to be honest in his campaigns. He would convert a company's weak point into its strength by making it the heart of the advertising campaign. He suggested to PAL that they have a little fun with the one thing that most airlines never mention-fear of flying. Most of the executives were fearful of the idea, but PAL's president, Matthew McCarthy, gave the go-ahead.

Freberg went ahead-full steam ahead. He originated full page ads that PAL placed in New York and Los Angeles papers that read: "Hey there, you with the sweat in your palms. It's about time an airline faced up to something—most people are scared witless of flying. Deep down inside, every time that big plane lifts off that runway, you wonder if this is it, right? You want to know something, fella? So does the pilot, deep down inside."

Freberg and PAL carried their campaign even onto the aircraft. Flight attendants handed out tongue-in-cheek survival kits that included a copy of Norman Vincent Peale's *The Power of Positive Thinking*, a rabbit's foot for luck, and a fortune cookie that contained the message, "It could be worse. The pilot could be whistling 'The High and the Mighty.'" Freberg also had the flight attendants announce on landing, "We made it; how about that?"

This comic campaign infuriated other carriers. They felt these shenanigans would frighten travelers away from airlines altogether. PAL's president McCarthy said, "Nonsense. Lot's of people are afraid of flying and we thought it was time we cleared the air."

They cleared the air of Pacific Air Lines planes. Within a few months the company folded.

BANKERS

It's easy to tell this is a Banker's Convention. I asked someone in the lobby how to get to the banquet hall. He wouldn't give me an answer without a co-signer.

■

It's easy to tell this is a Banker's Convention. I asked someone in the lobby how to get to the banquet hall and he immediately set up a series of red ropes that led right here.

That's why I'm a little late. He wouldn't let me move until someone hollered "Next."

Of course, you know the old saying: "Give a man enough red rope and he'll open up a bank lobby."

I always enjoy speaking to bankers. I can always use the free toaster.

■

Most groups that I speak to ask for a photograph and a biography. This group asked for the first page of last year's tax return.

■

I'm glad so many of you stayed for my talk. Of course, with this group, I understand there is a substantial penalty for early withdrawal.

■

It's nice to be around a group of people who are financially responsible and know the meaning of money. I spend most of my time around my wife and kids.

■

I asked my branch manager what I could do to get laughs from a bunch of bankers. He said, "Show them some of your loan applications."

I don't know what terminology some bankers use for approving or rejecting a loan, but at my branch, I'm listed as A.Y.K.–Are You Kidding?

■

Bankers advertise on TV that they want our business, they trust us, they want to help us. Then we get there and find that all the pens are chained down.

How much can they love us if they think we're going to steal their pens?

■

Some banks require that you leave two signature cards—one for how your signature looks normally, and one for how it looks when the chain on their pen isn't long enough.

■

Here's a good way to get even with your bank branch for chaining the pens. When you make a deposit, staple the money together.

■

If you want to drive the people at your bank branch crazy, leave the pens and steal the chains.

■

There are very few sit down strikes at banks. That doesn't necessarily signify good management. It could be the marble floors that account for that.

■

Bankers are the ultimate establishment workers. Even the ring around their collar is white, too.

Bankers are traditionally conservative. Sports clothes to them are any that are not grey.

■

One banker had to do business at a nudist colony, so he had his entire body tattooed with pinstripes.

■

Even on a binge, bankers remain conservative. One went out on a wild spree and got a tattoo that read, "Born to raise interest."

■

One bank recently went through a major reorganization. They discovered they had more vice-presidents than depositors.

■

"A banker is a person who is willing to make a loan if you present sufficient evidence to show you don't need it."—*Herbert V. Prochnow*

■

Will Rogers said it a long time ago, but it seems to apply today:

"Every one of us out here in the land of sunshine and second mortgages is hustling from bank to bank, trying to renew our notes. A man has to be careful nowadays, or he will burn up more gasoline trying to get a loan than the loan is worth."

■

Comedian-curmudgeon Groucho Marx couldn't tolerate meaningless business correspondence. His banker once sent him a note that ended with the cliche, "If I can ever be of service to you, please don't hesitate to call."

Groucho wrote back and said, "Dear Sir, the best thing you can do to be of service to me is to steal some money from the account of one of your richer clients and credit it to mine."

COMPUTER EXPERTS

A computer expert is someone who can tell you logically why he doesn't know what to do about your problem.

■

There are almost as many computer experts in the world as there are computer problems.

Nowadays a computer expert is anyone with a keyboard.

■

Too many people are convincing us they're computer experts when they should be convincing the computer.

■

Calling some of the people who work with computers "computer experts" is like calling a boy scout with a first aid merit badge "Doctor."

■

Computers will do anything that anyone tells them, and therein lies their fault.

■

Lieutenant is a rank; Vice-President is a position of authority; Computer expert is a boast.

. . . often an unfounded one, at that.

■

You become a Senator by being elected; you become a lawyer by passing an exam; you become a computer expert by telling someone else you are.

■

Computer expert is a term that's often used loosely and without substantiation– much like the term "loving husband."

■

Computer expert is neither an approved certification, nor a regulated degree. Generally, it's more of an unfounded rumor.

■

A computer expert is someone who knows a lot of ways to say, "Well, then, let's try this."

■

Beware of computer salesmen who are also computer experts. When you buy a computer from them, all you can be sure of, despite what they tell you in the store, is that you are the new owner.

■

The word "computer" always seems to be heard with the word "expert" following it, or the word "damn" preceding it.

■

Everyone who owns a computer is an "expert" in the same way that everyone who owns a paint brush is an "artist."

The computer can't tell the difference between an expert and a novice, and many times neither can the expert or the novice.

■

As far as input is concerned, there's practically nothing you can do with a computer that can't be repaired–except maybe asking a friend for advice.

■

The difference between a computer expert and a computer novice is that the novice hesitates before doing something dumb.

■

Computers should be more like golf balls–if you do something dumb with them you have to go look for them.

■

A real computer expert has a healthy respect for the computer, and a confirmed distrust of other computer experts.

■

A real computer expert is someone who can make a mistake and not get mad at the computer.

CONSULTANTS

Them that do, do. Them that did but now don't, consult.

■

There are two types of consulting. One is to sell a service. The other is to convince the buyer that what you sold him was a service.

■

Farmers talk about a bull "servicing" the cows. Keep that in mind. When you buy a service from a consultant, you'll know what you're getting.

■

Consultants sell their expertise. One wonders if they're so expert, why they can't get regular work.

■

Some people say if your pet has an accident in the house, rub her nose in it and put her out. That's sort of what consultants do in the business world.

Consultants are like the hookers of the business world. They sell you something for a considerable price, and after they sell it, they've still got it.

■

A consultant has been described as a guy who knows 138 different ways of making love, but can't get a girl.

■

There was a tom cat who used to roam the streets every night sowing his wild oats. His owner finally had him fixed. He still roams the streets every night, but now as a consultant.

■

Consultants change procedures in your office and then go to their next client. That's kind of like voting a town dry and then moving to another city.

■

If you had to jump out of an airplane, would you let a consultant pack your chute?

■

Some say a consultant is somebody who knows nothing and sells that information to someone who knows less.

■

Specialists are people who know more and more about less and less.
. . . If that's true, the perfect consultant is someone who knows everything there is to know about absolutely nothing.

■

One rule of thumb is: Anyone who makes a business decision to hire a consultant needs a consultant to help with their business decisions.

■

You know who grow up to be consultants? The kid who used to offer to hold your coat while you fought the schoolyard bully.

■

A consultant is someone who studies what you're doing, analyzes it, and suggests alternatives. If they did it while you were playing chess, you'd punch them in the nose.

■

Of course many consultants are brought in after the damage has been done. It's like being hired by a guy who just jumped off the Empire State building to reassure him on the way down that this won't happen to him again tomorrow.

It's like General Custer hiring an expert to speak to his men at Little Big Horn on "Subtle Signs of Indian Unrest and What to Do about Them in the Future."

■

A consultant is often like a Monday Morning Quarterback who's not hired until late Sunday night.

■

It's like being hired as a plane spotter the day after Pearl Harbor.

■

Dr. Larry Hunt said, "As a rule, clients will recognize the obvious much sooner than professionals."

■

Charles Steinmetz, the electrical genius, who worked for the General Electric Company, was called in as a consultant after his retirement to help out with a baffling problem.

A complex battery of machines had failed and none of the GE engineers could solve the problem or even find the source of the trouble.

Steinmetz looked over the machinery, walked around it, tested electrical output in various parts of it, and finally put a chalk mark on one part of the machinery.

The workers dissassembled the machine and discovered that the problem was right there where Steinmetz said it was.

Later, the company received a $10,000 bill from Mr. Steinmetz for consulting fees. The company officials were shocked and demanded that the bill be itemized.

Steinmetz agreed and sent back an itemized bill that read:

Making one chalk mark $1.00
Knowing where to make it $9,999.00

■

Sometimes consulting work is merely pointing out the obvious to the client.

Sir Laurence Olivier worked on the motion picture, *Marathon Man*, with Dustin Hoffman. It's reported that when they worked on the dramatic scene where Dustin Hoffman is being tortured by Olivier, there were many problems on the set. Olivier played a dentist who is trying to extract (no pun intended) information from Hoffman by drilling a tooth down to the exposed nerve.

Hoffman supposedly had a lot of trouble with the lines. He finally apologized to Sir Laurence saying that he had gone without sleep for the past two days.

When Olivier asked why he would do such a thing, Hoffman said that such a traumatic scene required that he look haggard and worn. He said, "How else could I have prepared for it?"

Olivier said simply, "Didn't it occur to you to just try acting?"

A consultant answered an ad to work with a businessman. At the interview the proprietor said that his business wasn't going well. He was losing money. He was worried about it but he didn't have time to both worry and do the work that was necessary to save the business.

He wanted to just devote himself to his business and pay this consultant to just do all the worrying—about quality control, about payments due, about profit and loss ratios, about anything at all that needed worrying.

He was willing to pay handsomely for the consultant's time. They settled on an annual fee of $67,000 plus a liberal expense allowance.

The consultant agreed, but said, "If you're in such trouble, where are you going to get the $67,000 to pay me?"

The man said, "That's your first worry."

DOCTORS

M.D. used to stand for "Medical Doctor." Now it stands for "Medicare Documentation."

■

Doctors can't cure all the ailments of the world. Even if they could, they wouldn't have time for the paper work.

■

Doctors don't even like to play golf on Wednesdays anymore because keeping score just feels like more paper work.

■

A doctor today is a pencil pusher with a prescription pad.

■

Doctors will tell you there's no disease known to man that the government can't devise some form for.

■

Doctors have to fill out so many forms that it's hurting the profession. Who wants a surgeon with writer's cramp?

■

An MD today is nothing more than a government clerk who's allowed to wear a caduceus on his ring.

The caduceus is the symbol of the medical profession. It's two snakes intertwined. One snake's the government, the other is a malpractice insurance salesman.

■

Doctors keep a lot of people alive and happy–especially those who sell malpractice insurance.

■

They don't even try to hide it anymore. One insurance company sent a letter to a doctor that read:

Dear Goose:
    Next year your malpractice insurance is going to cost a few more golden eggs.

■

If doctors had their way, they'd return to the simpler times of long, long ago– when the magazines in their offices were new.

■

Doctors should be required by law to stay current and so should the magazines in their waiting rooms.

■

There are two places where you'll never see a clock–in Las Vegas casinos and in Doctors' waiting rooms.

A lot of gambling goes on in both places.

■

A doctor's waiting room is where God got the idea for Limbo.

■

After a certain amount of waiting time the words "The doctor will see you now" sound exactly the same as "Congratulations, you've just won the lottery."
    . . . and the odds *are* about the same.

■

That's one blessing of Alzheimer's disease–you keep forgetting how long you've been waiting there.

■

Doctors don't really prolong your life. But when you're stuck in the waiting room, it seems that way.

A good doctor can add 10 years to your life, but 8 of those years are spent in his waiting room.

■

British actor, William Macready, had atrocious handwriting, completely illegible. While on an American tour, he wrote a complimentary letter of admission to the theatre for a friend. It looked like it was a prescription written by a doctor . . . riding in the back of a cab . . . driving along a cobblestone street . . . and going over railroad tracks.

It was that illegible.

The friend decided to see if it did indeed resemble a doctor's scribbling. He took it to a pharmacist to have it filled.

The assistant pharmacist read the note briefly then immediately began to pull down bottles of chemicals.

As the young man mixed the compound he was puzzled by one ingredient. He called the head pharmacist out to confer. The older man studied the note, smirked at his assistant's inexperience, pulled down a bottle from the shelf and completed the mixture.

He handed the "filled prescription" to the customer and said, "A cough mixture, and a very good one, I might add. That'll be fifty cents, please."

■

A gentleman went to the doctor with many complaints. The doctor examined him in the office and advised that his patient abstain totally from tobacco and alcohol.

The patient dressed quietly and began to leave the office.

The doctor said, "Wait a minute. My advice is going to cost you $35."

The man said, "Why? I'm not going to follow it."

■

A patient in his mid 80's visited his doctor and was told that if he gave up smoking and drinking he might live another ten years.

The old fellow said, "You call that living?"

He left the office, lit his pipe, and stopped at a bar for a drink.

■

My Dad received a warning from his doctor. He was told to give up rich foods, tobacco, and alcohol. The doctor warned, "I'm giving you only six weeks to change your way of life."

In five weeks my father had changed doctors.

■

A lawyer was questioning a witness in court. He wanted to discredit the witness as quickly as possible.

The lawyer asked, "What is your occupation?"

The witness answered pompously, "I employ myself as a surgeon."

The lawyer asked, "But does anyone else employ you as a surgeon?"

■

Samuel Morse, the inventor, was also a competent and successful artist. He once painted a picture of a dying man. He showed it to a physician friend and asked, "What do you think?"

The doctor said, "Probably malaria."

■

One old-timer went to see his doctor.

The doctor said, "Any problems?"

The man said, "I'm getting a little deaf."

"Have you been doing some drinking?" the doctor asked.

The guy said, "Yeah, I have a little shot every now and then...for medicinal purposes."

The doctor said, "You have to lay off that stuff or you might lose more of your hearing."

The guy said, "I'll tell you, Doc. I like what I've been drinking a heluva lot better than what I've been hearing."

■

Someone once defined a doctor as a person who acts like a humanitarian but charges like a TV repairman.

■

The kid who pumped gas came in to the owner of the service station and said, "There's a guy out there with a flat tire. He said I should fix it fast because he's a good friend of yours. He says he's your doctor. What should I do?"

The owner said, "It's just a flat?"

The kid said, "Yeah."

The service station owner said, "Fix it. Diagnose it as flatulancy of the perimeter, and charge him a whole bunch of money. That's what he does."

■

Dr. Robert Andrews Milliken was a United States physicist who was awarded the Nobel Prize in 1923. One of his many accomplishments was the first measurement of the charge on the electron.

His wife once overheard the maid answering the phone. She said, "Yes, this is where Dr. Robert Milliken lives . . . but he's not the kind of doctor who does anybody any good."

LAWYERS

Behind every great business deal is a company lawyer advising against it.

∎

Corporate lawyers are people who know hundreds of legal terms for the word "no."

∎

Company lawyers know a lot of Latin phrases but all of them boil down to "status quo."

∎

My boss said, "Go ahead. Take it to the Legal Department," not fully realizing that those are contradictory statements.

∎

Sign in the Legal Department: "The buck stalls here."

∎

God created the world in 6 days simply because He didn't have to wait for a legal opinion.

∎

In the average office, more things get jammed up running through the legal department than running through the copying machine.

∎

The legal department in any company is a bottleneck with diplomas on the wall.

∎

Legal departments don't like to take chances. If they had been running the Old West, there would have been no gunfights. The combatants would have died of boredom exchanging letters.

Billy the Kid would have had 12 notches on his briefcase.

The gunfight at the OK corral would have been settled out of court.

∎

The Legal Department thinks its job is to prevent trouble before it starts. They do that by preventing everything before it starts.

∎

A corying "I'll get rying "I'll get right back to you" is like Zsa Zsa Gabor saying "Till death do us part."

The legal department is very arrogant. Nobody else has a size of paper named after them.

■

Legal size paper is necessary for corporate lawyers. All the B.S. doesn't fit on an 8 1/2 x 11 sheet.

■

In the world of business innovation, the legal department is the Bermuda Triangle.

■

Lawyers study things for a long time. No wonder it takes them nine years to get through school.

■

If corporate lawyers were undertakers, no one would be buried until the first anniversary of their death.

■

"The check's in the mail" and "the Legal Department is working on it" are interchangeable statements.

■

It's easy to learn how to converse intelligently with lawyers. All you have to do is nod in all the right places.

■

The prosecuting attorney said, "Ladies and gentlemen of the jury, the defendant was seen trying to leave the country under an assumed name. He was apprehended going through the detection devices at the airport when the security personnel noted a human thumb protruding from his luggage. He was caught transporting his murdered and dismembered wife out of the country. We shall prove that he is the premeditated murderer of his late, unfortunate wife."

The defending attorney responded. He said, "Ladies and gentlemen of the jury. Is my client a vicious killer? No. Is he a cold-blooded murderer? No. A lousy packer . . . maybe."

■

A worker was injured on the job and had to miss several weeks of work. His boss called to inquire about his health. The boss said, "How are you doing?"

The worker said, "Good and bad."

The boss said, "I don't understand."

The worker said, "Well, the doctor says I can do without the crutches, but my attorney says I still need them."

There was a dedicated young man who worked hard to put himself through law school. On graduation, he moved back to the small town where he was born and grew up. He looked forward to a prosperous practice because he was the only attorney in town.

But things didn't go so well. Business was bad. Even though he was the only lawyer in the town, there wasn't enough business to support him and his young family.

He talked things over with his wife and they decided that they would have to move. As much as they loved their birthplace, they simply couldn't make a living there.

Then, just before they abandoned the practice, another lawyer hung his shingle out in town. Now there's plenty of work for both of them.

■

Someone once said if there had never been any lawyers, there would never have been a need for them.

■

Abraham Lincoln was a common-sense lawyer who discouraged his clients from unnecessary litigation. One man, though, came to him once and demanded that he prepare a suit against another for $2.50.

Lincoln argued against it. Not only was it a waste of time, but it would be fruitless. The man he wanted to sue was penniless.

That didn't deter the angry client. He wanted to sue. When Lincoln realized he was getting nowhere with his advice, he quoted a legal fee of $10, which the client gladly paid. Lincoln gave half of his fee to the defendant who then willingly confessed to the debt, and paid the $2.50.

■

Doctors and lawyers in one city had a professional feud going on for some time. It arose out of several lawsuits that had polarized the two professions. One group of doctors, though, hosted a "bury the hatchet" type of dinner at a nearby Country Club.

The cocktail party was less than warm, and things heated up when the doctor who made the welcoming remarks delivered a condescending speech to the guest attorneys.

One attorney stood up to toast his hosts, and make a rebuttal to those opening remarks. He raised his glass and said, "I feel compelled to remind our hosts that while their professional ancestors were bleeding George Washington with leeches and teaching that the night air was unhealthy and poisonous, my professional ancestors were drawing up the Constitution of the United States–as noble a document as known to the minds of men or angels. I thank you and enjoy your dinner."

A high-powered attorney in Washington D.C. was consulted by a corporate president whose firm had a difficult problem. The lawyer listened and gathered information, then offered his advice. He said, "Don't do or say anything at all about this."

A few days later he sent a bill for $10,000.

The president called him and said, "This bill seems to be way out of line, and why should I keep quiet about this anyway?"

The lawyer said, "Because I told you to, and now I'm telling you again." Then he sent a bill for another $5,000.

■

A certain lawyer was willing to accept work for a client who couldn't afford his hourly fee on a contingent fee.

The client said, "What's a contingent fee?"

The attorney said, "It's very simple. I work as your attorney, but if I don't win your lawsuit, I get absolutely nothing."

The client said, "What if you do win the suit?"

The attorney said, "Then you get absolutely nothing."

■

A businessman and an associate were attending a funeral. As they were leaving, they stopped at a grave site. It was an acquaintance of the businessman.

He glanced down at the tombstone and said solemnly and sincerely, "There lies a fine attorney and a very honest man."

The associate said, "Why did they bury the two of them together?"

■

An eager young office boy began working for a corporate attorney. The lawyer lectured the kid every chance he got.

One day another young office boy asked this youngster how much he was making.

The kid said, "I make $22,000 a year."

The other kid was astounded. He said, "Wow! That much?"

The kid said, "Well, I get $25 a week in cash, the rest is in legal advice."

■

A corporate attorney was being bothered by a bill collector. It had nothing to do with work; it was a private matter.

The bill collector kept calling and calling, but the lawyer never called back.

Finally, one day he did get through and he berated the attorney. He said, "I've called you six or seven times, and you never return any of my calls. Frankly, I'm getting pretty fed up with it."

The lawyer said, "Please don't take it personally. I'm just trying to give the impression to other people around the office that you're a client."

NURSES

Some nurses are mean. I had one who they called "The Mr. T of R.N.s."

She had a black belt in Nursing.

She used Nursing as a stepping stone to her real goal in life—to be the Warden at a Turkish prison.

She was once in charge of the exercise room at a Cardiac Rehabilitation unit. She made those patients pedal their bicycles for the full 30 minutes. One gentleman kept yelling and screaming and trying to dismount, but she was inflexible. She made him pedal that bike no matter how much he yelled.

Finally when the half hour was up, we discovered what the problem was. The seat had fallen off his bicycle.

It took his mind off his heart problem, I'll tell you that.

■

In one primitive village in earlier times the men would prove their fitness by having a tug-o-war with a burro. The warrior would pull and tug until the animal would fall exhausted and die from the exertion.

Then to show how manly he was, the tribesman would drag the carcass of the donkey through the village.

There are some nurses who still subscribe to that theory. They think you're not healthy unless your ass is dragging.

■

Nurses can be executives today. It's a rare blending of briefcase and bedpan.

■

Nurses make tough executives. There's nothing more powerful than authority backed up by a syringe.

■

Nurses make decisive leaders. It comes from years of ripping bandages off of hairy men.

■

Nurses make calm executives. Anyone who has spent that much time around hospital gowns has seen it all.

Nurses can approach a problem head on, which is different from the way they approach many of their patients.

■

The title, "Head Nurse," has nothing to do with where she gives her needles.

■

Nurses are good at executive decisions. They deal with life and death situations constantly, so what color chair to get for the office is a snap.

■

Nurses have seen organs removed, so hiring and firing is nothing to them.

■

They've seen transplants, so they know what a lateral move is all about.

■

They've seen dead tissue cut away, so corporate belt-tightening doesn't frighten them.

■

They've worked with people under anesthesia, so working with reluctant unions doesn't bother them.

■

They've drawn a lot of blood in their day, so they think nothing of asking people to work overtime.

■

They've witnessed brain scans, so they understand the corporate mind.

■

They've worked for practically nothing, so they can empathize with their fellow workers.

SALES

We need salesmanship in the world. The only thing that sells itself is illegal and leans against a lamppost.

■

Selling is not the world's oldest profession, although the comparison has been made.

I like to meet a good salesman. It's how I got my set of electric forks.

■

A good salesman is one who can ask a woman for a kiss, get slapped in the face, and accept that as a down payment.

■

I knew a great salesman who once sold a refrigerator to an Eskimo. He told him it was a doghouse for his pet penguin.

■

I had a friend who believed the sign of a great salesman was the closing. He closed 14 branch stores.

■

I knew one salesman who had his foot in so many doors he used to buy shoes with brass knockers on them.

This guy firmly believed that there was a better way of selling than sticking his foot in the door. He experimented with other body parts.

. . . He never had any children.

■

One salesman firmly believed that if he could sell two of an item, he could just as easily sell three. It nearly killed him. He worked in a shoe store.

■

I did know the greatest salesman in the world.

. . . he could sell Sparklett's water to Dean Martin. (Of course, Dean would buy anything if it came in a big enough bottle.)

. . . he could sell *Brides* magazine to Zsa Zsa Gabor.

. . . he could sell Sprint to Ma Bell.

. . . he could sell paternity suit insurance to Mr. Rogers.

. . . he could sell sleeping pills to Perry Como.

. . . he could sell a training bra to Dolly Parton.

. . . he could sell a "Save the Whales" bumper sticker to Dom DeLuise.

. . . he could sell dancing lessons in Salt Lake City.

. . . he could sell a grieving widow a burial suit for her husband, and talk her into two pair of pants.

■

Some sales people enjoy making cold calls. They're the ones who also enjoy root canal work and getting their lip caught under a manhole cover.

Cold calls are to sales people what a butcher's rubber mallet is to a long horn steer.

■

A cold call is contacting someone you never heard of and trying to sell him something he never heard of.

... often he calls you names you never heard of.

... and never want to hear again.

■

Cold calls are the labor pains of good salesmanship.

■

I don't know what you call salesmen who go through the initiation ritual of cold calling, but when horses go through a similar ordeal, they're called a "gelding."

■

A snappy, fast-talking guy walked into an office and said, "You can't afford not to hire me. I'm the greatest salesperson in the world. I'm super. I'm colossal. I'm dynamite."

The boss said, "We'll see."

He said, "I've been trying to sell to my neighbor across the street. We've been doing business here for years. We're good friends, but I can't get him to buy from me. You sell to him, you're hired."

The salesman said, "It's a snap."

He went out and came back about 20 minutes later. The boss said, "How'd you do?"

He said, "I got two orders."

The boss said, "Really?"

He said, "That's right. 'Get out' and 'Stay out.'"

■

A fellow was using all of his sales techniques to sell Charlie a horse. Charlie was weakening.

"Is he fast?" Charlie asked.

"Fast?" The salesman said. "I guarantee if you get on this horse at midnight, he'll have you in Oxnard by two in the morning."

Charlie said, "Hmmm. I'd like to think it over. I'll let you know in the morning."

Next morning he said, "I don't want the horse. I've been up all night and I can't think of one good reason why I'd want to be in Oxnard at two o'clock in the morning."

A salesman strode back into the office looking cocky and smug. He said, "I made some pretty valuable contacts today, boy."

Another weary salesman doing paper work at his desk said, "Yeah, I didn't get any orders today, either."

∎

Mark Twain offers a valuable lesson on closing a sale. He was at a meeting where a missionary had been invited to speak and to take up a collection to aid in his valuable humanitarian work. Mark Twain tells it:

> "The preacher's voice was beautiful. He told us about sufferings of the natives, and he pleaded for help with such moving simplicity that I mentally doubled the fifty cents I had intended to put into the plate. He described the pitiful misery of those savages so vividly that the dollar I had in mind gradually rose to five. Then that preacher continued, and I felt that all the cash I carried on me would be insufficient, and I decided to write a large check. Then he went on, and on, and on and on about the dreadful state of those natives and I abandoned the idea of the check. And he went on. And I got back to the five dollars. And he went on, and I got back to four, two, one. And he still went on. And when the plate came around, I took ten cents out of it."

∎

In 1936 an American business executive arrived in France. He carried a sample case of cosmetics. The customs inspector asked incredulously, "You're bringing cosmetics to sell in France?" The businessman said, "Yes." The inspector said, "You haven't got a chance."

"Well, you may be right," said Davis Factor, Max Factor's son, "but my father is convinced we have something women want."

∎

An elderly woman was taking her first airplane ride. She wasn't too enthused about it. Fortunately, though, she was seated next to a clergyman. She thought that would help, but it didn't.

After they were up for awhile, the plane hit some pretty traumatic turbulence. They bounced around and she got whiter and whiter.

Finally, in anger she turned to the clergyman and said, "You're a religious person. Can't you do something about this."

He said, "I'm sorry, Madam. I'm in sales; not management."

∎

A man came back to the auto dealer's showroom and asked for the salesman who sold him his car.

The salesman showed up and the man said, "You sold me a new car two weeks ago."

The salesman said, "Yes."

The man said, "Tell me all over again what you said about it then. I'm getting discouraged."

■

A hotel maid was talking to her supervisor. She said, "Excuse me, M'am, but there are a half a dozen vacuum cleaner salesmen downstairs. They say they have appointments to give demonstrations."

The supervisor said, "That's right. Put them all in separate rooms and tell them to get busy."

■

Salesmen have to be trained to observe. One salesman called on a private home. On his way to the front door he noticed that a youngster was at the piano practicing the scales.

The salesman knocked and the piano playing stopped. The young boy answered the door.

The salesman said, "Good afternoon, young man. Is your mother at home?"

The kid said, "Would I be busting my chops at the piano if she wasn't?"

■

A salesman was demonstrating unbreakable combs in a department store. He was impressing the people who stopped to look by putting the unbreakable comb through all sorts of torture and stress.

Finally, to impress even the most skeptical, he bent the comb completely in half . . . and it snapped with a loud crack.

He quickly and calmly held both halves up for the onlookers to see and said, "And this, ladies and gentlemen, is what an unbreakable comb looks like on the inside."

■

Robert Louis Stevenson summed it up pretty well: "Everyone lives by selling something."

PART TEN

HINTS ON USING HUMOR IN BUSINESS

*If you aren't having some fun, you might wonder just what
you are doing in your business life. . . . If employees,
customers, and vendors don't laugh and have a good time
at your company, something is wrong.—Paul Hawken*

THE VALUE OF HUMOR IN BUSINESS COMMUNICATION

In business speaking, the message is paramount. Speeches take time and time is money, therefore every talk you give has a purpose. Then why bother with humor at all? Why not just make the point as forcefully as possible and get on with it?

Marshall McLuhan probably answered it best with this: "Those who draw a distinction between education and entertainment don't know the first thing about either."

In the business world your speech is worth very little if it doesn't have a message to convey, (One worker once described his local union meeting: "Most of the members had nothing to say, but they all insisted on standing up and saying it.") but it's worth nothing at all if that message is not heard, understood, and remembered. That's where humor can help.

Abraham Lincoln was the first President who used humor as an effective communication device. In fact, he used it well as a leadership tool. He used it powerfully. Of the famous Lincoln-Douglas debates Douglas once said, "Every one of his stories seems like a whack upon my back . . . Nothing else—not any of his arguments or any of his replies to my questions—disturbs me. But when he begins to tell a story, I feel that I am to be overmatched."

Because of his effective use of folksy tales, many people think of Lincoln as a rustic lawyer who happened into the Presidency of the United States.

Lincoln was the consummate politician, and he was a capable attorney. In fact, it was in the 1840's, while practicing law on the Eighth Judicial Circuit, when Lincoln honed his story-telling abilities. After the courtroom would close for the day, everyone would go to a nearby tavern to hear the greatest raconteurs of the day—the courtroom barristers. Lincoln's law partner, William Herndon, describes it:

> "The barroom, windows, halls, and all passageways would be filled to suffocation by the people eager to see the 'big ones' and to hear their stories told by them. Lincoln would tell his story in his very best style. The people, all present, including Lincoln, would burst out in a loud laugh and a hurrah at the story. The listeners would cry out: 'Now, Uncle Billy (William Engle), you must beat that or go home.' Engle would clear his throat and say: 'Boys, the story just told by Lincoln puts me in mind of a story I heard when I was a boy.' . . . Lincoln would tell his story and then followed Engle and then came Murray and thus this story-telling, joking, jesting, would be kept up till one or two o'clock in the night, and thus night after night till the court adjourned for that term."

The tall tale telling was more than just an evening's relaxation, more than fun and games. These were circuit riding lawyers who constantly opposed one another in court. Their tasks each day were to ridicule each other's forensic logic, impress judges, explain complicated legal issues, and convince jurors of their arguments. The humor of these folk tales was a major weapon in their arsenal.

Lincoln saw the power of humor during these years and capitalized on it in his political pursuits.

First of all, there was the perception of the person. Lincoln was speaking to a jury of peers. They were plain folks who sat on those panels. Lincoln spoke to them as one of them. He spoke in their language, using their way of life as his parables. He didn't try to overwhelm them with high-powered oratory. He didn't dazzle them with legal expertise. No, he told humorous anecdotes that they understood, but that contained a message—a powerful message that got his point across. So Lincoln became known as a down-home, folksy kind of character.

This is a speaker's first duty—to impress the audience. To have your message be convincing, listeners must feel that you're a worthy bearer of the message.

But wouldn't Lincoln have been more imposing if he appeared learned and eloquent? Not when he was speaking to groups of local farmers and ordinary townspeople. He appeared wise because he could reach them in their vernacular. He could reduce intricate issues to images that they could easily grasp.

They called Will Rogers the "Cowboy Philosopher." They might have nicknamed him the "Cowboy Comic" or the "Country Comedian," but philosopher explained more how the common people felt about his humor. It was funny, but it said something that everyone understood.

We often hear the terms "wit" and "wisdom" used together because they are so closely interwoven. It's often hard to separate one from the other. Wisdom often contains a touch of wit, and wit exudes wisdom.

A speaker who can quickly cut to the heart of the matter with humor is perceived as aware, knowing what's going on, worth listening to.

Laughter has a certain universal appeal. Some sage said, "Laugh and the world laughs with you; cry and you cry alone." Would the townspeople have crowded into the saloon after court closed to hear pure oratory or to listen to depressing stories or even educational lectures? Not nearly as many. They came to listen to entertaining stories.

But they *did come to listen.*

That's another attribute of humor—it gets people to listen. Pay attention to some of the comments you hear circulating at conventions and seminars about the speakers. You'll often hear, "That speaker was really funny," or "The luncheon speaker was very entertaining." That's usually what sets the effective speakers apart.

Presumably, all of the lecturers are qualified. Otherwise, they wouldn't have been invited in the first place. They know what they're talking about. That's not enough, though. If it were, then all students would get As in their classes because the professors certainly know what they're talking about.

The speakers have to get the audience to know what they're saying, too. This means that first they have to get the audience to listen. Humor accomplishes this.

Notice at cocktail parties how everyone seems to be glancing toward the one conversation group that is laughing. People are distracted from their own pedestrian conversations to try to hear "What's so funny?"

Listeners in an audience do the same. They may be distracted with their own notes or thinking their own thoughts, but a good hearty laugh, or even a delicate chuckle, perks up their ears. They want to know "What's so funny?" Because they missed that laugh line, they'll pay attention so they won't miss the next.

For the same reason, humor has a rejuvenative effect on listeners. Regardless of how accomplished an orator is, people weary of listening. It's like studying or work. The mind reaches a saturation point and stages a sit-down strike; "I demand some refreshment or I'll absorb no more."

A tidbit of comedy can be that recess. It relaxes the mind and refreshes it, so that it can get back to the work of listening to the important message of the speaker.

Humor, also, is incisive. It cuts to the heart of a situation, tearing away any irrelevant matter in the process. It's economical. It says much with very little.

One of the most eloquent sayings of all time was spoken over 2000 years ago. Some people were plotting to embarrass Jesus before his followers. Their ploy seemed foolproof—ask him if we should pay taxes. A yes answer would be unpopular since these people despised the Romans. A no answer would be a rejection of legal authority, possibly cause for his arrest. When they asked the question, he asked them, "Whose likeness is on the coin?" They said, "Caesar's" Jesus answered, "Render to Caesar the things that are Caesar's and to God the things that are God's."

That little bit of irony, which didn't amuse the questioners but probably Jesus' followers, was the perfect reply. The harassers had no reply to it, since there could be none. The statement was brief, concise, and powerful. It said exactly what had to be said and was understood by all who heard it.

That very economy makes humor a fine educational tool, and business speaking is basically informational. The incisiveness and compactness of comedy make it easy to understand. Humor cuts to the essentials.

Consider this story. See if it doesn't convey a simple message effectively:

"A policeman stopped a traffic violator for going through a stop sign. The man argued, 'But I slowed down.' The officer said, 'You're supposed to stop.' The gentleman insisted, 'Slowing down is the same thing.' The patrolman said, 'But the law says that you have to stop.' The man said, 'Slowing down is the same thing.' Finally, the policeman ordered him out of the car. Then he started beating him over the head with his night stick. The man yelled, 'Hey, you're hitting me over the head with a club.' The officer said, 'That's right. Do you want me to slow down or stop?' "

Lincoln realized the value of this attribute of humor, too. This one-liner of his told all those who heard it that America was in a time of peril and that all who wanted to defend the Union had better realize that they must be strong in their belief in right.

A clergyman said to the President, "I hope the Lord is on our side." Lincoln said, "I'm not at all concerned about that for I know that the Lord is always on the side of the right, but it is my constant anxiety and prayer that I and this nation should be on the side of the Lord."

Humor, too, is graphic. An anecdote is not just a collection of words; it's a raconteur planting an image in an audience's minds. It's not really the story-teller getting the laugh; it's the image the listeners create.

That's one reason why it's so difficult to explain what's funny about a joke—because it's so subjective. Each listener envisions a different scene. For instance there's a joke about Abraham Lincoln who is about to review his troops. When he mounts his horse, the animal begins to rear and buck. It jumps and kicks so violently that it throws Lincoln's legs out and gets its own hind leg caught in one of the stirrups. Lincoln sees this and says, "Well, if you're getting on, I'm getting off."

All listeners see that joke in their own heads just as they would see a movie. No two people see it the same way.

That visualization, though, that graphic image, also helps the speaker. Why? Because visualization is a great memory aid. Because the humor is graphic, it helps the listeners remember better and longer.

Practically every memory device created relies on visualization. Instead of remembering the number one, you picture the word "gun." For the number two, you see a "shoe," and so on. The picture burns into the memory better than an abstract concept such as the number one. One manager wanted to impress his employees with the need for meeting their commitments, for being on time with their deliveries. His basic premise was that it's easy for workers to put things on the "back burner" and not get around to them until someone complained. He didn't want any customers complaining.

He illustrated his point with this tale:

"Once I was helping my parents move. As we were going through some of the junk that had piled up in the house, I found a ticket for some shoes that my Dad had sent to the shoemaker around the corner for repairs. The yellowed ticket was about 22 years old. Since the shoemaker's shop was still there, I just thought I'd go around, you know, and see . . . well, see if the shoes were still there. I handed over the ticket and said, 'Are these shoes still here?' The old shoemaker looked at the ticket, went in the back, came out and said, 'Yeah, I have those shoes. They'll be ready next Tuesday.' "

The story got a nice laugh, but it also made an important point. It made a point that the employees remembered. Some of them had rubber stamps made with a cartoon drawing of a pair of shoes. When that was put on a requisition form or on a work assignment everyone knew that it meant, "Get this done. Don't tell me when I ask that it'll be ready next Tuesday." Others collected paper weights in the form of shoes or booties that were placed on top of those documents that were not to be postponed.

Most got and remembered the message.

Some business speeches are confrontational. Humor has the capacity to disarm an opponent. Comedian David Brenner used to do a routine about Superman in the movies. You would often see him confronting one of the "baddies" who would fire at him with a gun. Superman would smirk and throw his chest out; the bullets would bounce harmlessly away. Brenner said, "And then when the guy ran out of bullets, he would throw the gun at Superman. And Superman *ducked*."

It's funny that Superman wouldn't flinch at the bullets, but would when the gun was tossed.

However, that's the kind of power that humor can give one in a confrontational exchange. It enables a speaker to face the opponent's ammunition and deflect it harmlessly away.

The classic example of paralyzing an opponent's offensive was Ronald Reagan's handling of the age problem in his 1984 re-election campaign against Walter Mondale.

There was a suspicion that Reagan might be too old for another four year term. Reagan's staff knew it was a potential problem, but to debate it would only bring more focus to it in the media. So Ronald Reagan attacked it head on with humor. He joked about his age every time he spoke.

His own offensive took the weapon out of Walter Mondale's hand. How could Mondale launch an effective attack against Reagan's age, when the President had already been kidding himself about the same thing. It wasn't a substantive issue; it was something people were kidding about.

In the second Presidential debate, reporter Henry Trewhitt asked Reagan a question about age. Reagan answered, "I want you to know that I will not make age an issue in this campaign. I am not going to exploit for political purposes my opponent's youth and inexperience."

His one-liner won the evening. The audience laughed, then applauded. Mondale smiled. Reagan won the debate and later the election.

Verbal attacks like that can hurt if you let them. If you stand like Superman with your chest out and parry the thrusts with humor, they become ineffective.

Sometimes, too, speakers can use humor as an offensive weapon, a counter-punching tool. Like some of the martial arts, a clever use of wit can turn opponents' strengths against them.

It's a precarious use of humor, but often an effectual one. Winston Churchill is the source of some excellent examples.

Once Lady Astor dined with Sir Winston. They weren't friends. During the formal dinner she said to Churchill, "Winston, if you were my husband I would put poison in your tea." Churchill said, "Madam, if I were your husband I'd drink it."

At another function Churchill exchanged words with a female MP. She said, "Mr. Churchill, you are drunk." Churchill said, "And you, madam, are ugly. But tomorrow I'll be sober."

That is one other valuable attribute of humor that, although it doesn't apply to speeches, should be mentioned. It can be useful for executives. That is the therapeutic, relaxing, stress relieving capacity of a sense of humor.

Abraham Lincoln, again our mentor, knew of this and used it extensively throughout his tumultuous years in office. Lincoln said of his anecdotes:

"I often avoid a long and useless discussion by others or a laborious explanation on my own part by a short story that illustrates my point of view. So, too, the sharpness of a refusal or the edge of a rebuke may be blunted by an appropriate story, as to save wounded feeling and yet serve the purpose. Story-telling, as an emollient, saves me much friction and distress."

Ohio Congressman James Ashley, who was one of those demanding some decisive action from the President, tells this account of his meeting with Lincoln. Although some historians consider it tainted with myth, it nevertheless makes a valid point.

"You have come to see me about McClellan?"

"Yes, sir."

"Well," said he, "That reminds me of a story."

I was determined to have a solid talk with him. So I said, rising to my feet: "Mr. President, I beg your pardon, but I didn't come this morning to hear a story."

He looked at me and said, with such a sad face: "Ashley, I have great confidence in you, and great respect for you, and I know how sincere you are, but if I didn't tell these stories, I would die. Now you sit down."

As we said in the beginning of this chapter, though, in business speaking, the message is paramount. Humor has many admirable virtues, but it shouldn't overpower the speaker's information.

All of the above applies with the caveat that wit should be used wisely and sparingly in business communications. It should complement and enhance the speaker's message; not overshadow it.

HOW TO TAILOR MATERIAL TO THE SPEAKER AND THE AUDIENCE

At least two people should be pleased with every story you tell—you and the person you're telling it to. You should be happy with it, otherwise why would you repeat it? Also, your own enjoyment of the story enhances your delivery. Your enthusiasm blossoms through your telling of it.

It should delight the listener because that's the reason for recounting it in the first place. There's little point in reciting an amusing story if the listener won't find it amusing.

This means that most stories have to be adapted–adjusted to the speaker and the audience. One writer on *The Carol Burnett Show* staff told a story of how his mother described his work to her friends. She said, "My son takes jokes that he hears from some people and sells them to other people."

This wasn't what he did. However, it is in a sense what you should do. You should take humor that you collect, read, hear, have told to you, or write yourself, and change it to suit your style.

A French dramatist and novelist named Tristan Bernard once told a story to a friend. The friend enjoyed the story and complimented Bernard on his wit. Bernard then admitted that he had read the comment in that morning's paper. "But," the friend said, "you told it as your own." The novelist said, "Of course. To make it sound authentic."

Good humor has a spontaneity to it, a sort of ad-lib quality. Even when we know that professional comics like Jay Leno and Johnny Carson have writers working eight hours a day on their monologues, we like to believe that they're top-of-the-head comments.

Tom Dreesen, the comedian who opens the show for Frank Sinatra's concerts, told us that he likes to keep all of his material conversational. He wants the audience to feel as if he's just out there talking to them about things that interest both him and them.

Your material should sound the same way. It should sound like you talking. It shouldn't sound like you repeating an anecdote word-for-word as you heard it. It shouldn't sound like you reading a humorous story from the pages of a book or magazine. It should sound like *you* telling a story the way *you* would tell it.

You have definite speech patterns that you're comfortable with. You have a vocabulary, expressions, and gestures that are peculiar to you. We all have them. Bill Cosby is particularly recognizable in his comic gestures, and has an expressive style of speaking. They not only enhance his humor, but also stamp it with an indelible mark. His comedy becomes Bill Cosby comedy.

You should incorporate your style into your humor. Your style needn't be flamboyant, graceful, or even skillful. It simply has to be you.

Early in his career Bob Newhart guested on the Johnny Carson Tonight show. Carson said that when he first heard Newhart's records he thought the material was great, but Newhart's delivery was nothing. Then he listened again and realized that the delivery was everything.

Newhart didn't sound like the comedians of the time. He sounded laid back, almost apologetic. But that was Newhart's style. That was Newhart.

That's what you want to put into your humor.

You can accomplish this by experimenting with your humor. First know the story you're telling, then put it into your own words. Experiment with the telling of the story. Try it this way, then that way. Find the most comfortable and the most effective way that *you* can tell it.

That way it will sound like your story. People will feel like you're relating it with enthusiasm and not just reciting it from a written or memorized script.

You also have a point of view, an outlook on any topic. Any humor you do should be consistent with your philosophy. If your anecdotes contradict your message, you'll confuse your audience.

If your principle and your humor don't complement one another, one must go. It should be the humor.

You have standards of good taste, too. No joke, regardless of how funny, should be allowed to violate them. Some stories can be funny, well-constructed, and surefire laugh-getters, but they are also offensive. They may be racial, ethnic, or sexist. If they breach your standards in any way, omit them.

These hints will help tailor material to you, the speaker, but that's only part of the task. You also have to adjust your material to your audience. Remember, your humor must please you and your listeners.

This doesn't imply that you have to water down your message or bow down to a kind of audience "mob rule." Not at all. You can still deliver a forceful, firm presentation. You can even antagonize your listeners if that's the purpose of your speech. However, any humor you use to deliver that presentation still should be adapted to that audience.

Abraham Lincoln often used humor to win a debate. He wasn't surrendering. He wasn't being wimpish. He was being powerful. His humor was more powerful because it was aimed directly at the people he wanted to overpower.

Lincoln himself said, "I don't tell my stories to amuse the people; I want to convince them." To convince people, you have to be sure they get the point, they understand the point. That means you have to bend, adjust, alter your presentation to a form that they will understand.

That's the first question you must ask: "Will the audience understand this?" Will they understand the point of the humor? A great anecdote about the executive washroom won't go over very well if you're talking to a group of farmers. Nor will a fantastic story about the cow caught in the barbed wire fence do much good at a convention of robotics engineers.

Will they understand the language of your story? Almost every profession has a corresponding lingo. The military has terms that only they understand. So do folks in show business, politics, computer sciences, teachers. Even high school and college kids have their own code words.

These can be used quite effectively. Bob Hope used to pepper his wartime monologues with military slang that the service men and women understood and appreciated. However, they could only be used with military audiences.

You have to be careful that the listeners can interpret your story. If they can't, you must change the vocabulary. Substitute new words or ideas for the obscure ones. If not, you're speaking to people in a foreign language.

Next you should ask what your audience wants to hear. This might sound like a concession, but it isn't. Remember, the humor is only a part of your presentation. It's only a tool to make your speech more effective. Your speech can say anything you want it to say. It's message can be an unpleasant one if that's what you want it to be. The humor part of it, though, is designed to help get your message across. It's a brief respite from the seriousness of your talk. For that reason it should be pleasant and not antagonistic.

If the listeners rebel even against the humor, they'll be even more inclined to reject the message.

You can also adapt your anecdotes to include the audience, making them a part of your speech. People love to be included. Again, Bob Hope's military monologues were fine examples. He would open his routine with a joke about *their* base. It was a joke that only someone familiar with the base would be able to tell. Throughout his joke routines, Bob Hope would imply that he ate the same food they did, slept in the same sort of bunks, got in the same kind of trouble with the authorities. He was just one of the guys.

He used expressions that they used. He claimed to have visited the same off-limits bars that they snuck off to.

You can do the same thing by incorporating the audience's lingo into your humor. Tell your stories about people they know. Use local references. Instead of saying "two guys went into a bar," use the name of the bar that all these people know.

I once heard a speaker get a giant laugh and a standing ovation simply by localizing a bit of humor. He spoke to the sales force of a particular computer software company. He said, "I've been invited here for two reasons. First, I've never owned a Sony appliance, and second I have never in my life used the words 'seven' and 'forceout' in the same sentence."

That doesn't sound too funny, does it? To that audience, it was hilarious. Why? Well, that company had some contractual disagreements with Sony, and also, they had a project known as "Seven Forceout" that was a horrible flop and particularly devastating to the sales department.

It applied to them. It was funny to them. It worked fantastically to the speaker's advantage.

In all of your humor, consider your listeners. Hear your material the way they will hear it. Judge it the way they'll judge it. If there is anything in your material that you suspect might jeopardize your relations with your audience, omit it.

HINTS ON CREATING YOUR OWN HUMOR

Mark Twain once advised writers "The difference between the right word and the almost right word is like the difference between lightning and lightning bug." The difference between the right joke and the almost right joke is like the difference between laughs and confused stares.

Many of the selections in this book may be "almost right" for you. They may fall into the "close, but no cigar" category. Don't dismiss them too quickly. They may be the raw material that you can temper and tamper with, reshape or retool, reword and rework to get the perfect joke for you and your situation.

Even in the above example, if Mark Twain will forgive us, there's room for rewriting. I've heard someone change that admonition to this:

> "The difference between the right word and the almost right word is like the difference between chicken and chicken pox."

Another variation on the same theme might be:

> "The difference between the right word and the almost right word is like the difference between Mother and Mother-in-Law."

In addressing a medical association, the rewrite may read:

> "The difference between the right word and the definitely wrong word is like the difference between hospital and hospital bill."

Hollywood comedy writers in pitch sessions, which are the writers' version of brainstorming sessions, are constantly rewriting each other's jokes. As soon as a joke is offered to the room, someone else tries to improve it. Someone may suggest the line:

> "He's really a cheater at golf. Anytime he gets a par, he writes down a birdie."

Another may build on that theme and offer:

> "He keeps score in golf like my agent. He takes 10 percent off the top."

Another variation may be submitted like this:

> "He takes so much off his golf score, I may get him to do my tax returns."

Finally, another writer may go back to the original suggestion and rewrite it to read:

> "He's really a cheater at golf. One time he got a hole in one and wrote down a zero."

We recommend you use this book as a research tool the same way those Hollywood gag writers use that initial suggestion. Use each line as a springboard to other ideas. Start with the printed word and build on it. You may generate additional lines to use with the original. You may replace the original. You may discover that the original is the one you want to keep.

In any case, you've brought the page to life. Humor is an ever changing art. If it stagnates, it becomes unfunny. That's why we groan at an old joke. It doesn't mean it's not funny; just that we've heard it before. It has lost it's freshness.

By working with some of the lines in this book, adapting them to your own style and situation, you breath freshness into the comedy. You create original humor.

We'll discuss three methods of producing new humor: (1) Switching; (2) Springboarding; (3) Writing New Material.

SWITCHING MATERIAL

Switching material means to convert humor that was originated for one application to a second application. If a joke was written about accountants, we make it apply to engineers.

Switch the Application

The simplest switch is to simply change the titles or change the application. For example, a line reads:

> "What does it mean when you find 6 lawyers buried up to their necks in sand? It means they didn't have enough sand."

That exact same joke might apply if you're speaking to a management group in the middle of a strike.

> "What does it mean when you find 6 shop stewards buried up to their necks in sand? It means they didn't have enough sand."

Obviously, the opposite applies, also. If you're speaking to union representatives, change "shop steward" to "managers" and you've made the switch.

We once heard a speaker addressing a group of stock brokers use a story that was easily switchable. He said:

> "How many people are there in the room with an I.Q. over 175? Don't be bashful; I want to see. OK, there are a few hands up. After this talk, I'd like to get together with you and get your thoughts on Einstein's theory of relativity.
> How many with an I.Q. between 125 and 175? OK. I think we can discuss later how computers might be used to generate artificial intelligence.
> How many have an I.Q. below 50? I see a few hands. What do you folks think the market's going to do?"

The story worked well because it was obvious kidding of the group being addressed. You can see, though, that just changing that last line would make this story apply to practically any group.

Switch the Set-up; Keep the Punchline

Another way to convert a story that you like is to use the same punchline with a different set-up. These generalized jokes serve as an illustration:

> "This guy's breath was so bad he had to buy breath mints by the 6-pack."

The idea here, of course, is that "6-pack" denotes a lot of something—more than any normal person might use. That same punchline can be used with other applications. For example:

> "I have a friend who is so heavy, when he goes to the beach he brings along a 6-pack of suntan lotion."

> "I don't think I did very well on my exam. Before the teacher began to correct it, he pulled out a 6-pack of red pencils."

Switch the Punchline; Keep the Set-up

Sometimes a joke or story may have the ideal set-up for your application, but the wrong punchline. Fine. Generate a new punch, and you've got a new, usable, gag. For example:

> "It's easy to tell this is an insurance salesmen's convention. I asked a gentleman in the lobby how to get to the banquet hall and he said, 'You just go down this corridor and turn to the right. You can't miss it, but

God forbid if anything should happen to you, how's the little woman going to get there?'"

It's a nice joke to recognize the group you're addressing and also kid them gently. So the set-up works. The form of the joke is usable, but obviously you can't just change "insurance salesmen" to "doctors." The punchline doesn't apply. That's what you have to switch.

To apply to physicians the ending might now read like this:

"... You can't miss it. He was so sure of himself that I immediately got a second opinion."

Speaking to a management convention, the gag might be switched to read:

"It's easy to tell this is a management convention. I asked a gentleman in the lobby how to get to the banquet hall and he immediately appointed a committee to get back to me in two months with an answer."

Switch to a Parallel Form

Sometimes you can switch both the set-up and the punchline to create a new joke, yet retain the basic form. The following jokes were originally written for Phyllis Diller's routine about her mother-in-law. Phyllis called her Moby Dick because she was the size of a whale.

The joke form is consistent. It has to do with her dress color, and what happens when someone her size wears that color.

"When she wore a white dress, we showed movies on her."

"Once she wore a green dress with white stripes and two college teams played football on her."

"She wore a red, white, and blue dress one day, stood on the corner, and a man threw a letter in her mouth."

"One day she wore a grey dress, and an admiral boarded her."

SPRINGBOARDING

Springboarding goes beyond switching. It is using the basic humor content of a joke to inspire new jokes. The new jokes may be in an entirely different form and style.

Topping a Joke:

A topper is a joke added onto a joke. The original gag remains unchanged.

Toppers are usually stronger than the original because they build on its humor. They are more economical and they come quicker because they need no exposition. That was taken care of with the original set-up.

They also have an added element of surprise. The audience thought the joke was completed. This additional line seems to come from nowhere.

Then, too, if the first line was effective, the topper is coattailing on existing laughter. The resulting laughter is bigger because the effect is cumulative.

Following are some examples of toppers. Notice in each one that the first part of the story seems to stand on its own. It is a laugh getter. The last line is an additional punch line. It builds on the previous line.

This first is a line Bob Hope did on the telecast of his 80th birthday from Washington, D.C. He sat in the Presidential Box with Ronald Reagan during the entire show. At the end he delivered a short monologue and he commented on sitting with the President:

> "Ladies and gentlemen, you've got to know what a thrill it is to sit in the Presidential Box with the President of the United States, Ronald Reagan. You know when we first walked in, there were only two chairs in there. One was marked "Number One American," and the other was marked "Washed Up Actor."

(topper)

> "Boy, did we fight over those."

This second is a line Phyllis Diller did after hurting her shoulder in an accident in Australia. She had to wear an upper body cast, and she wanted some lines that she could use to explain the cast and dismiss it so she could do her regular act in Las Vegas. She was opening there within the week.

Here's the line she did, along with the two toppers:

> "Ladies and gentlemen, I'd like to explain away this cast and also make a public service announcement. If there are any people in the audience who have just bought the new book, *The Joy of Sex* . . . "

(topper)

> "There's a misprint on page 205."

(topper)

"It may break your arm, but it's worth it."

Express the Same Comedic Thought in Various Ways

An original joke or story may contain a comedic idea that appeals to you. You can springboard into other jokes by expressing that same comedic thought in different ways.

For example, consider this joke about a worker who had a very loud telephone voice:

> "He's the only guy I know in this whole plant that you can hang up on without losing volume."

Using that same idea—that he has a loud, booming telephone voice—we might generate these other lines:

> "They disconnected his phone three weeks ago and none of the people he's called since have realized it."

> "He's gone through three phones already this year. The mouthpiece keeps melting."

> "His telephone voice is so loud he can say 'Hello' before you even pick up the receiver."

WRITING NEW HUMOR

One of the best ways to find fresh, funny material is to write your own. It's not nearly as difficult as you might imagine for several reasons.

First, if you truly know your subject and your audience, you can localize your material. You can hit right on the target. The more specific you make your material, the easier it is to be effective.

Second, your jokes don't have to be top-notch, professional quality lines. Your material won't be judged with the same critical eye that an audience might turn to a Johnny Carson, Joan Rivers, or Jay Leno. You can get big laughs with less.

Third, an audience will appreciate humor that is original. If what you write is obviously not "store-bought," they'll know and respond.

We attended a convention once over the fourth of July. There was a big waterfront fireworks display on the holiday. The next night there was a lunar eclipse. The speaker on the last day of the convention commented:

"You people really know how to throw a convention. On the Fourth of July, you had a giant fireworks display that was magnificent. I said to myself there's no way you can top that. You did. The next night, you turned off the moon."

That line got a giant laugh. First, it was funny; and second, the listeners knew that the only place he could have gotten that one-liner was from his own inventive mind.

Here's a step-by-step procedure that might help you to write funny.

Step One: Decide What You'll Write About

No one, regardless of their talent, can write a joke without first knowing what they're going to talk about. It's impossible. You can't offer an opinion until you know what the subject matter is. You can't deliver an extemporaneous speech until you decide what you'll talk about.

So the first step in writing a joke is to decide what you're going to joke about, and what you're going to say about your topic.

For example, let's say your topic is "the boss." That's a start. You do have something to talk about, but it's too general. What are you going to say about the boss? Is he a slave-driver? Is he hard-nosed? Does he hand out impossible deadlines? Is he too easy? Any of these can generate lines, but you must decide before the lines will form in your head.

Decide what you're going to write about and find your point of view, your angle of attack.

Of course, you may decide on several different areas you want to kid about. That's fine, but you have to decide on them before the jokes flow.

Step Two: Do Some Research

Most jokes are generally two different ideas tied together by some similarity. For instance in this joke of Phyllis Diller's:

"When I go to the beauty parlor I always use the emergency entrance. Sometimes I just go for an estimate."

Phyllis is relating going to the beauty parlor to going to the hospital and to going to a body and fender shop. The beauty parlor was her basic premise and the others were what she related that to.

You can build up a catalogue of references or relationships before you generate any comedy. If "the boss" is your topic, list those things that apply to him. You needn't be funny; simply list references. He smokes cheap cigars, his hobby is woodworking, he plays guitar badly, his favorite expression is "Trust me," he used to work in marketing, and so on.

These references may be used later when you get down to looking for the second half of your joke line.

Step Three: Write the Jokes:

Now that you've done all the preparatory research, it's time to be funny. It's time to get the jokes flowing. We recommend two ways of thinking funny:

1) Make declarative statements and caption them.
2) Ask questions.

You know what you're going to talk about and what you want to say, so begin by making basically true statements and then searching through your own mind or your list of references for the punchline, the caption to that statement.

Let us illustrate. We will use your boss as our example. These are the declarative statements:

"The boss smokes smelly cigars."
"He buys them for five cents each."
"He smokes them everywhere."

Those statements might lead to these punchlines:

"The boss smokes smelly cigars, which is good for us workers. We always know when he's in the area."

"Yesterday he bought a nickel cigar. He couldn't buy his regular brand because the guy didn't have four pennies change."

"He smokes those cigars everywhere. He rides to work in a car pool where the driver charges him five dollars a week. Twenty five dollars if he lights the cigar."

The second way of stimulating funny thoughts is to ask questions about your topic. Ask about anything relating to your topic. Extend the situation out to the limits of believability–maybe beyond. In your replies, exaggerate, distort, do whatever you have to do to be funny. But do ask "what if?"

Again, using the boss and his cigars as an illustration, ask how you can get him to smoke better cigars. Ask what the company thinks about his cigars. Ask what his wife thinks. Ask if he'll ever give up cigars. Ask anything at all and see what sort of answers you get.

The answers to some of these have generated the following punchlines:

(How to get him to smoke better cigars) "One guy in the office has decided that he and his wife should have another baby. They want to be able to offer the boss at least one good cigar."

(What the company thinks about them) "The company likes having him smoke smelly cigars. It confuses the inspectors from the Environmental Protection Agency."

(How does his wife feel about them?) "Actually his wife says she'll follow him anywhere when he's smoking one of his cigars. She's says that's easier than kissing him good-bye."

There's another advantage to generating comedy of your own. It's fun.

HINTS ON TELLING A JOKE

Henny Youngman uses a joke that has become his trademark. It reads:

"Take my wife...please."

It's perfect joke structure.

First, because it has a punchline. It's funny. Of course, humor is subjective, so some may object. "It's not hilarious," they might say. Others might object that it's sexist or that it's a gratuitous put-down of spouses. Still others might fail to see any humor at all in it. Fine. All the objections are valid and we'll discuss them later in this chapter, but for now, for the sake of our discussion, let's agree that it has a punchline.

Second, it misleads the audience. The wording of the gag leads the audience along one path and then suddenly switches directions on them.

"Take my wife" is a well-known figure of speech. We interpret it to mean, "Let's use my wife as an example." Our minds begin to translate the joke on that basis. The very last word tells us that's not what the comic meant at all. He was using the phrase literally. He wants us to "take" his wife. "Please," he says; he's begging us to take her off his hands.

We realize we've been had; we've been tricked.

Third, the surprise, the trick, the gimmick is hidden until the end. We don't see the switch until the final word.

Fourth, the punchline, the laugh-producer comes at the end of the thought. It's the final word of the sentence. The audience is free to laugh because they have nothing more to listen to and nothing other to think about.

Fifth, the joke wording is economical. The meaning is clear and concise, yet presented with as few words as possible. It doesn't need any more than those four words, and in fact, would be weakened by any additions.

Sixth, the wording of the gag is precise. It's actually tamper proof. You can't substitute. You can't say, "Let's use my wife as an example...please." You can't change it to "Take my wife...if you don't mind." It uses the exact words for both clarity and for effect.

Seventh, the humor in the gag is readily recognizable and easily explained. The comic misleads the audience into thinking he's simply using a figure of speech. When we find he isn't, we realize we've been had and we laugh.

Plus, the comedian is begging this audience to solve his marriage problems for him. He wants someone, anyone, to "take his wife."

All of the above is a lengthy explanation of a joke that is so perfect it needs no explanation. However, the analysis serves as a reference for us. It provides a good example of what a good joke, story, or anecdote should accomplish.

"Take my wife . . . please" has one flaw. Practically everyone knows it. It's been heard; it's been done. That's a lesson to us also. Even a perfect joke with a solid punchline is useless to us as speakers if too many in the audience have heard it.

That's the first step in telling a good joke . . .

1. SELECT A GOOD JOKE

You can tell a good joke badly, but you can rarely tell a bad joke well. In Hollywood they say, "It has to be on the paper." That means a good screenplay, a good teleplay, a sketch, a monologue, all begin with the script. Good material is a prerequisite to a fine finished product.

On the *Carol Burnett Show*, the writing staff delivered a simple sketch that Carol and Harvey Korman performed beautifully. It was about a solicitous husband who was taking his wife home from the hospital. She had been there with a nervous breakdown. He took her to dinner and during the meal we discovered that his annoying habits had driven her bats in the first place and they were doing it again.

The sketch played to big laughs in the studio and good reaction from the viewing audience.

Later, one of the writers of that sketch was auditioning performers for a variety show that he was producing. He made this piece of material available for any actors who didn't bring their own material. One couple performed it—very badly.

Disappointed, the young lady tossed the script across the room and shouted, "How can we get laughs with slop like this?"

She didn't get the job.

The point is that even though this couple didn't get laughs with this sketch, Carol Burnett and Harvey Korman could not have either if it weren't a good piece of material to begin with. All of us can sometimes destroy a good story with a bad telling—all performers have—but we can't get a good reaction with a bad piece of material.

Be very selective. If you want to tell a joke well, pick a good joke to tell.

2. UNDERSTAND THE JOKE YOU TELL

Know why the joke, story, or anecdote you're going to tell is funny. You might wonder why that's important to the delivery of your story. If it's funny, why is it necessary that we know why it's funny?

You should know the logic behind the humor because *you* have to tell it. *You* must emphasize the right word. *You* have to provide the correct voice inflection. *You* have to misdirect the audience. *You* have to know what *you're* talking about.

This doesn't mean that you have to be able to dissect the anecdote and write a treatise on why listeners should laugh. Sometimes you can't verbalize what's funny about a story. But you should have that "seat of the pants" feel for why a story is humorous. Sometimes we can't find the words that describe the warm feeling and the lump in the throat when they play "America, the Beautiful" on the Fourth of July, but we know what it means. That's the kind of knowledge you should have of your jokes.

If you don't have that kind of faith in your story, perhaps you shouldn't be telling it.

A story that one speaker tells in his banquet speech illustrates how understanding the joke helps in the telling of it. The story is about a man who got in an argument with his wife. In his anger he said something he shouldn't have said, wished he hadn't said, and wished he could pull back. He said, "I don't understand how anyone like you can be so beautiful, and at the same time so stupid." His wife said, "I think it's God's will." She said, "I think God made me beautiful so that you would be attracted to me. And I think he made me stupid so I would be attracted to you."

In delivering the wife's last sentence, this speaker always emphasizes the word "attracted." The temptation is to accent the word "me" because the comparative words are "me" and "you." However, if the comic does accent "me," it immediately tips the punchline of the joke. By emphasizing "me," the audience can infer the rest of the joke.

Stressing the word "attracted" in the first part of the sentence, hides the joke without hurting the punchline. Read the joke aloud both ways and see and feel the difference for yourself.

Remember we said with Henny Youngman's joke that the surprise was saved until the very last word. If we tip this joke too early, we destroy the surprise. It would be like Youngman saying, "Please...take my wife."

The more you understand the humor of your joke, the better you'll be able to tell it.

3. BELIEVE IN YOUR JOKE

This means more than just believing it's funny; it means believing the premise, agreeing with what the story says. To tell a joke effectively, you have to stand behind it. You have to practically sell it like a politician selling his platform. To do that, you must believe in it. If you don't, it affects your performance.

We once watched a game of Scrabble. One player had a high-scoring play, but refused to put the tiles down. Why? Because they spelled out an obscene word. This person preferred to take the lower score rather than allow that word to be spelled out on the board. Writing that word out in Scrabble tiles would have ruined the fun of the game for this player.

Comedian Steve Allen admitted in one of his books that he dislikes the word "ass." It's unpleasant for him to hear it and especially repulsive for him to say it. Consequently, he won't do any jokes that use that word.

But this goes beyond naughty words. You also have to believe in the concept of the joke. If you don't buy the idea, you can't properly deliver the joke. Subconsciously you hold back. You might hold back enough to destroy the telling of the story.

Here are two examples:

Lawyer-rapping is an "in" kind of humor today. There are many jokes circulating about that profession. Here's one that we've heard, but probably wouldn't tell to an audience:

> "A rich lawyer, a poor lawyer, and Santa Claus are walking down the street and they spot a ten dollar bill on the ground. Who picks up the money?
> "The rich lawyer. The other two are figments of your imagination."

It's not a bad joke, and certainly not off-color or distasteful. We simply won't tell it because we don't agree with the philosophy. What's wrong with being rich? Attorneys pay for a good education and are entitled to whatever fees they can get. Now that may be nit-picking and perhaps being overly sensitive. That's all right. We don't have to justify our reasons for disagreeing with a story.

The point is, if we feel that way, we can't do justice to the telling of the story. They say that animals can sense your fear. Well, audiences can sense your disagreement with an anecdote. They'll know your heart's not in it.

Now here's a lawyer joke that we would tell to an audience—especially an audience of attorneys:

"I was coming to this dinner tonight and I asked an attorney how to get to the banquet hall. He was very nice about it. He gave me a clear, concise, direct answer just like that—pro bono."

We can deliver that story with a clear conscience and in good humor. Whether you see the difference or not is immaterial. We see the difference, and that's what's important.

You must be able to see, know, or feel the difference in any jokes that you tell. Then only deliver the ones you believe in.

4. BE ABLE TO TELL THE JOKE

That sounds simplistic, but it isn't. Many of us, even professionals, try to tell stories that we can't tell—physically can't tell.

Just yesterday we heard a friend tell a joke that demanded an Italian dialect. His Italian accent sounded more like a cross between a German, an Armenian, and an American Indian.

Some stories demand shouting and screaming, and many of us feel uncomfortable raising our voices. We can't do it well.

A vaudeville comedian used to tell a story where the punchline was a front somersault. Neither one of the authors would risk telling that joke.

On Johnny Carson one night Buddy Hackett told a story about a hunter who shot a duck. When he went to retrieve it, though, the farmer claimed that since the duck fell on his property, it belonged to him. The hunter argued that it was his—he shot it. The farmer offered the settlement that he claimed was traditional for this region. They'd have a contest. They'd kick each other in the groin. Whoever kicked the hardest would claim the duck. So the hunter agreed and the farmer hauled off and kicked him, with all his might, in the groin.

At this point, Buddy Hackett acted out the hunter's reaction. He grabbed his crotch, screamed, yelled, rolled on the floor in agony, tried to get up, screamed some more, fell down again, rolled around the floor some more. He continued these antics for about two minutes.

Then he stood up, regained his composure, and said, "Okay, now it's my turn." The farmer said, "It's all right. You can have the duck."

The audience laughed explosively, and Carson fell off his chair.

But could you tell that joke? Could you give it that kind of physical commitment? If you can't, perhaps you shouldn't tell that story.

Sometimes we think we can tell a tale, but we can't. Oh, we can tell it in our head. In there it sounds perfect. But we can't tell it aloud. In the perfect acoustics of our own mind, we can hit every high note in music, but we can't when we try to sing out.

To test yourself, practice your jokes aloud. Hear yourself say them. Try them on friends. Make sure you can do whatever is necessary to deliver that particular joke.

If you can't tell the story, it's better to find out privately rather than after you get to the lectern.

5. BE ABLE TO TELL YOUR JOKE WELL

There's a difference between being able to tell a joke and being able to tell a joke well. Some musician made the same comment about the guitar. He said it was an instrument that many people could play, but very few could play well.

Sure, you may be able to scream, yell, do an Italian dialect, roll around on the floor like Buddy Hackett, perhaps even do a front somersault. Can you do them well? Well enough to get the joke across?

If not, you'd better either drop the joke, or practice the telling of it. Tell it to friends, experiment with the wording and the delivery.

The good comedians make comedy look spontaneous. They do that by practice, practice, and practice. You owe your jokes the same devotion.

6. KEEP YOUR JOKE ECONOMICAL

For an audience, listening to a humorous story is like buying an appliance. They want something good, but they want it at a bargain price.

Each punchline has a price tag. The price the listeners pay is the amount of time they invest listening to the build-up. If you waste a lot of time and words telling your story, the punch line has to be worth it.

Your safest bet is to keep your story-telling economical. "Brevity is the soul of wit," Shakespeare advised. However, you do have to tell enough to properly set up the punchline. You can't tell a joke and not have people know what you're talking about.

A writer on the Carol Burnett show once said, "Give me a good ending and I can write a sketch that leads up to it." The producer called his bluff. He said, "Okay, Tim Conway falls out a window. Have the sketch on my desk by 4:30 this afternoon."

Don't be chintzy with your set up, but don't ramble either. The more you do, the more jeopardy you place your punchline in.

Again, the Henny Youngman line was ideal. It said it all in four words. Five words would have hurt it.

7. KNOW WHERE THE LAUGH IS

The punchline, the joke, the laugh is your reason for telling the story. Everything in the telling should support the ending and lead up to it. Everything in your story should be there simply because the ending demands that it be there.

Yet, how many times have you heard people get two or three minutes into a story and then say, "Now let me see. I forget how this ends"?

Before you begin a joke, know where the laugh is and how to get to it. It's the only way to properly tell a story, yet it's the one rule that people violate most often.

To me, this is like getting in the car, driving the freeways for an hour, and then saying, "OK, let's see where we want to go." You find out where you're going before you start the trip. Likewise, know where you're going before you start telling a joke.

If you learn only one thing from this entire essay, let it be that the punchline is the essence of the joke. Know where it is and how to get to it.

HOW TO USE INSULT HUMOR WITHOUT INSULTING

Insults have become an American way of showing affection. You can almost tell how close people are by how "vicious" their playful insults get. Look at a rack of greeting cards in any store and you'll notice that a goodly percentage of them are "studio" cards—cards with a little barb attached to the greeting.

Are we offended by these? No. In fact, when a person opens a greeting card at his birthday celebration and sees the wacky drawing and the put-down inside, he laughs and then immediately passes the card around so others can enjoy the joke, too.

When show business people want to honor one of their own, they "roast" that person. They write offensive, derisive gags. It's their way of paying tribute.

So the insult has become an accepted form of compliment to those we care for.

Insult humor has become respectable. You can say embarrassing things about your friends, you can blaspheme the company and management, you can attack your audience, and remain in good graces with them all.

However, this doesn't mean that you should use it. It simply means that you're permitted in today's society to use it . . . *if it fits your personality on the podium.* That's the bottom line in any humor you do, and is even more important in deciding whether to use insult humor or not.

Are you comfortable with it? If you are, then go ahead (with cautions that we'll discuss in a few paragraphs). If you're not at ease with it, ignore it.

Two close show business friends are Don Rickles and Bob Newhart. Their families socialize; they vacation together. They're close. On stage, though, they're about as far apart as two comics can get. Rickles is raunchy and aggressive. He attacks anyone in sight. His one-liners have venom in them and he spits them out like a viper.

Newhart is laid back, easy-going. His stage persona is almost apologetic. He'd like you to listen to him if it's not too much trouble.

Each admires the other's talents, but neither one would trade. Newhart doesn't do insult humor; Rickles thrives on it.

Neither one is better than the other. They're just different.

So you have the choice, too. Insult humor, nowadays, is not ruled out as too offensive for any speakers–performers, banquet professionals, or business speakers. It can be utilized effectively by all of them.

However, the respectability of insult humor doesn't give each speaker carte blanche to use it indiscriminately. It's accepted, but it's still volatile. It's dangerous. It can still backfire. It can still hurt.

No one who's using humor to enhance the message, wants to alienate an audience, or even part of an audience, with inappropriate put-down humor.

How do you avoid that catastrophe? By applying these three principles when using insult humor:

1) Be sure your insults are obviously not believable.
2) Kid about things that are of no consequence.
3) Kid about things that people kid themselves about or don't mind being kidded about.

In other words, don't hit an open nerve.

NOT BELIEVABLE:

We attended a wedding reception and party where a proud father took the microphone to offer a toast to his newly married daughter.

He said, "This may the third proudest day of my life. The first was when I finally got out of the fifth grade, and the second was when I got married."

The bride, who was standing by her Dad, chimed in, "And they were both in the same week."

Certainly this remark is insulting, but it got laughter and applause from the listeners. More importantly it got a hearty laugh and a warm hug from her Dad. There was no sting, no malice, to the comment because it was obviously not true. Everyone knew the remark was fabricated and offered in a sense of fun.

KID ABOUT THINGS THAT ARE OF NO CONSEQUENCE:

Bob Hope has joked about every President from Franklin D. Roosevelt on.

He said of Harry Truman: "He rules the nation with an iron fist. The same way he plays the piano."

Eisenhower," he said, "switched from golf to oil painting to relax. For him, it's fewer strokes."

He kidded Kennedy about raiding Harvard: "There are so many professors in the cabinet you can't leave the room without raising your hand."

Hope teased Nixon when he emceed a gala in New York's Waldorf-Astoria. He said, "I really didn't expect President Nixon to be here. He doesn't have a White House in this state."

Ford was and still is the object of Hope's comedy because of his hazardous golf. Hope says, "When I play with Jerry, I don't have to keep score. I just look back along the fairway and count the wounded."

At Bob Hope's 75th birthday bash at the White House, President Carter turned the tables, kidding the comedian. He said, "I've been in office 489 days . . . In three weeks more I'll have stayed at the White House as many times as Bob Hope has."

Reagan and Hope were friends from their Hollywood days. Hope says, "Ronald Reagan is a politician who doesn't lie, cheat, or steal. He's always had an agent to do that for him."

Notice in all the gags that the heart of the joke is about something not important. Truman's piano playing, Ike's golf, Kennedy's Harvard friends, Nixon's many vacation places, Ford's erratic golf, Reagan's show business ties. None of them came close to an open wound.

It's a matter of taste and self-censorship. Every person, every association, every audience has some sensitive area. They don't want you to "mess with it." So don't. Kid about other areas.

All of us have plenty that we can be kidded about without getting too personal. Use those.

It's kind of like what football players say: "Sure, I play to win. I hit hard. I want the opponents to know I'm on the field. But I also hit clean." There's a difference on the football field between a hard hit and a cheap shot.

There is at the podium, too.

WHAT THEY KID THEMSELVES ABOUT:

This is the governing rule in using insult humor inoffensively. You may diligently adhere to the first and second, but you're in danger if you don't positively follow rule three–this one. If people don't want to be kidded about something, don't kid them.

It's really as simple as that.

You might say, though, how about Don Rickles? How about some of the night club comics who insult from the stage. They get away with it. They can't possibly be sure that people will accept it.

True. They probably can't. In most cases, though, they're professional enough and experienced enough to guess when they can. They have a feel for the audience and sense just how far they can go.

However, they don't have as much at stake as you do. They are there to entertain. Offending someone in the audience occasionally isn't going to kill their careers, or even hurt their show that much.

Business speakers are trying to do more than "put on a show." They're trying to get a message across—to these listeners. They're trying to impress this audience. Remember Lincoln said he didn't want to amuse the listeners, he wanted to *convince* them.

Will Rogers probably said it best when someone asked him how he could tease all the well-known people that he did without alienating any of them. Rogers said, "Heck, if there's no malice in your heart, there can't be none in your jokes."